Important HTML Tags

HTML consists of tags, surrounded by **<** and **>**. Each tag has an open tag that ⸺
and a close tag, with a slash (**/**), that goes after it. Some important tags include

<b></b>	This tag makes text appear bold.
<i></i>	This tag italicizes text.
<img />	This tag inserts an image into your description. The **src** attribute tells the browser where to find the image file. For example **<img src="http://www.nicholaschase.com/ebaystuff/ mypicture.jpg" alt="Item Photo" />**
<h1></h1>	This tag creates a separate line of large, bold text.
<h2></h2>	This tag creates a line of slightly smaller, but still large, bold text.
<p></p>	This tag creates a paragraph of text, adding a blank line before and after.
** **	This tag adds a line break to the page.
<hr />	This tag adds a horizontal rule, or line, to the page.
<a></a>	This tag lets you create a link. For example, you can create a link that lets users email you with questions: **<a href="mailto:easyhtml4ebay@nicholaschase.com?Auction+ question">Email me</a>**
<table></table>	This tag, along with the **<tr>**, **<th>**, and **<td>** tags, creates a grid of information, such as this: **<table border="1">** **<tr><th>Heading 1</th><th>Heading 2</th></tr>** **<tr><td>Information 1</td><td>Information 2 on tw lines</td></tr>** **<tr><td>Information 3, slightly longer</td><td>Information 4</td></tr>** **</table>**
<tr></tr>	This tag creates a row of data cells.
<th></th>	This tag creates a column heading. The text is bold and centered in the cell.
<td></td>	This tag creates a table data cell of content. You can put virtually any HTML inside this tag. You can use the **colspan** and **rowspan** attributes to expand the box vertically or horizontally.
<ol></ol>	This tag, along with the **<li></li>** tag, creates an ordered, or numbered, list.
<ul></ul>	This tag, along with the **<li></li>** tag, creates an unordered, or bulleted, list.
<li></li>	This tag defines list items for ordered or unordered lists.
<div></div>	This tag creates a block of content. You can also use this tag to add styles such as backgrounds and borders to a block of text.
<span></span>	This tag enables you to add styles to smaller, individual sections of text.

eBay Custom Tags

eBay has created a selection of tags that are not HTML, but that can be used within the About Me and store pages. These tags are an easy and automated way to add information such as current listings and feedback to your pages.

About Me page tags include

<eBayUserID>: This tag adds your eBay user ID and, optionally, your feedback rating and email.

<eBayFeedback>: This tag adds a designated number of recent feedback comments to your page and enables you to control properties such as the color, border, and caption.

<eBayItemList> This tag lets you automatically list your current items. It also lets you control the appearance and order of the list, as well as enabling you to limit items to a specific category. eBay store tags take a slightly different form, using brackets (**{}**) instead of the less-than and greater-than signs (**<>**) HTML tags take. They include

{eBayUserID} This tag adds your user ID; feedback score; and applicable icons, such as the sunglasses or Me Page icon.

{eBayFeedback}: This tag adds your most recent feedback items and enables you to control their appearance.

{eBayStoresItemList}: This tag displays a list of the items in your store. It also lets you control the items shown (by category, keyword, or type), how they're displayed (in a list or as a gallery), and how they're sorted and displayed.

{eBayStoresItemShowcase}: This tag gives you an easy way to feature up to four items, automatically including a photo and other information about the items.

{eBayStoresItem}: This tag shows a single item of your choice as though the user were pulling it up in the search results.

{eBayStoresItemDetail}: This tag lets you pull a specific item property, such as its title or current price.

{eBayStoresSearchBox}: This tag lets you easily add a search box so users can search other items in your store.

CSS Style Properties

You can add style information directly to an element by using the **style** attribute in the tag, or you can add style rules to the page itself using the **<style></style>** tag. Either way, here are some useful properties:

font-family: This property controls the font, such as Helvetica or Times New Roman.

font-size: This property controls the size of the text, either in point size or by height in terms of pixels.

font-weight: This property lets you bold the text with a little more control over just how bold it becomes.

float: This property enables you to take an item such as an image and float it to the left or right side of the page, allowing text and other content to wrap around it.

text-decoration: This property enables you to control the appearance of text. It's most often used to remove the underline from links.

color: This property controls the color of an item. You can set it by name or using the red, green, and blue values.

border: This property lets you set the color, thickness, and style of a border. You can also use properties such as as **border-bottom** and **border-right** to set a partial border on an object.

background: This property lets you choose an image file to use as a background image for an item or even for the page page itself.

background-color: This property sets the background color for an item. You can use it as a backup for the background property or on its own.

easy

HTML
for eBay®

Nicholas Chase

Contents

Easy HTML for eBay®
Copyright © 2005 by Que Publishing

International Standard Book Number: 0-7897-3231-9

Library of Congress Catalog Card Number: 2004107075

Printed in the United States of America

First Printing: December 2004

07 06 05 04   4 3 2 1

Trademarks

Warning and Disclaimer

Bulk Sales

Que Publishing offers excellent discounts on this book when ordered in quantity for bulk purchases or special sales. For more information, please contact

U.S. Corporate and Government Sales

1-800-382-3419

corpsales@pearsontechgroup.com

For sales outside the United States, please contact

International Sales

international@pearsoned.com

Associate Publisher
Greg Wiegand

Acquisitions Editor
Michelle Newcomb

Development Editor
Kevin Howard

Managing Editor
Charlotte Clapp

Project Editor
Tonya Simpson

Production Editor
Megan Wade

Technical Editor
Patti Rich

Publishing Coordinator
Sharry Lee Gregory

Interior Designer
Anne Jones

Cover Designer
Anne Jones

Page Layout
Bronkella Publishing

Additional Photography
Sarah Chase

Dedication

To Eric, for your friendship and your patience—and for dragging me out of the house once in a while.

Acknowledgments

First and foremost, I want to thank my wife, Sarah, for being my co-author on this book. Sarah has helped me every step of the way, from designing sample auctions to doing artwork to running interference to finding me food at 3 a.m. Sarah, I literally couldn't have done it without you.

I also want to thank my family, both immediate and extended, for putting up with me hibernating in the office to get this book finished. Thanks to Sean, and thanks to Cheyenne, Dakota, and Running Wolf Ferrett.

I'd especially like to thank Patti Rich for guiding me through some of the intricacies of eBay that are only visible to those who make a living at it. Your experience and wisdom have been invaluable. And thanks to Eric Lowery for offering to get us together, and for following through until it happened.

I also want to thank Michelle Newcomb for asking me if I'd be interested in the first place and for guiding me through the intricacies of this series. And thanks for that time dilation at the end there—it really helped.

Finally, I want to thank the entire team. Kevin Howard, thanks for helping me through the organizational obstacles and for helping me to make it all flow right. Tonya Simpson, thanks for as much flexibility in the production process as you were able to provide. Megan Wade, thanks for nitpicking to see what you could find in my copy that needed fixing.

Overall, this book has been a blast, and I hope you have as much fun with it as I'm having.

About the Author

Nicholas Chase has been involved in website development for companies such as Lucent Technologies, Sun Microsystems, Oracle, and the Tampa Bay Buccaneers. Nick has been a high school physics teacher, a low-level radioactive waste facility manager, an online science-fiction magazine editor, a multimedia engineer, an Oracle instructor, and the chief technology officer of an interactive communications firm. He has written more than 100 tutorials and articles for IBM's developerWorks and serves as InformIT.com's XML and web services reference guide. He is the author of several books on XML and web development, including *XML Primer Plus* (published by Sams Publishing). He's currently trying to buy a farm so he and his wife can raise alpacas and mutant chickens. He loves to hear from readers and can be reached at nicholas@nicholaschase.com.

We Want to Hear from You!

As the reader of this book, *you* are our most important critic and commentator. We value your opinion and want to know what we're doing right, what we could do better, what areas you'd like to see us publish in, and any other words of wisdom you're willing to pass our way.

As an associate publisher for Que, I welcome your comments. You can email or write me directly to let me know what you did or didn't like about this book—as well as what we can do to make our books better.

Please note that I cannot help you with technical problems related to the topic of this book. We do have a User Services group, however, where I will forward specific technical questions related to the book.

When you write, please be sure to include this book's title and author as well as your name, email address, and phone number. I will carefully review your comments and share them with the author and editors who worked on the book.

Email: feedback@quepublishing.com

Mail: Greg Wiegand
Associate Publisher
Que Publishing
800 East 96th Street
Indianapolis, IN 46240 USA

For more information about this book or another Que title, visit our Web site at www.quepublishing.com. Type the ISBN (excluding hyphens) or the title of a book in the Search field to find the page you're looking for.

Each step is fully illustrated to show you how it looks onscreen.

It's as Easy as 1-2-3

Each part of this book is made up of a series of short, instructional lessons, designed to help you understand basic information that you need to get the most out of your computer hardware and software.

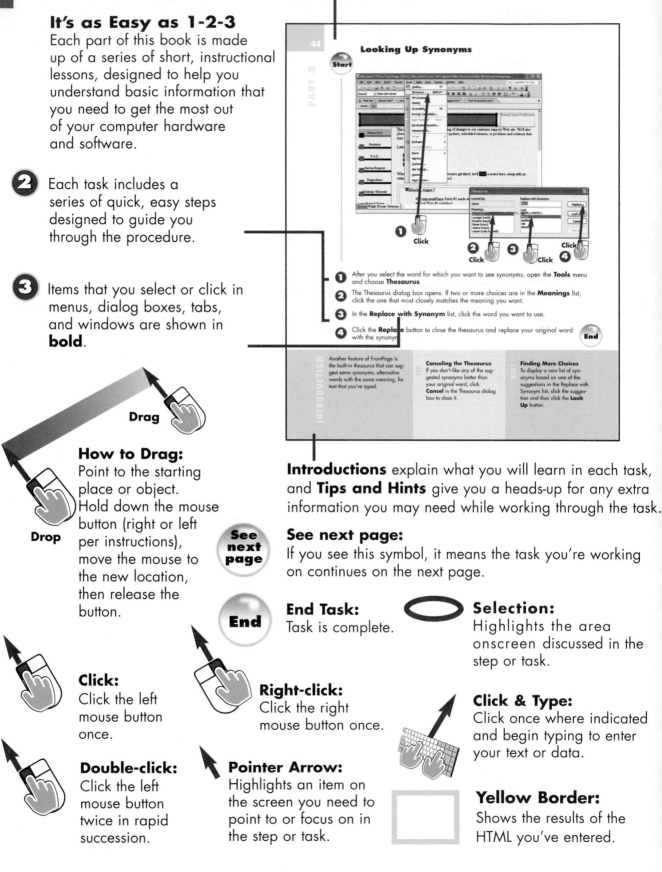

2 Each task includes a series of quick, easy steps designed to guide you through the procedure.

3 Items that you select or click in menus, dialog boxes, tabs, and windows are shown in **bold**.

Drag

How to Drag:
Point to the starting place or object. Hold down the mouse button (right or left per instructions), move the mouse to the new location, then release the button.

Drop

Introductions explain what you will learn in each task, and **Tips and Hints** give you a heads-up for any extra information you may need while working through the task.

See next page

See next page:
If you see this symbol, it means the task you're working on continues on the next page.

End

End Task:
Task is complete.

Selection:
Highlights the area onscreen discussed in the step or task.

Click:
Click the left mouse button once.

Right-click:
Click the right mouse button once.

Click & Type:
Click once where indicated and begin typing to enter your text or data.

Double-click:
Click the left mouse button twice in rapid succession.

Pointer Arrow:
Highlights an item on the screen you need to point to or focus on in the step or task.

Yellow Border:
Shows the results of the HTML you've entered.

Introduction to
Easy HTML for eBay

Are you one of the millions who've discovered eBay? Do you pour through listings looking for that one piece of treasure? Or do you have a pile of treasures you've pulled out of your attic to sell? Maybe you've decided to make eBay the storefront for your new business. If so, you've probably discovered something: You have to make your listings look good.

But there's a problem. Maybe you'd be perfectly capable of creating a beautiful listing as long as you could use a paper and pencil, but the idea of designing something that will appear on the World Wide Web has got you stuck. After all, this isn't like a Word processor, where you can just type and drag items around on the page. No, if you're going to take full advantage of the capabilities at hand, you need to know how to write Hypertext Markup Language (HTML), the language your browser understands.

This book takes you by the hand and explains how to use HTML in your listings, About Me page, and eBay Store. You'll start with the basics such as paragraphs and lists, which you can also accomplish using eBay's editors. Then you'll move on to more advanced HTML, such as adding images to your description and controlling its layout and appearance, which is well beyond what you can do with eBay's editors. Later in the book, I'll show you how to notch up the "cool factor" for your listings with special effects. And all along the way, I'll try to provide you with some tips for making sure your listings don't go from looking professional to looking overdone and amateurish.

This book has 10 parts:

Part 1, "Creating an Auction Listing," starts by showing you what things look like for a buyer and then takes you through the process of actually adding a simple listing.

Part 2, "Creating a Simple Description," gives you practice in using the basic HTML elements such as headings, paragraphs, and horizontal rules.

Part 3, "Adding Pictures," talks about one of the most important aspects of your listing: the photo. It shows you some techniques for getting good photos of your items and explains how to make the photos you take available on eBay as part of your description.

Part 4, "Arranging the Page," shows you how to use tables and divisions to control the layout and placement of items in your description.

Part 5, "Decorating the Page," uses borders, background colors, and background images to liven up the display of your page.

Part 6, "Styling the Text," explains how stylesheets work and shows you how you can control just about every aspect of your text's appearance.

Part 7, "Creating Links," demonstrates the types of links that are, indeed, permitted under eBay's rules, such as one that automatically creates an email with the auction number in the subject.

Part 8, "Adding Sound, Video, and Animation," teaches you how to take things one step further and create and add sound, video, and animations to your page. (Subtly, I hope!)

Part 9, "About Me Pages and eBay Stores," starts by explaining how to create your own About Me page and customize it using eBay's custom tags. It also explains how to create your own store and perform the limited customization that eBay allows there.

Part 10, "Making Your Listings Stand Out," is a catchall chapter, filled with techniques for enhancing your listing.

Throughout the book, I've used Microsoft Internet Explorer because at the time of this writing it's more commonly used, but these techniques have been tested to work in other common browsers such as Netscape and its derivatives.

This book should teach you what you need to know, but eBay is an ever-changing place. As I write this, eBay is restructuring how it displays descriptions. So if you still have questions, or if you just want to check in to see what's new, I'll be maintaining a section for this book on my website at http://www.nicholaschase.com/easyhtmlforebay/.

All right, then, on to Part 1!

Creating an Auction Listing

In this first part of the book, we'll concentrate on the basics with an introductory chapter on eBay. Oh, I know, you already know eBay; that's why you're here. In this chapter, we'll simply make sure we're all on the same page, so to speak, while we do two things.

First, we'll look at eBay from the buyer's point of view. Which parts of your listing does a buyer see? In other words, you never get a second chance to make a first impression, but which parts of your listings actually make up that first impression?

From there, we'll get into the actual creation of a listing. We'll cover the mechanics of creating a listing and then move on to the description of your item, including how to enhance your listing with different colors, fonts, and graphics and using HTML coding. As to applying that HTML, you have several options, such as built-in editors available directly on the eBay site—although the capabilities they provide are pretty basic compared to what we ultimately want to accomplish.

Creating a Listing

Choose a category

Enter item information

Create an item description

What the Buyer Sees: Browsing Categories

Start

① **Point your browser to http://www.ebay.com.**

② **Scroll down and click Collectibles.**

③ **Click Holiday, Seasonal to see a list of holiday-related items.**

HINT

Related Categories
Looking for something similar? Related categories are listed beneath the list of subcategories.

TIP

Item Specifics
In many categories you can narrow down the list of items by choosing one or more item specifics in the left column.

4 Click **Christmas: Vintage (Pre-1946)** to narrow down the list to vintage Christmas items.

5 When the next page of listings appears, click a specific item.

See next page

TIP

Gallery Items
eBay places "gallery" items at the top of the listing for each category. These are items for which the seller paid extra to have his items come to the top.

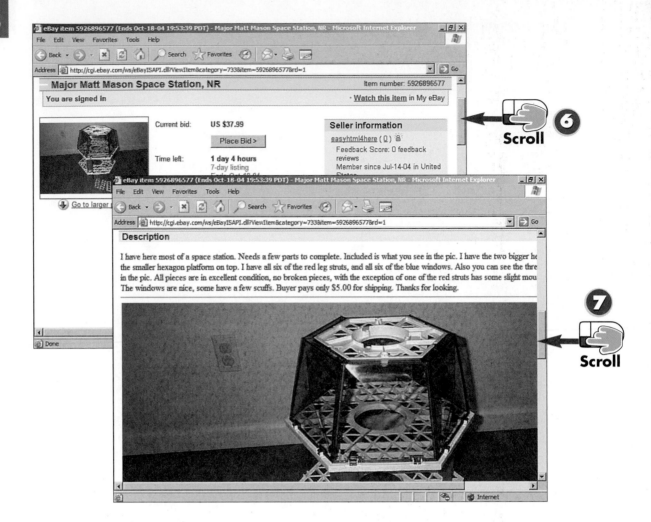

6 The first view of an item provides basic information, such as the title, price, and seller. Scroll down to see the description.

7 The middle section of the listing provides a description of the item, and sometimes a picture. Scroll down further.

TIP

Above the Fold

Items that show up in the initial view of a web page, before the user scrolls, are called *above the fold*, a term left over from newspapers. Unless the buyer has a large monitor (and resolution set higher than 800 × 600), all your description is below the fold.

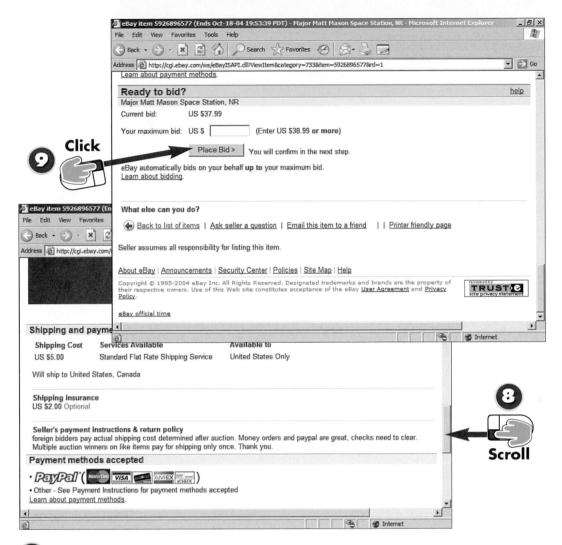

Click

9

8

Scroll

8 Below the item description are the shipping and payment details. Scroll down further.

9 The very bottom of the page is the Ready to Bid? section. Click the **Place Bid** button to enter a bid.

End

Standard Information
TIP
Most of the customizing you'll do will be in the Description section. You can't use HTML anywhere else in the item listing.

Registering As a Seller

Start

① Click

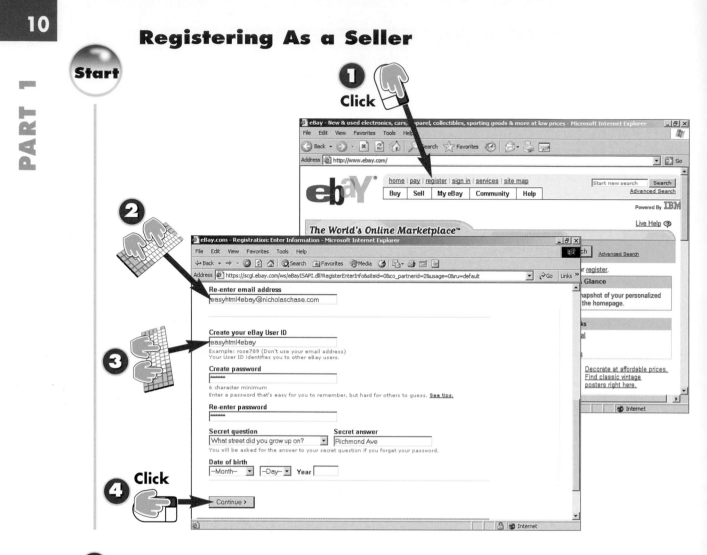

②

③

④ Click

① From the top of the eBay home page, click **Register**.

② Enter your personal information.

③ Choose a login name and enter the rest of your information.

④ Click **Continue**.

How Personal?

TIP

eBay requires you to be truthful when registering as a user to protect all users from fraudulent sellers (and buyers). In fact, if you try to make up a nonexistent address or phone number, the system tells you the information's invalid.

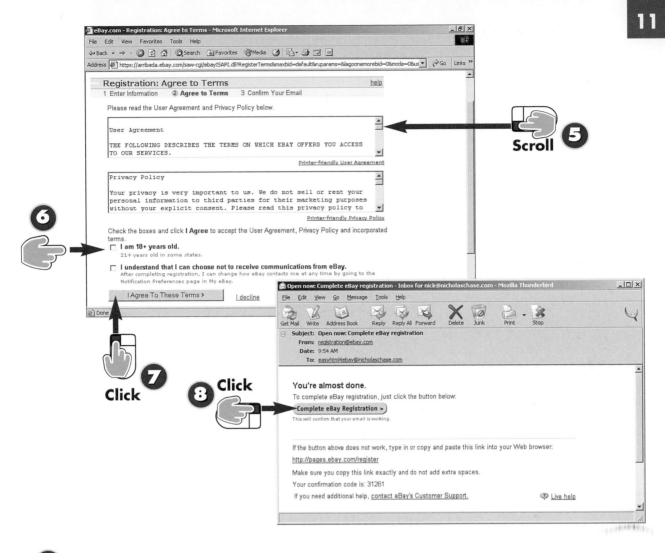

5 Scroll the agreements to read them in their entirety.

6 Read the check box information and check the appropriate boxes.

7 Click **I Agree to These Terms**.

8 Check your email and click the **Complete eBay Registration** button to complete your registration.

See next page

Good Names
You can choose any username you want, as long as it isn't already chosen by another user. If you plan on becoming a seller, think of a name that reflects positively on what you'll be selling.

TIP

Click 9

eBay.com - Microsoft Internet Explorer

File Edit View Favorites Tools Help

Back · → · ⊗ ⊠ ⬆ | Search Favorites Media | ⊗ | ⬇ · ⬆ ⊠ ⬜

Address http://cgi4.ebay.com/ws1/eBayISAPI.dll?RegisterSuccess&ommakebid=0&qachoice=0&userId=easyhtml4here&ssPageName= | ⬇Go | Links »

ebaY®

home | pay | register | sign out | services | site map | help

| Browse | Search | Sell | My eBay | Community | Powered By **IBM** |

Congratulations, easyhtml4here
You can now bid and buy

See the item you last looked at:

Welcome to eBay

View Last Item >

Want to sell something? You need to
account on eBay.

Announcements | Register | Security Center

Copyright © 1995-2004 eBay Inc. All Rights Reserved.
Designated trademarks and brands are the property of their respec

eBay.com: Seller's Account: Verify Information - Microsoft Internet Explorer

File Edit View Favorites Tools Help

Back · → · ⊗ ⊠ ⬆ | Search Favorites Media | ⊗ | ⬇ · ⬆ ⊠ ⬜

Address https://scgi.ebay.com/ws/ebayISAPI.dll?SellerRegistrationEnterContactInfoShow& | ⬇Go | Links »

Please have the following ready, as you'll need both to sell on eBay.com:
- Credit or debit card   If you don't have these available,
- Checkbook (checking account)   please use **ID Verify** instead ($5 fee).

First, verify that your information below is correct.

First name   **Last name**
Nicholas   Chase

Street
4997 Richmond Avenue

City
Staten Island

State   **Zip code**   **Country**
New York   10314   United States
                                    Change country

Primary telephone
(718) 555 - 2254 ext.:

Date of birth
March   07   Year 1960

Continue >

Internet

10

11 **Click**

9 If you plan on becoming a seller, click **Sell**.

10 Verify that the information is correct.

11 Click **Continue**.

Fee Information

HINT

To become a seller, you have to
provide eBay with financial
information so you can pay
your fees. (Sellers pay eBay
fees; buyers don't.)

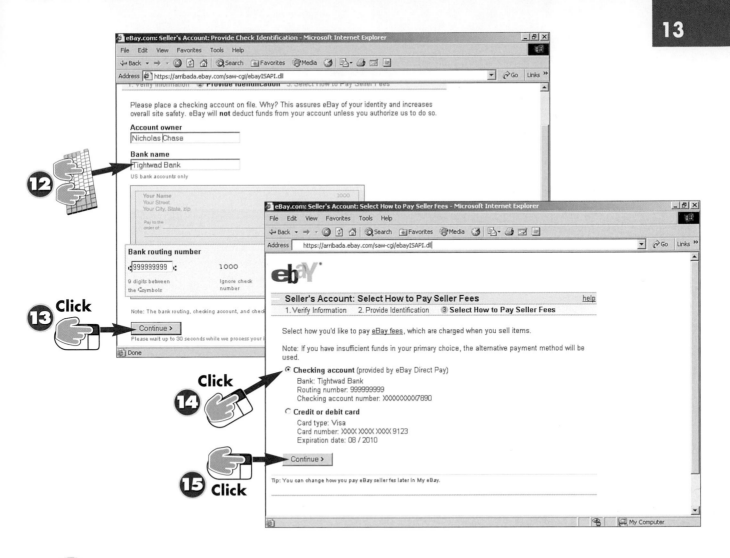

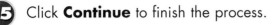

12 Enter your credit card and checking account information to verify your identity.

13 Click **Continue**.

14 Click the radio button next to your preferred payment method.

15 Click **Continue** to finish the process.

End

ID Verify

TIP

If you don't want to divulge your financial information, you can sign up for eBay's ID Verify program instead. For a $5 fee, you can sign up to sell without providing a credit card, although you do have to answer some other personal questions and provide your driver's license number.

Creating an Auction

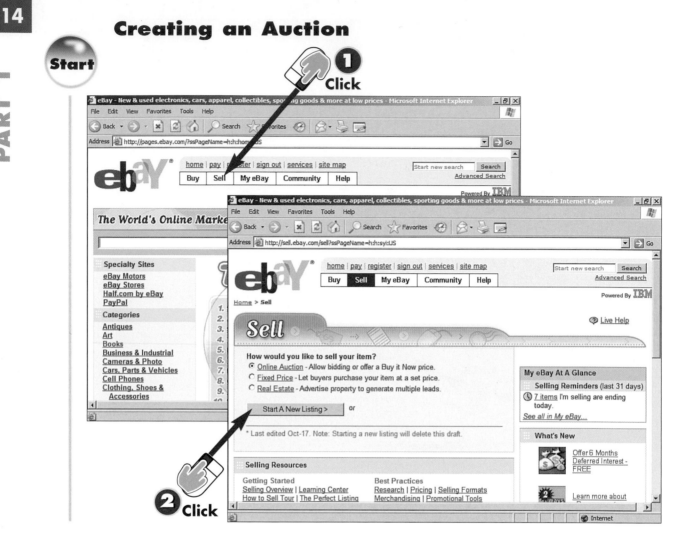

1. From the main page, click **Sell**. (If prompted, enter the username and password you created when you registered.)

2. **Online Auction** should already be selected. Click **Start a New Listing**.

This book is about HTML, so I won't go into the business of choosing an item, picking the right category in which to sell it, pricing it correctly, and so on. You can check out *Absolute Beginner's Guide to eBay* for that information. In this case, we'll just create a simple auction to see how it's done.

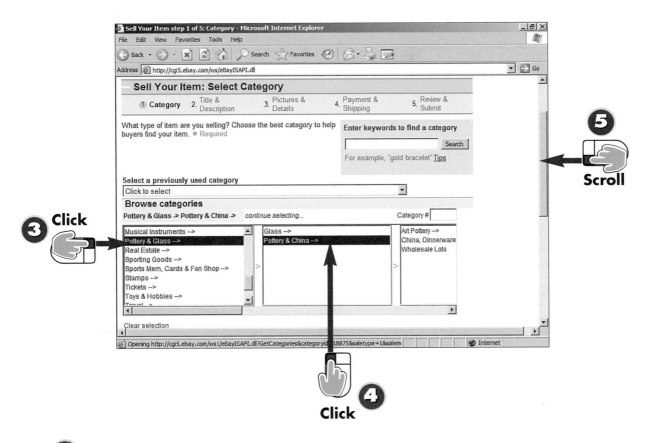

3 Under **Browse Categories**, click a main category.

4 Keep clicking additional subcategories until the last box says **Main Category Selected**.

5 Scroll down and click **Continue**.

See next page

Multiple Categories

TIP You also have the option of choosing a second category by following the instructions in the List in a Second Category section. Just be aware that choosing this option increases your fees.

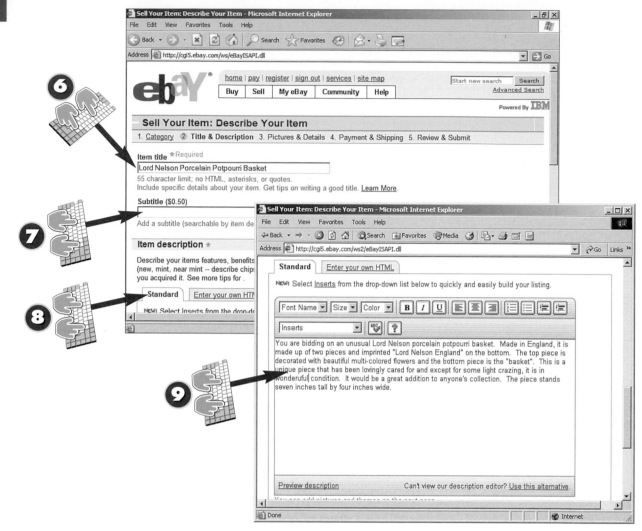

6 Enter a title for your item.

7 Enter a subtitle (additional fee), if desired.

8 Enter any item specifics for your item, if applicable.

9 Scroll down to the description box and enter the basic description of your item.

What Specifics?
Not all categories have item specifics, so don't panic if they don't appear for your auction.

TIP

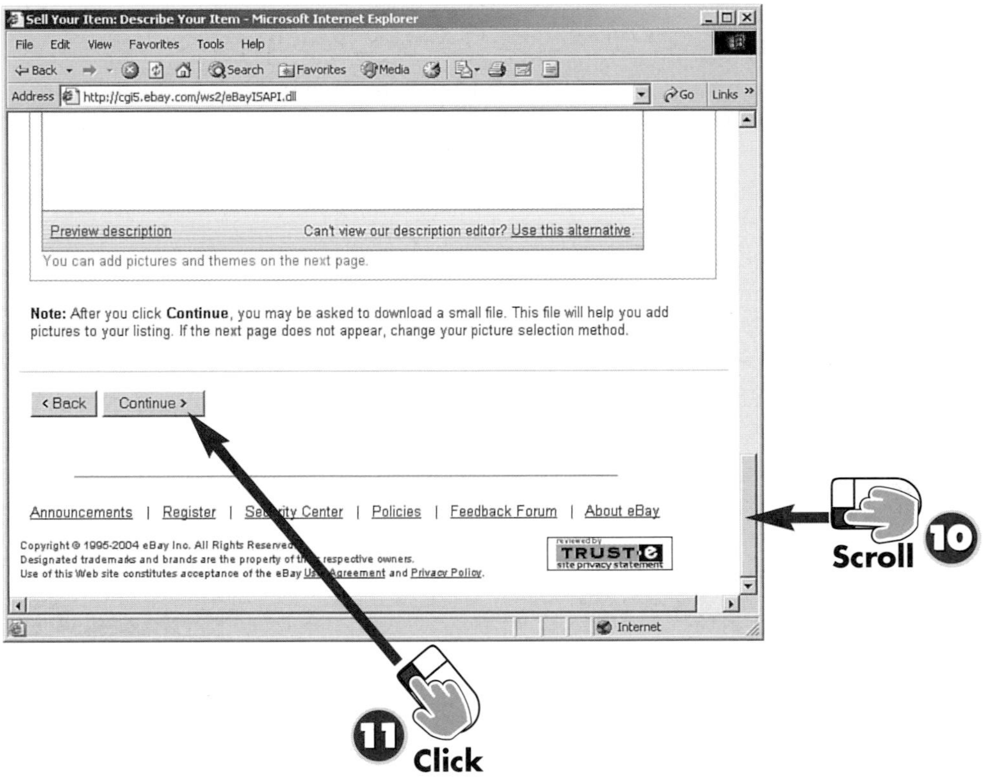

Scroll (10)

(11) **Click**

(10) Scroll down to the bottom of the page.

(11) Click **Continue**.

See
next
page

eBay Picture Services

If you're prompted to install the new version of eBay Picture Services, do so. Downloading the offered version of eBay Picture Services provides you with additional functionality, such as the ability to rotate, crop, and preview your photos without needing an extra application.

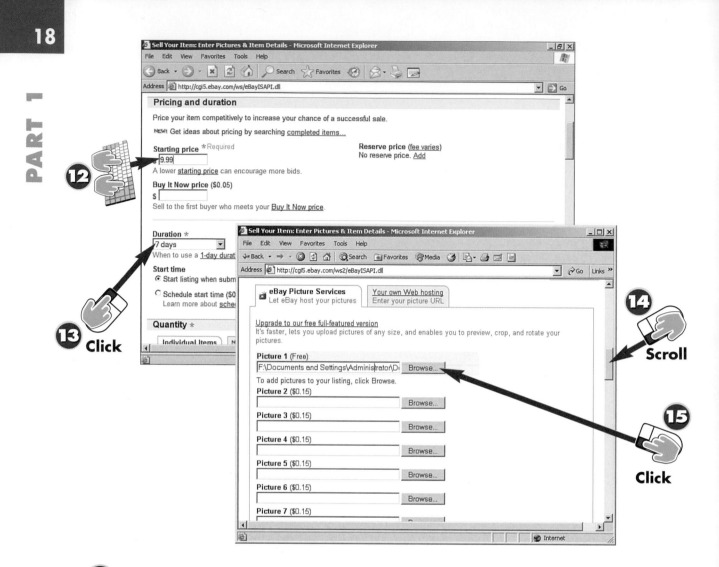

 12 Enter your starting price.

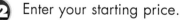 **13** Select your auction duration.

14 Scroll down to eBay Picture Services.

 15 Click **Browse** to add a single photo.

Quantity and Location
In most cases, you can accept the default settings and skip over the Quantity and Item Location sections of this page. If you're selling more than one item, however, enter a larger number in the Quantity field.

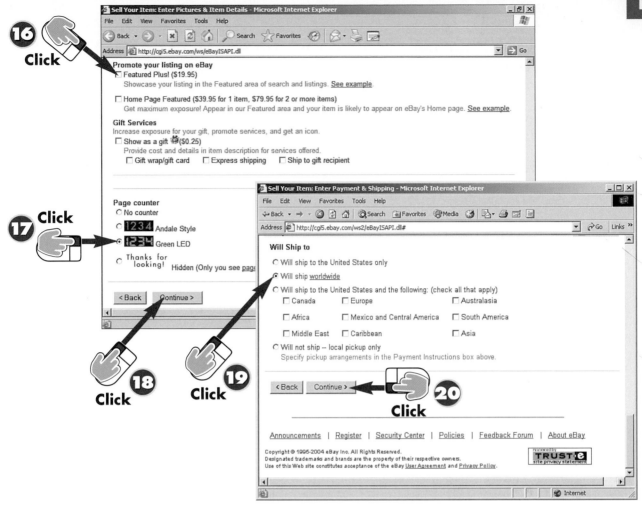

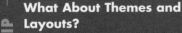

16 Select any item enhancements (for a cost) in the **Increase Your Item's Visibility** section.

17 Select a page counter style.

18 Click **Continue**.

19 Enter the appropriate payment and shipping information.

20 Click **Continue**.

See next page

TIP

What About Themes and Layouts?
Right now we're just creating a basic listing. See page 22 for a look at themes and page 24 for layouts.

TIP

The Shipping Calculator
In general, the shipping calculator is the best way to go.

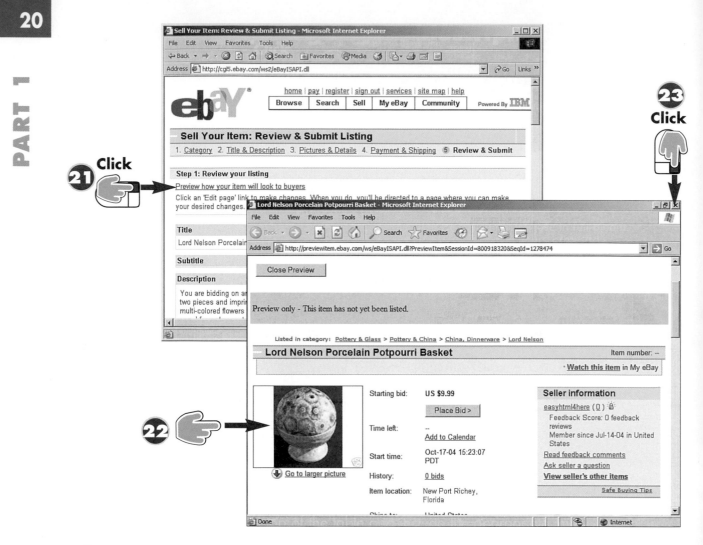

Click 21

Click 23

22

21 Click **Preview How Your Item Will Look to Buyers** to see the potential listing.

22 Verify all the information in the listing.

23 Click the **x** at the top of the window to close it.

HINT

Fancier Listings with HTML
The plain-text listing you see here is just that—plain. You can jazz up the listing (with different colors, fonts, and such) by adding HTML code to your item description. We'll talk more about this in Part 6, "Styling the Text."

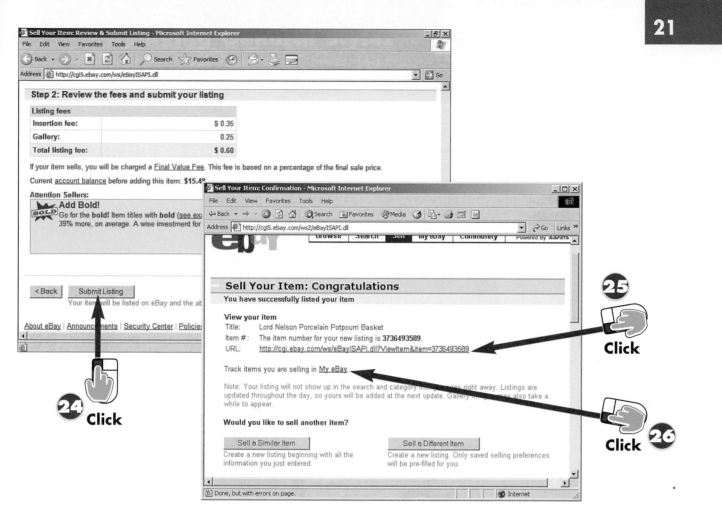

24 In the original window, scroll down to verify all your information and then click **Submit Listing**.

25 Click the **URL** link to see the actual listed item to verify that you haven't missed anything.

26 Click **My eBay** to track the items you're selling.

End

My eBay

TIP
You can track all your auction activity—selling, buying, and watching—on the My eBay page. It's a great auction management tool.

Editing an Auction

Start

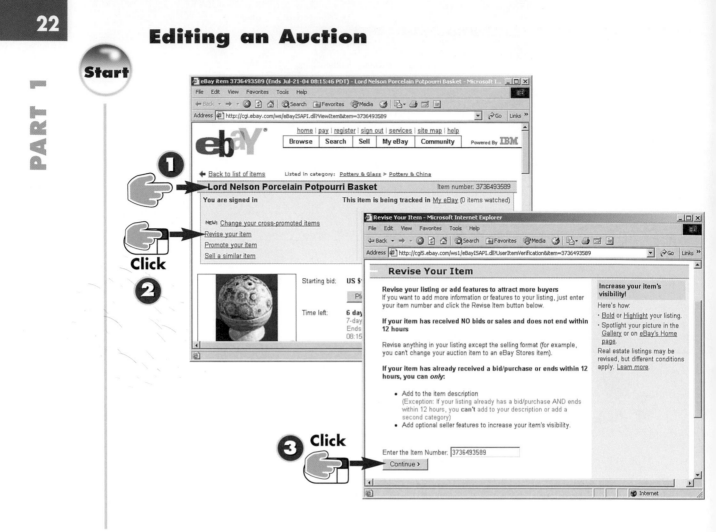

Click

Click

1. From within eBay, navigate to the item listing that you want to revise.

2. Click **Revise Your Item**.

3. The item number should already be entered in the text box, so click **Continue**.

INTRODUCTION

Everybody makes mistakes. If your item has no bids and has more than 12 hours to go, you can change anything about your listing. If it has a bid, you can't change anything, but you can add something to the description.

HINT

Too Late to Change

If your auction has less than 12 hours to go, you can't change anything about it, except to add features (such as bolding) or a second category. This prevents sellers from posting an item with false information and then correcting it after they have bids.

Click 4

Click 5

Click 6

4. Click the link for the section you want to revise. For example, to revise the description, click **Edit Description**.

5. Make any necessary changes and click **Save Changes**.

6. Verify the information once more and click **Submit Revisions**.

End

Make More Changes

TIP

You can change or amend your item listing as many times as you like—or as you need.

Choosing a Theme

Start

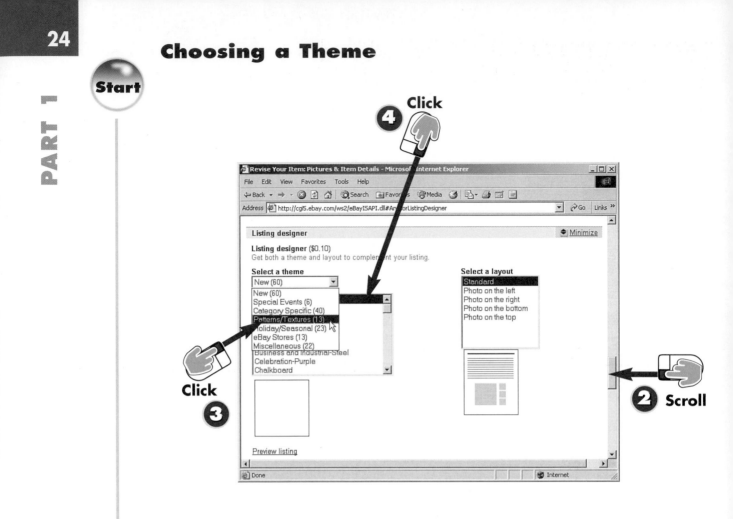

① Click

④ Click

③ Click

② Scroll

① Create a new auction, add your description, and then click **Continue**.

② On the Pictures & Item Details page, scroll down to the **Listing Designer** section.

③ Under **Select a Theme**, click the arrow and drag the mouse to select a group of themes.

④ Click a theme, such as **Green Squares**.

INTRODUCTION

The item we've posted is about as plain as you can get—just text, no extra images, no fancy design. The easiest way to upgrade the look is with eBay's Listing Designer, which lets you specify a predesigned theme and layout. It's not as versatile as using HTML, but it's a lot easier for the novice.

HINT

It's Not Free
It costs 10¢ per listing to use eBay's Listing Designer themes. (Using your own HTML is free!)

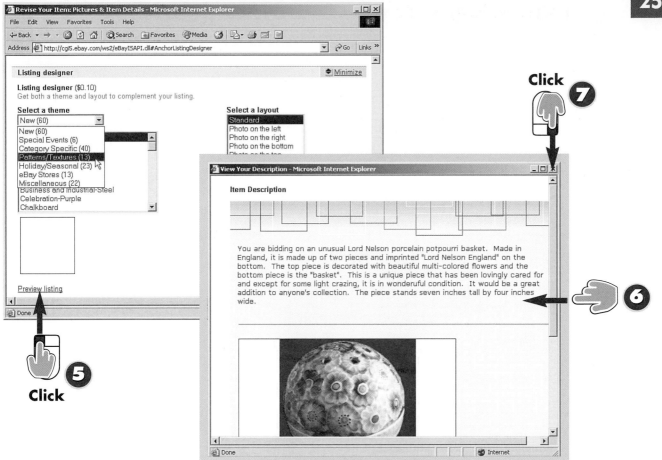

Click

Click

⑤ Click **Preview Listing** to see what it looks like.

⑥ Observe the way your description looks with the new theme.

⑦ Click the **x** to close the preview and continue adding or revising your auction.

End

Available Themes
eBay has dozens of themes available, and the Preview Listing link makes it easy to see whether any of them are to your liking.

Your Text Doesn't Change
Notice that your description and image are intact after you apply the new theme. The only things that change are the background behind both of them and a graphic at the top and bottom of this section.

Choosing a Layout

Start

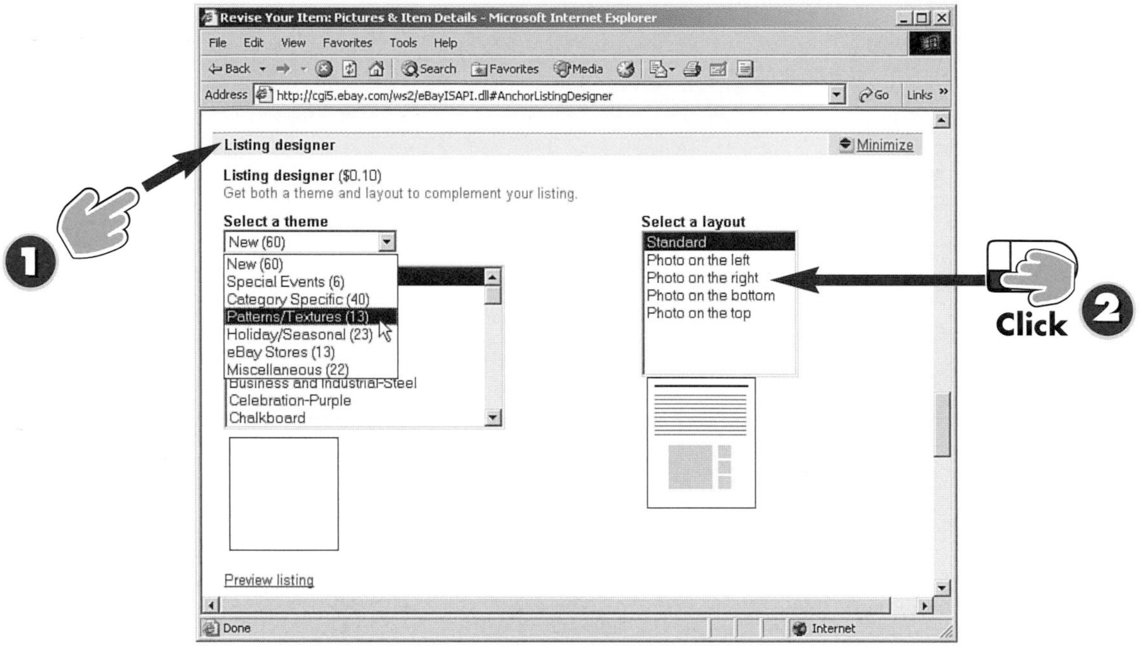

1 Create a new auction. On the Pictures & Item Details page, scroll down to the **Listing Designer** section.

2 Under Select a Layout, click one of the alternative layouts, such as **Photo on the Right**.

Unless you tell eBay otherwise, your auction appears with the description above your main image. When you use eBay's Listing Designer, however, you get several picture layout choices. For example, you can specify that the image appears to the right of the text.

HINT

Standard Layout
The Standard Layout puts a single large picture below the text of your item description.

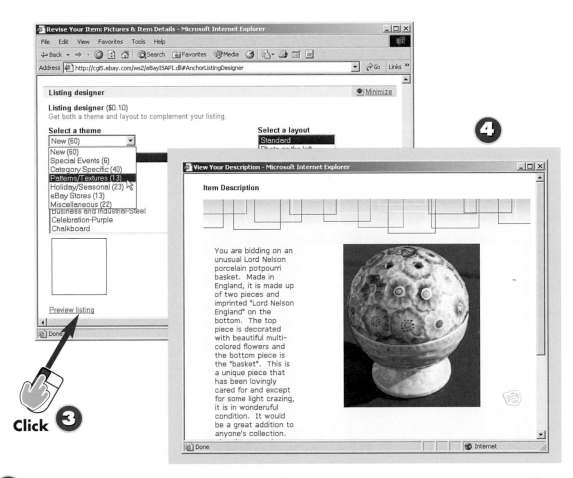

3 Click **Preview Listing** to see the results.

4 Find a layout that's to your liking and finish adding or revising your auction.

End

Creating a Simple Description

Now you know how to add a new listing to eBay and what you need to look out for, so let's talk about formatting. In this part, we'll look at simple formatting issues, such as line breaks, headlines, and bolding and italicizing text.

eBay is special in that it provides an easy way to put content on the Web, but aside from that, the description you add to your auction works just like any other web page. That means you control the look of your auctions through the use of HTML tags.

If you've never worked with it before, you might be intimidated by the thought of having to use HTML, but in this part you'll see that you don't have to be afraid of it. HTML is made up of simple *tags*, such as **<b>** for bold, and most of them are pretty straightforward. You're just *marking up* text to tell the browser what you want it to look like; you're not programming a computer.

Although there are plenty of them around, you don't need any special programs to write HTML. Instead, you just type it directly into the Item Description box eBay provides.

In this part, we'll create a complete, formatted listing by typing the description and adding HTML tags to control the formatting. In future parts, you'll learn more powerful HTML tags and other ways to control the appearance of your eBay pages.

Formatting Text with HTML Tags

Add formatting such as headlines and text treatment.

Add the basic text of the description.

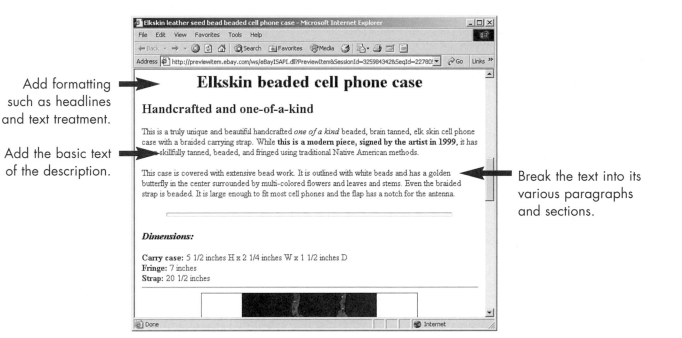

Break the text into its various paragraphs and sections.

Writing and Previewing Your Description

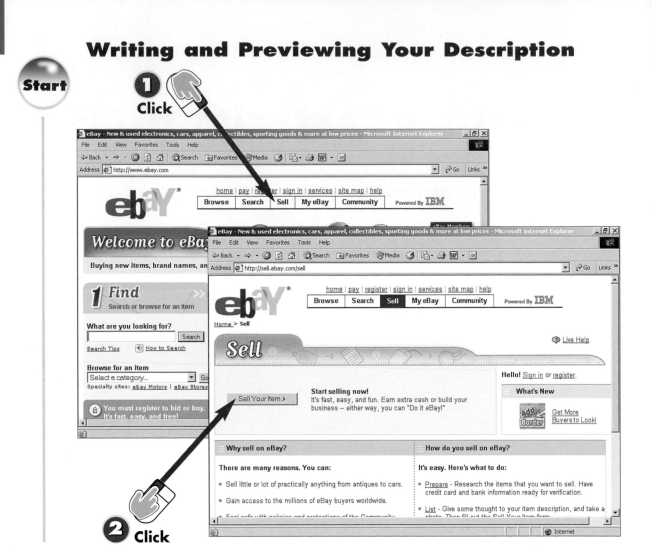

Start

① Click

② Click

① On the eBay home page, click **Sell**.

② Click **Sell Your Item**.

The first step in creating any description is to add the actual descriptive text. You can either type it directly into the description box or type it into a program such as Notepad and then copy and paste it into the description box, as we're doing here.

INTRODUCTION

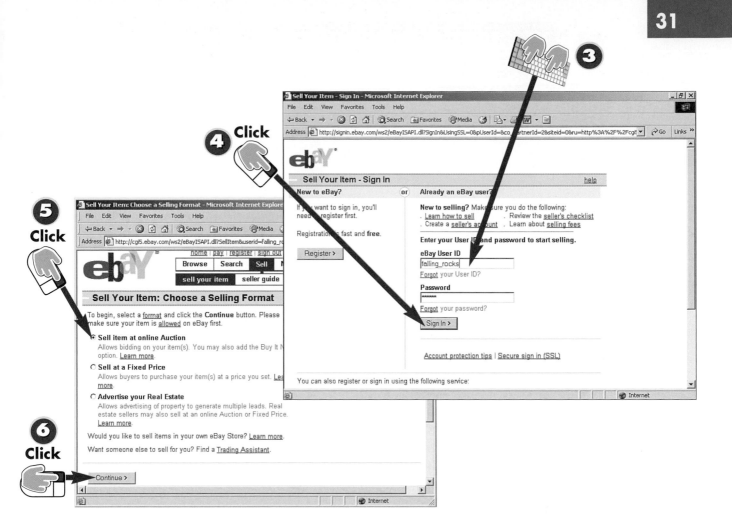

3 Enter your username and password.

4 Click **Sign In**.

5 Select **Sell Item at Online Auction**.

6 Click **Continue** to move on.

See next page

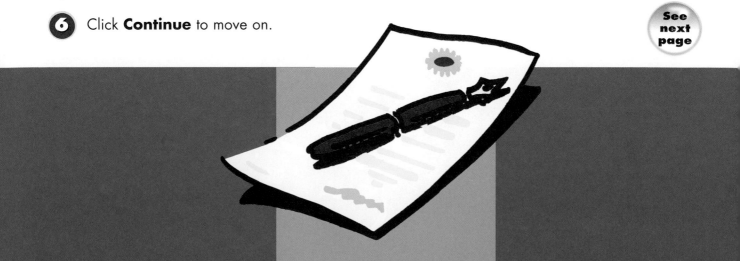

PART 2

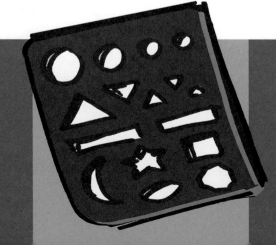

Sell Your Item step 1 of 5: Category - Microsoft Internet Explorer

File   Edit   View   Favorites   Tools   Help

Back • → • ⊗ ⊘ ⌂ | ⊘Search ⊞Favorites ⊛Media ⊛ | ⊞- ⊜ ⊠ ⊟

Address ⊞ http://cgi5.ebay.com/ws2/eBayISAPI.dll | ⊘Go Links »

○	Click to select ▼	
○	Antiques	Antique silver, furniture, ceramics, textiles & other décor
○	Art	Paintings, prints, photos, posters, folk art & sculpture
○	eBay Motors	Cars, boats, aircraft, motorcycles, parts & accessories
○	Books	Books, textbooks, collectible books, children's books, magazines & more
○	Business & Industrial	Equipment & supplies for Construction, Farm, Restaurant, Retail, Healthcare, Manufacturing, Office and much more
○	Cameras & Photo	Cameras, camcorders, lenses, memory, accessories & more
⊙	Clothing, Shoes & Accessories	Apparel, footwear & accessories
○	Coins	Coins, paper money & numismatic supplies
○	Collectibles	Decorative Collectibles, Coin-Op & Casino, Comics, Militaria, Advertising and more
○	Computers & Networking	Laptops, Desktop PCs, Apple/Macintosh, Printers, Monitors, Software, Wireless & Home Networking, Servers, Routers, Switches, Telephone Systems, Components
○	Consumer Electronics	Cell Phones, Home Theater, MP3 Players, TVs
○	Crafts	Craft supplies of all kinds: Needlearts, Scrapbooking, Painting, Ceramics, Woodworking and more!
○	Dolls & Bears	Barbies, figures, miniature houses & Cherished Teddies

Click

Insertion and most listing upgrade fees will be doubled. Final Value fees will not be doubled. Learn more.

Click to select ▼

Second category # [   ]

< Back   Continue >

Click

8

Announcements | Register | Security Center | Policies | Feedback Forum | About eBay

Copyright © 1995-2004 eBay Inc. All Rights Reserved.
Designated trademarks and brands are the property of their respective owners.
Use of this Web site constitutes acceptance of the eBay User Agreement and
Privacy Policy.

TRUSTe
site privacy statement

Internet

7 Select a main category for your listing.

8 Click **Continue**.

9 Click the appropriate subcategory. For example, we're going to list a hand-beaded cell phone case, so I'll select **Women's Accessories, Handbags: Handbags, Bags**.

10 Click **Continue**.

11 Type the title, such as **Elkskin leather seed bead beaded cell phone case**, in the **Item Title** field.

See next page

TIP

Title Length
eBay limits the number of characters you can use in a title. At the time of this writing, that limit is 55 for the main eBay site and 45 for eBay UK.

Click 12

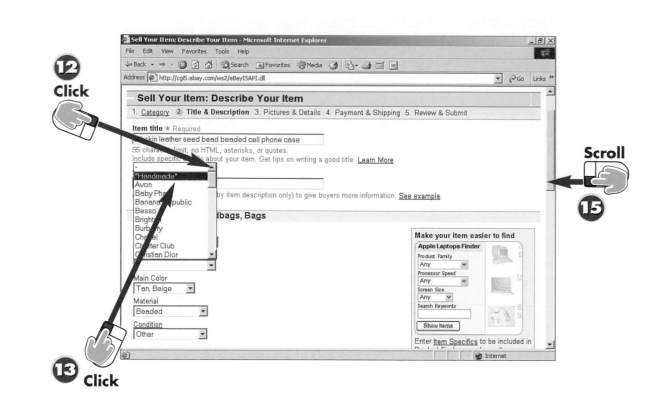

Scroll 15

13 **Click**

12 If your category includes **Item Specifics**, click the arrow next to one of the specifics.

13 Click the appropriate value.

14 Repeat steps 13 and 14 for each **Item Specific**.

15 Scroll down to the **Item Description** field.

16 Click

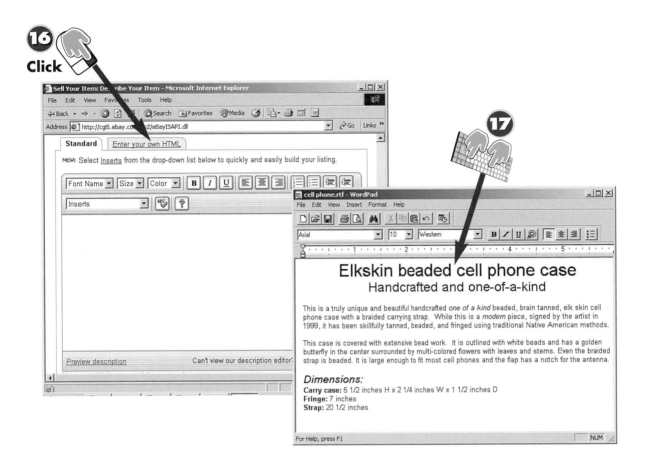

17

16 If the standard editor is showing—you can tell because you see a toolbar with formatting options—click **Enter Your Own HTML** to get the HTML editor.

17 Type the description, complete with desired line breaks, into a text editor such as WordPad or Notepad.

See next page

Standard Versus HTML
The Standard option might not appear at all if you are behind a firewall or are using a browser other than Microsoft Internet Explorer.

TIP

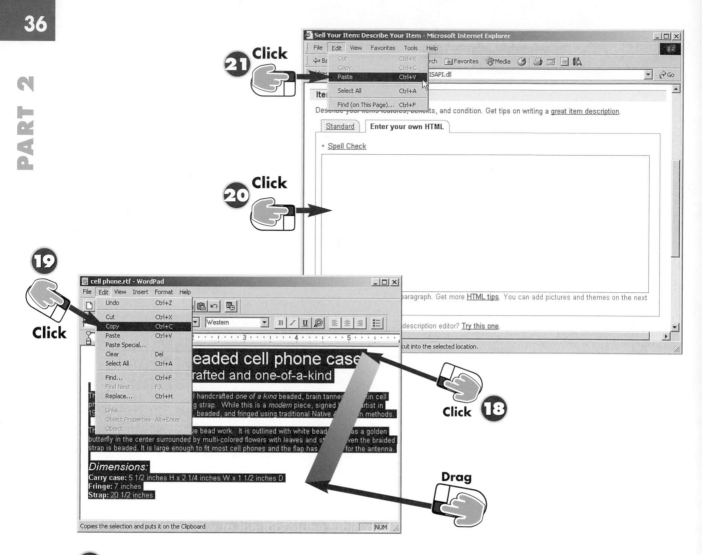

18 Click and drag the mouse to select all the text.

19 Click **Edit**, **Copy** to copy the text to the clipboard.

20 Click within the **Item Description** field in the browser.

21 Click **Edit**, **Paste** to add the text to the description.

TIP

Keyboard Shortcuts
You can also press **Ctrl+A** to select all the text, **Ctrl+C** to copy it, and **Ctrl+V** to paste it.

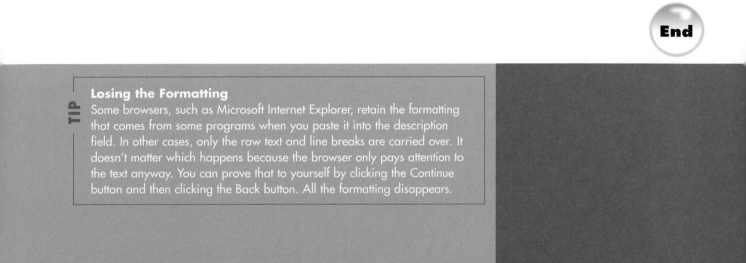

22 Click **Preview Description** to see the initial results.

23 Notice that the description in the Preview window is unformatted. We'll make it more presentable with HTML soon.

End

Creating a Heading

Start

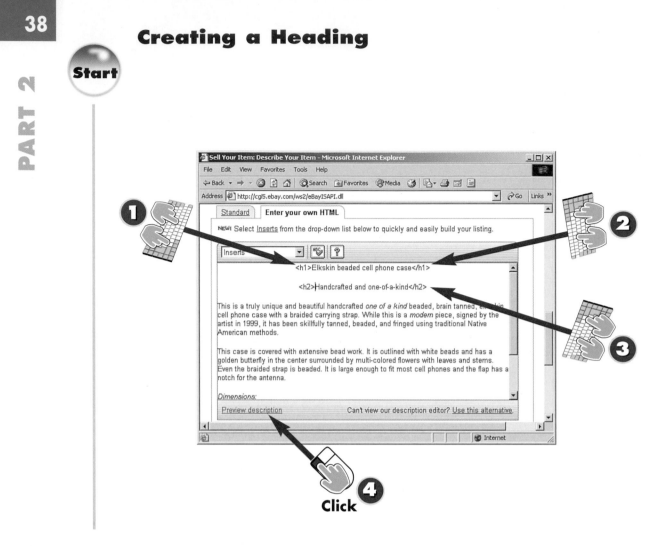

Click ④

① To create a heading, add the open heading tag **<h1>** before the heading. The brackets (**<>**) tell the browser that this is a tag, or an instruction.

② Add the close heading tag **</h1>** after the heading. The slash (**/**) tells the browser that this is a close tag.

③ Create the second heading by adding **<h2>** at the beginning and **</h2>** at the end of the text.

④ Click **Preview Description** to see the results.

INTRODUCTION

You've probably noticed that regardless of the white space or other formatting in the description, when you preview the description, all the text is shown in a single blob. Now we'll work on the appearance of the text, beginning with headings. We do that by adding HTML tags to the text.

TIP

What Is This "Tag" Stuff?
The browser uses a system of *tags* to tell it what to do with the text on the page. By adding these HTML tags, such as **<h1> </h1>** and **<h2></h2>**, you're telling the browser the text should be treated as a heading, or a paragraph, or bold.

TIP

Is That All There Is to HTML?
Simply put, yes. HTML consists almost entirely of adding tags to mark up your text. After you know which tags do what, you can do virtually anything on the page.

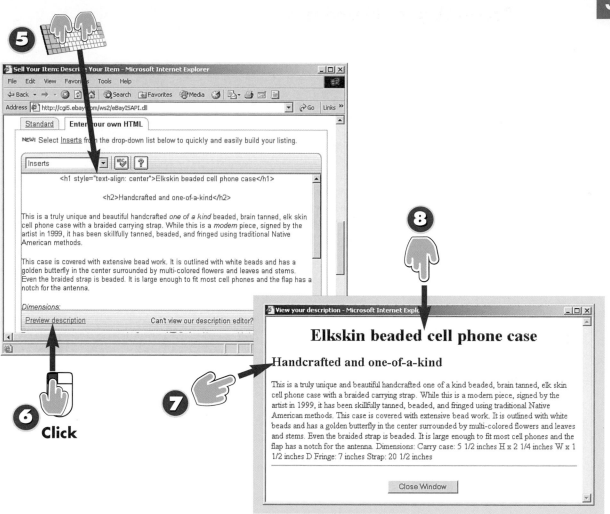

5 To center the headings, add a style attribute so the open heading tag reads **<h1 style="text-align: center">**.

6 Click **Preview Description** to see the results.

7 Notice that the **<h1></h1>** tags have created a large, bold heading and that the **<h2></h2>** tags have created a smaller, but still large, heading.

8 Notice that the heading to which you added the **style** attribute is now centered in the window.

End

Structure Versus Presentation

TIP

You could simply break the heading out into a block and adjust its look, but it's important to add meaning to the text through structural tags such as headings so search engines can tell what's important.

Heading Size and Importance

TIP

HTML defines six sizes of headers, **h1**–**h6**, with **h1** being the most important (and largest) and **h6** being the least important (and smallest).

Using Line Breaks

Start

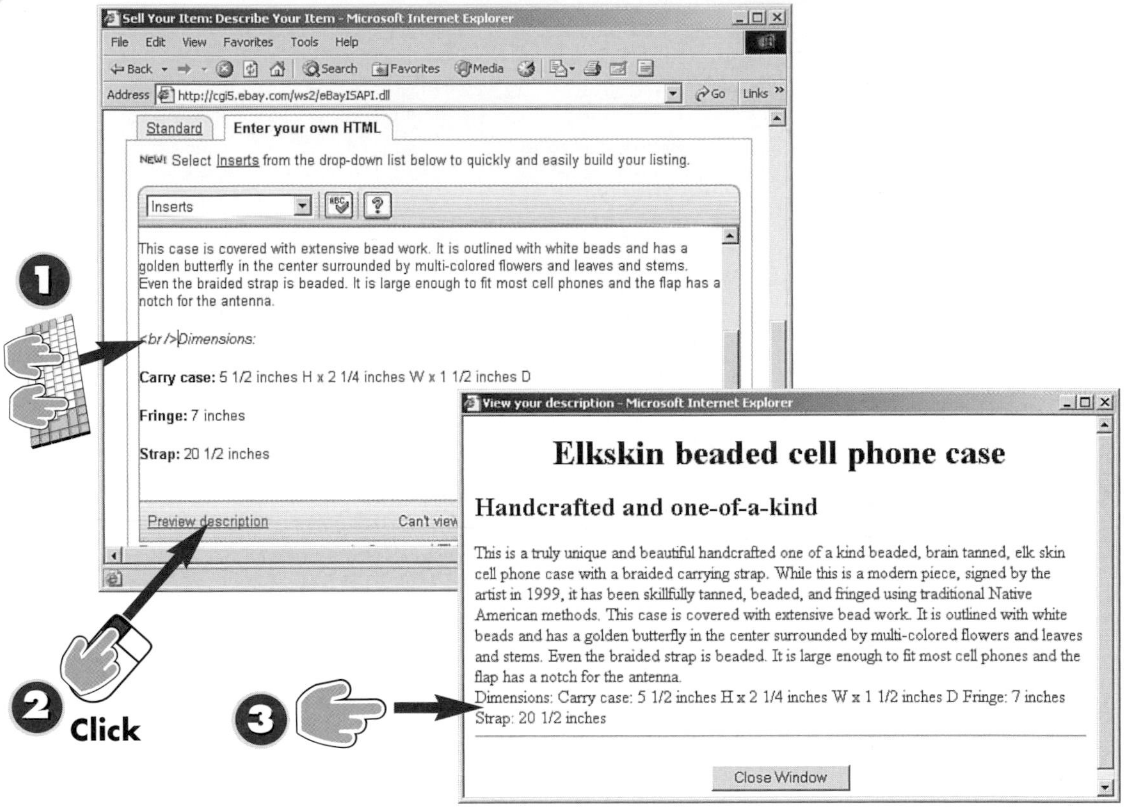

1. Add a break tag **
** before the **Dimensions** text.
2. Click **Preview Description** to see the results.
3. Notice that the dimensions are now on their own line.

INTRODUCTION

By now you've noticed that the browser ignores any white space (such as line breaks or extra spaces) in the description. That doesn't mean you can't tell it to add some, though. In this case, we'll add line breaks manually using the line break tag **
**.

TIP

Open Tags and Close Tags

Our first example had an open tag (**<h1>**) and a close tag (**</h1>**). Old-style HTML included several elements that didn't have a close tag, such as **
**. However, newer versions require you to include a shortcut version of the close tag by adding a space and slash to the open tag, as in **
**.

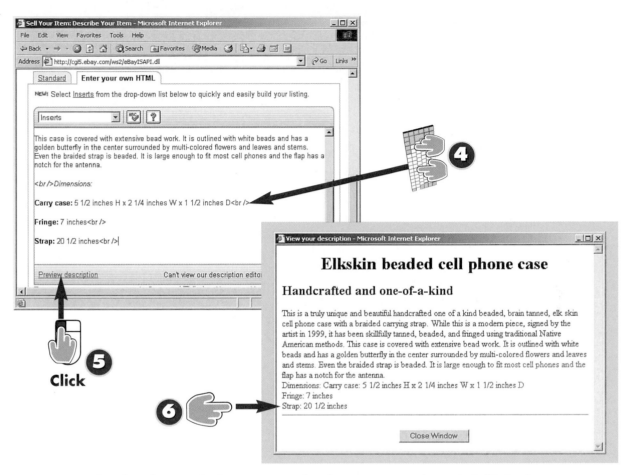

Click

4 Type **
** after each dimension in the description, such as **1 1/2 inches D
**.

5 Click **Preview Description** to see the results.

6 Notice that each break tag (**
**) forces the browser to start a new line for the text.

End

TIP

What's the / for?
Today every element must have an open tag and close tag. Some browsers, though, are used to the old-style **
** tag and are confused by **
</br>**, so you must use the **
** shorthand instead. Don't forget the space after the **br**; it prevents a problem in older browsers.

Creating Paragraphs

Start

1 Add an open paragraph tag **<p>** at the start of the first paragraph and a close paragraph tag **</p>** at the end.

2 In the same way, add a **<p>** at the beginning of the second paragraph and a **</p>** at the end.

3 Click **Preview Description** to see the results.

4 Notice that **<p></p>** tag automatically creates space between paragraphs.

End

One of the most common chunks of text is the paragraph. Although you could certainly use line breaks to create the space between them, it's better to create paragraphs because it gives you the option to style the text later, as you'll see in Part 6, "Styling the Text." You'll create paragraphs now.

TIP

Paragraph Spacing
By default, paragraphs have two line breaks between them. You can control this spacing with styles, as you'll see in Part 6.

Creating Separator Lines

Start

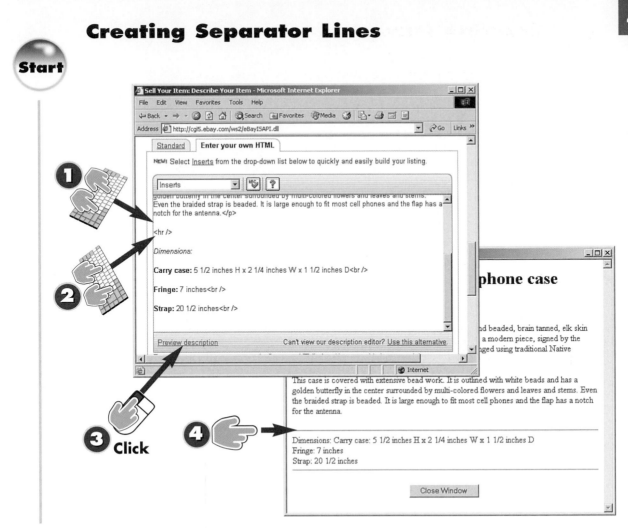

1 Remove the break tag (**
**) before the dimensions.

2 Add a horizontal rule **<hr />** before the dimensions in the description.

3 Click **Preview Description** to see the results.

4 Notice that the **<hr />** tag has created a horizontal line on a line all by itself.

See next page

INTRODUCTION

Often you want to visually separate different areas of your content. You can use a number of ways to create that separation, but the easiest is also one of the oldest: the horizontal rule, which creates a line on the page. Like the line break tag, the horizontal rule is a single tag, **<hr />**.

TIP

Horizontal Rules and Line Breaks
Like the paragraph and heading elements, the horizontal rule is a *block* element, which means the browser automatically gives it its own line. If you add a line break tag on either side of the rule, it produces extra space around the rule.

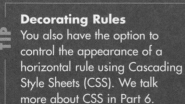

5 Adjust the width of the line so that it's always 85% of the available width by adding a style attribute, as in **<hr style="width: 85%" />**.

6 Adjust the height of the line so that it is 7 pixels high by adding the height to the style, as in **<hr style="width: 85%; height: 7px;" />**.

7 Click **Preview Description** to see the results.

TIP

Decorating Rules
You also have the option to control the appearance of a horizontal rule using Cascading Style Sheets (CSS). We talk more about CSS in Part 6.

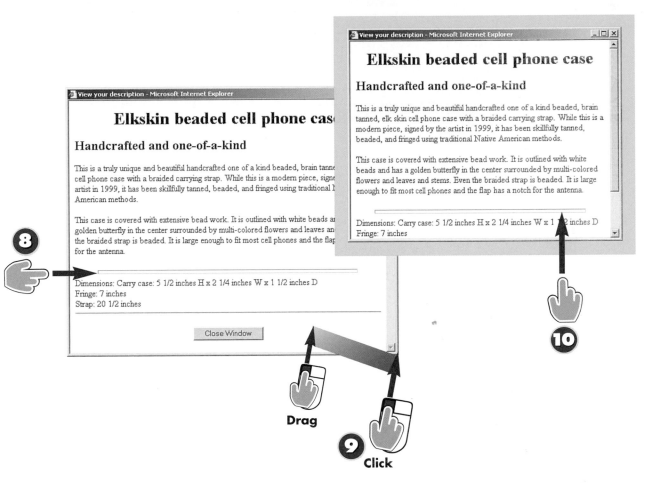

Drag

Click

8 Notice that the line now takes up only part of the window, and that it's now thicker than it was before.

9 Click and drag the lower-right corner of the window to resize it.

10 Notice that, as you adjust the size of the window, the line adjusts to stay at 85% of the window size.

End

TIP

Sizes
In this example, we looked at two ways to specify size: percentage and pixels. In Part 6, we'll look at all the units you can use to specify the size of an item on the page.

Basic Text Formatting

Start

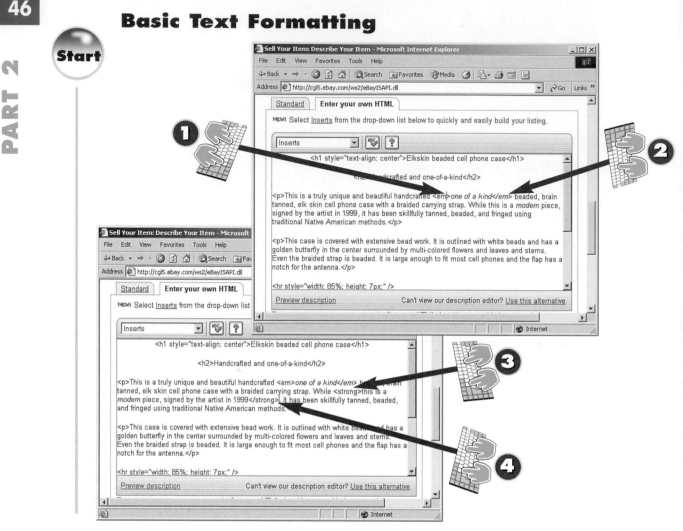

1 Add emphasis to the unique nature of the item by italicizing part of the description. Add the open emphasis tag, **<em>**, before the phrase **one of a kind**.

2 Add the close emphasis tag, **</em>**, after the phrase **one of a kind**.

3 Make sure the buyer knows this is not a historical item by adding the open **<strong>** tag before the words **this is**.

4 Add the **</strong>** tag after the words, **in 1999**.

INTRODUCTION

Now you can start formatting the text. In this part, we look at two methods of italicizing and bolding text. If you want to emphasize the importance of the text, you use the **<strong>** and **<em>**, or emphasis, tags. If you simply want to control the look of the text, you use the **<b>**, or bold tag, and **<i>**, or italics tag. Let's see how that works.

TIP

When Should I Use Which?
Use the structural tags, **<strong></strong>** and **<em></em>**, when you're making something bold or italic because it's important information. Use the presentational tags, **<b></b>** and **<i></i>**, when you're just making the text look pretty.

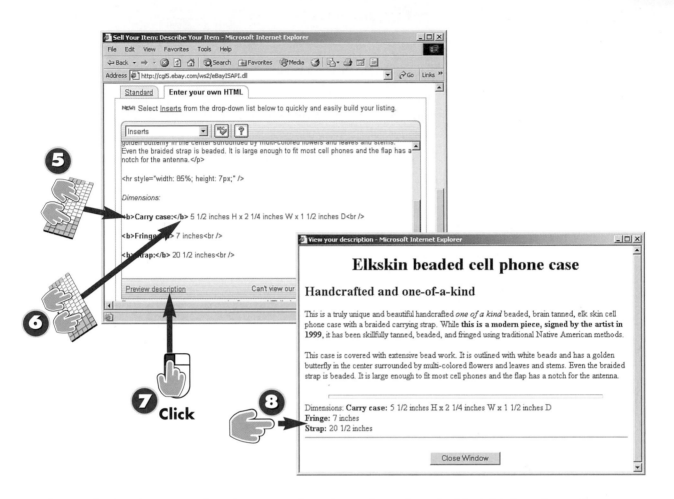

5 Help the dimension headings stand out by making them bold. Add the **<b>** tag before the **Carry case:**, **Fringe:**, and **Strap:** text.

6 Add the **</b>** text after the **Carry case:**, **Fringe:**, and **Strap:** text.

7 Click **Preview Description** to see the results.

8 Notice that the **<strong></strong>** and the **<b></b>** tags made the text bold and the **<em></em>** and the **<i></i>** tags made the text italic.

See next page

Inline Design Elements
TIP
Unlike all the elements we've dealt with so far, these are inline tags, which means the browser keeps them in the flow of content rather than breaking them out onto a separate line.

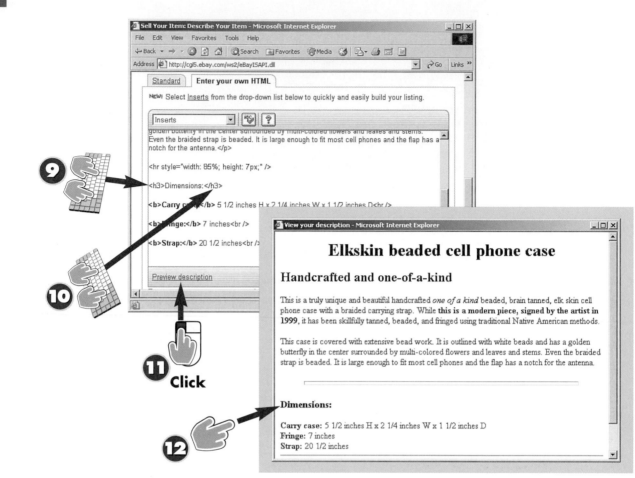

 Click

9 Make the dimensions text into a level 3 heading by adding the **<h3>** tag before the **Dimensions** text.

10 Add the **</h3>** tag after the **Dimensions** text.

11 Click **Preview Description** to see the results.

12 Notice that the **Dimensions:** text is now on its own line and is slightly larger and bolder than normal text.

Don't Abuse Your Headings

TIP

Heading tags are an easy way to make text stand out because they are automatically set apart from the rest of the text, but only use them for actual headings. If you have other information to emphasize, use styles, as discussed in Part 6.

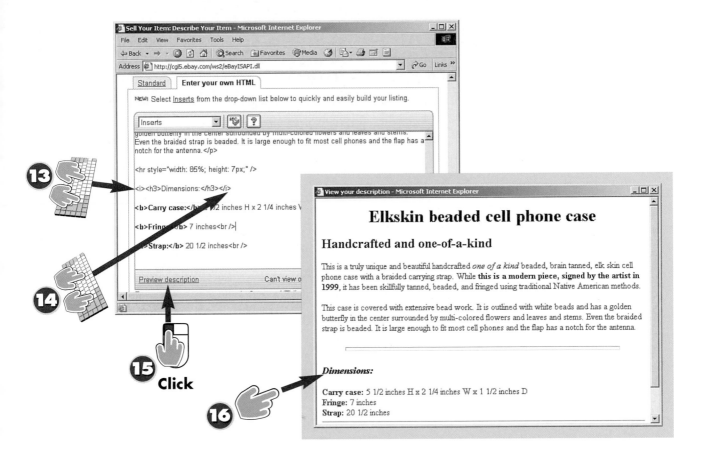

13 Italicize the new heading. Add a **<i>** tag before the **<h3>** tag.

14 Add the **</i>** tag after the **</h3>** tag.

15 Click **Preview Description** to see the results.

16 Notice that the text now has the effect of both tags. It's still bold text set apart from the rest of the content, but it's also italic.

End

Nesting Elements

You can apply just about any combination of tags to a single block of text, but you must make sure they're nested properly, with the inside tag both starting and ending inside the outside tag. For example, the code on this page, **<h3>Dimensions</h3>** is correct. **<h3>Dimensions</h3>** would be incorrect and could cause problems with some browsers.

Adding Pictures

On eBay, auction item photos serve several purposes. First, they provide the buyer a look at the goods. This way, the buyer can decide whether that knick-knack will look good on the shelf next to the glass swan or whether that comic book really is in "very fine" condition.

Photos also serve to protect you as a seller. After all, if there's no photo, it's easy to claim that you misrepresented the product, particularly if it's used. Photos give you a chance to show off both the features of the item and any defects—dents, scratches, holes, and so on. Sellers often try to hide these defects in an auction, but it comes back to haunt them when the buyer accuses them of misrepresentation, or worse, fraud. Also, when buyers can see the defects, they know they're not going to get any surprises.

On the other hand, photos can hurt you more than help you if they're unflattering to the item, so in this part we look at how to get the best photos for your auction. You don't need to be a professional photographer; you just need to consider factors such as lighting and backgrounds and know how to manipulate your photos.

As far as the camera itself, you can use something as simple as a drugstore disposable camera, but if you're serious about getting good photos, you should invest in a digital camera. You'll get virtually instant feedback as to the quality of the photo so you can reshoot if necessary, and you can easily make adjustments to the photo on your computer. This chapter examines all these issues, as well as adding the image to your auction.

Photos of Your Auction Item Are a Must

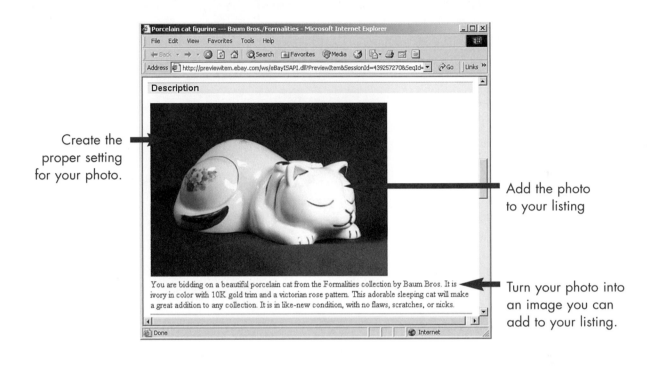

Create the proper setting for your photo.

Add the photo to your listing

Turn your photo into an image you can add to your listing.

Setting Up for Photos

Start

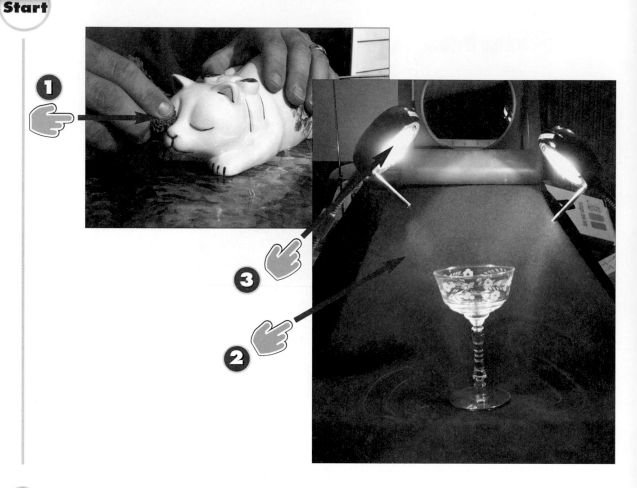

1 Get the item ready for sale, performing any necessary cleaning and so on.

2 Set up an appropriate background for the item. Solid colors are best.

3 Set up your primary lighting. Indirect sunlight is best, or use tungsten or halogen lights or household bulbs that filter out yellow light.

You don't need a lot of complicated equipment to take good pictures for your auctions. All you need is a decent camera and the proper environment. Investing in a digital camera is wise; you'll get instant feedback and save money on photo processing and film. Lighting can be as simple as a desk lamp or window.

TIP

Choosing a Background

The color of your background is entirely up to you, but be sure to pick one that enhances the item rather than distracting from it. Some people swear by white, but others feel it makes the item look washed out. I prefer a dark background for lighter items.

TIP

Curves, Not Corners

If possible, create a background that curves up around the item to avoid a sharp corner. Use seamless paper, poster board, or even a bed sheet.

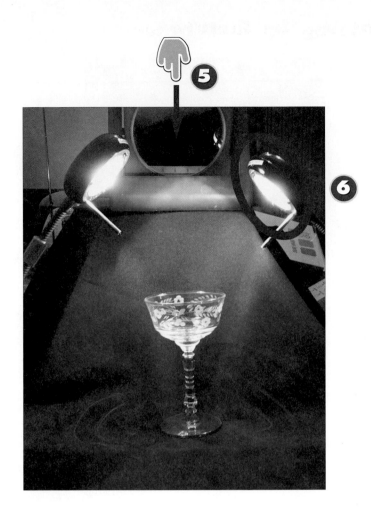

4 Diffuse any direct light by filtering it through a translucent material such as white plastic or tracing paper.

5 Add a hair light, a second source intended to make the item stand out from the background, with a reflector (such as a mirror) placed high and behind the item.

6 Soften shadows by adding a second light source opposite the first.

End

Softening Shadows
Your second light source can be as simple as a reflector made of a piece of white poster board or as complex as a second diffused light, farther away from the item than the primary light.

Lighting Glass or Other Clear Items
In some cases, you'll find it easier to light glass and other translucent items by bouncing the light off the background or creating a translucent background and lighting the item from behind and underneath, rather than lighting it directly.

Taking the Picture

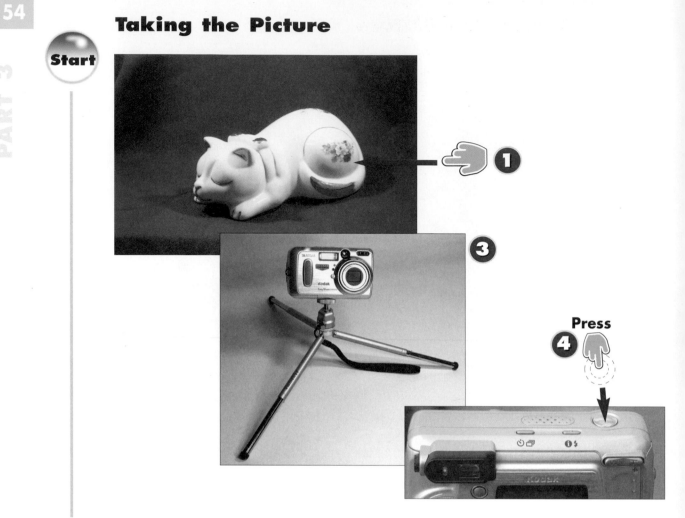

Start

Press

 Pose the item. Most items look best at a 45° angle to the camera, as though they were facing the primary light source.

 Position the camera so the item fills most of the frame.

③ Set the camera on a tripod, if possible, to prevent movement when you squeeze the shutter.

④ Press the button to take the picture.

End

INTRODUCTION

Your item is ready, and you've set up your background and all of your lighting. Now it's time to actually take the photo. A sharp, clear photo can only help you because it gives the buyer confidence that you're not trying to hide anything.

TIP

Stay Sharp
Even if you can't directly control the focus, most cameras have settings for close, midrange, and far away objects. If necessary, move the camera so the image is sharp and zoom in on the item. You can remove extra background later.

TIP

Covering All the Angles
Take pictures of the different sides, top, and bottom of your item, so the buyer can feel like she has seen all of it. Be sure to get photos of any defects so you can't be accused of misrepresentation later.

Saving the Picture

Start

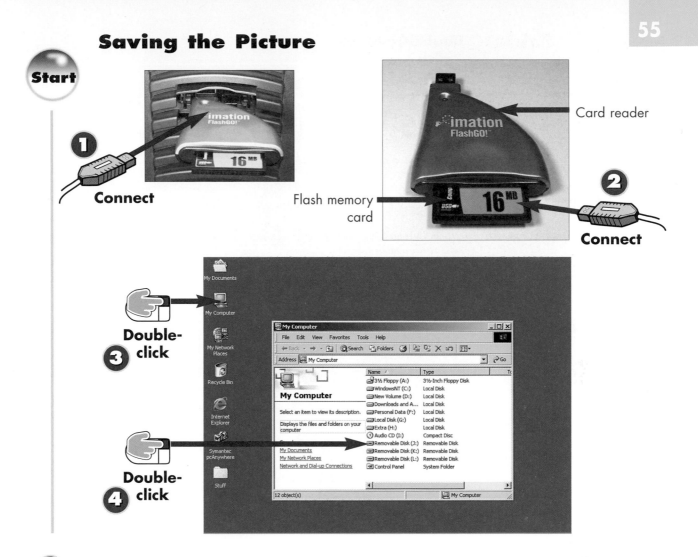

① **Connect**

Card reader

Flash memory card

② **Connect**

③ **Double-click**

④ **Double-click**

① Following the manufacturer's directions, install the card reader.

② Follow the instructions on your camera to remove its memory card and insert it into the card reader.

③ Double-click the **My Computer** icon.

④ Double-click the card reader as though it were another drive on your computer. (Your specific instructions might vary; check the instructions for your card reader.)

See next page

INTRODUCTION

You've taken your photos, and you're about to discover the advantage of a digital camera because you can skip processing and move right on to the next step: saving your pictures. How you do this depends greatly on the camera; we'll assume you're using a card reader.

TIP

Haste Makes Waste
Card readers are a lot like floppy disks; it takes time to save data to them. Make sure your camera is finished saving before you remove the card; otherwise, your photo will be gone forever.

TIP

Card Readers
Card readers are generally inexpensive and more convenient than having to connect your camera to the computer. Be sure you get one that works with your type of memory card, or get a multi-card reader that works with all three of the most common types.

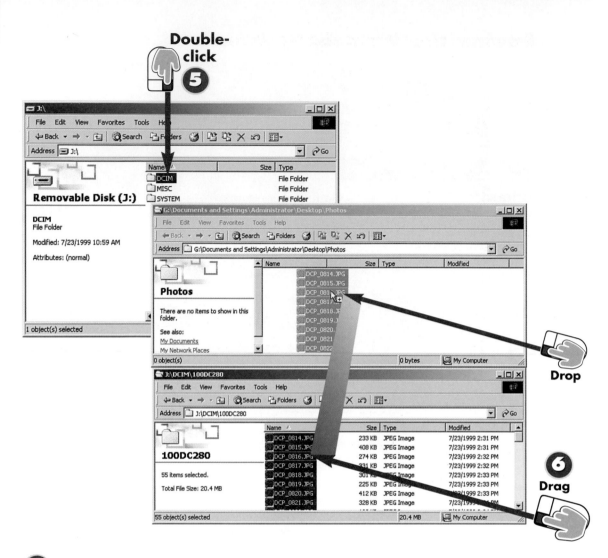

5 Double-click folders within the card reader until you get to the actual photo file(s).

6 Drag and drop the file to your hard drive.

End

Which Files to Copy?

If you take a lot of photos, you'll find that the files start to take up enormous amounts of drive space. You can use Windows's preview capability to limit the files you actually copy off the card, but for safety's sake, you should copy all the files and then delete those you're sure you won't need after you've opened all of them in your graphics program.

Removing Extra Background

Start

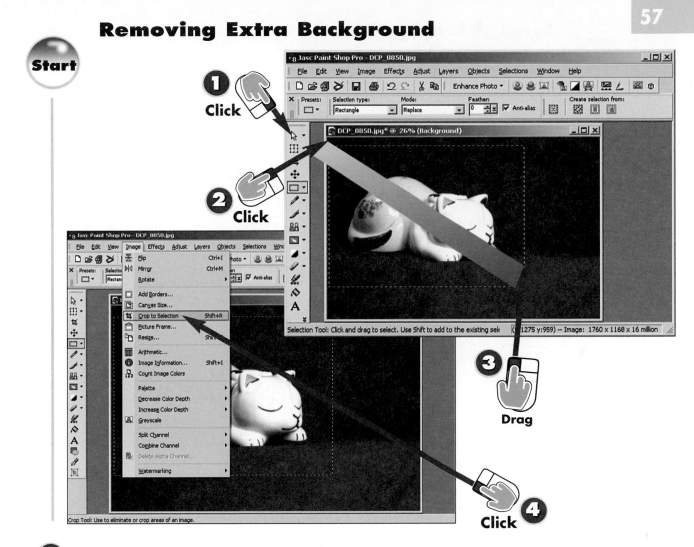

Click

Click

Drag

Click

1 In Paint Shop Pro, click the selection tool.

2 Click the upper-left corner of the area you want to keep.

3 Drag the cursor to the lower-right corner of the area you want to keep.

4 Crop the photo. In Paint Shop Pro, select **Image**, **Crop to Selection**.

End

INTRODUCTION

When you display your item, you should include as much detail as possible about the item itself. A lot of background around it in the photo is a waste. The first step is to *crop* the image. You have several choices of software. This part assumes you are using Paint Shop Pro, from http://www.jasc.com.

Other Software Programs
To see how to perform this and other tasks in a program such as the freely downloadable Irfanview (http://www.irfanview.com), check out my website at http://www.nicholaschase.com/easyhtml4ebay/photoinstructions.html.

Uniform Sizes
Multiple photos look better if they're the same size, so crop them to the same aspect ratio. For example, an image that's 400 pixels wide and 300 pixels high has an aspect ratio of 4:3. So does one that's 1200 pixels wide and 900 pixels wide.

Straightening the Photo

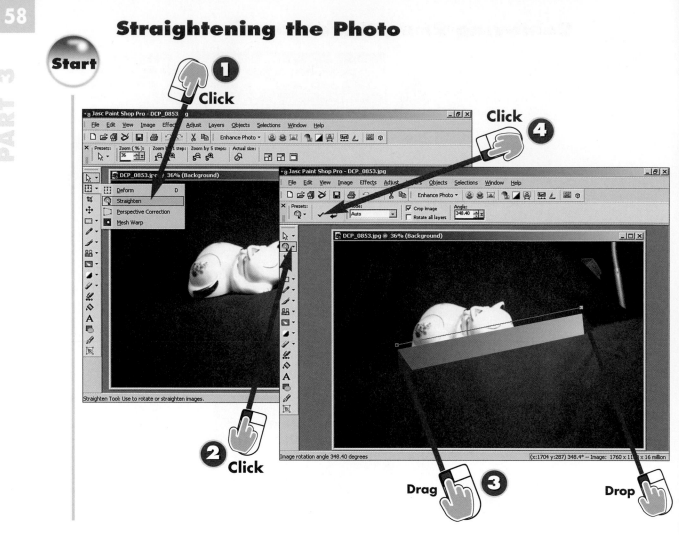

Start

Click ①

Click ④

Click ②

Drag ③

Drop

① In Paint Shop Pro, click the arrow next to the **Deform** button and select **Straighten**.

② Select **Crop Image**.

③ Click and drag the horizontal line to straighten the photo.

④ Click the **Apply** check mark.

End

When you don't have a tripod, it's common to take pictures that are just a bit (or perhaps more than a bit) crooked. Fortunately, straightening a crooked photo is easy, so users need never know the difference.

TIP

Leveling the Photo
To straighten a photo accurately in Paint Shop Pro, move the horizontal line so that it's parallel to the natural horizon line of the photo.

TIP

Cleaning Up After Rotation
If the image wasn't automatically cropped, you'll wind up with areas outside the actual photo after rotation. Follow the directions on page 57 to crop the image and remove them.

Color-correcting the Photo

Start

Click ① Click ②

Click ④

Drag ③

① In Paint Shop Pro, click **Enhance Photo**.

② Select **Automatic Color Balance**.

③ Click the slider and drag it to **Sunlight**. Adjust the slider as you prefer.

④ Click **OK**.

See next page

INTRODUCTION

Most of us aren't professional photographers, but fortunately we can correct a lot of lighting and other problems by adjusting the color of the photo after we've taken it. Even more fortunately, some graphics programs take care of it for us.

Seeing the Big Picture

Use the magnifying glass with the minus sign (–) in it to zoom out and see more of the photo in the previews.

Taking Shortcuts

If you don't care about controlling each of these steps, Paint Shop Pro provides the One Step Photo Fix option, which makes a best guess for each of these steps without requiring your intervention.

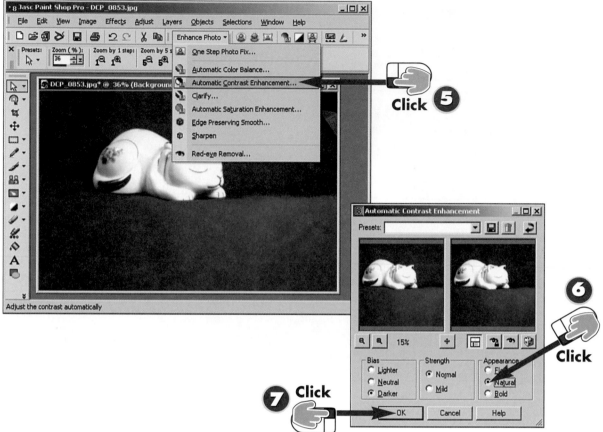

Click **5**

6

Click

7 Click

5 Click **Enhance Photo** and select **Automatic Contrast Enhancement**.

6 Adjust the appearance as necessary.

7 Click **OK**.

End

Accuracy, Accuracy, Accuracy
While you do want to make the item look nice, make sure the photo is still an accurate representation of what it actually looks like. If that plastic transistor radio has faded from black to gray, be sure you don't adjust out the fading just because it looks nicer.

Not All Monitors Are Created Equal
Computer monitors don't always provide true color; what looks red on your screen might look orange on almost everyone else's. If you can't get your monitor calibrated, have a friend check out the image to ensure that it looks as you expect it to before you add it.

Removing Photo Backgrounds

Start

Click ①

Click ③

② **Drag & drop**

① In Paint Shop Pro, click the arrow next to the rectangular selection tool and select **Freehand Selection**.

② Very carefully draw a selection around the item, excluding the background.

③ Click **Selections** and select **Invert** to select the background rather than the item.

④ Press the **Delete** key to remove the background.

End

INTRODUCTION

In some cases, you just don't have the option of creating a neutral background and getting a clear photo of an item. Maybe it's too big, or you were in a hurry, or you just didn't have the materials at hand. You can remove a background from an image after you've taken the photo with the appropriate image editing software.

TIP

Making It Easy
If the background is a solid color, most graphics programs enable you to select all the adjacent pixels of that color. This almost always gives a better result than selecting the item manually, but you might have to clean up extra pixels.

TIP

Do I Have to Remove the Background?
Just because you can remove the background doesn't mean you have to. In many cases, the background can enhance the image, providing a sense of scale or ambience.

Resizing the Photo

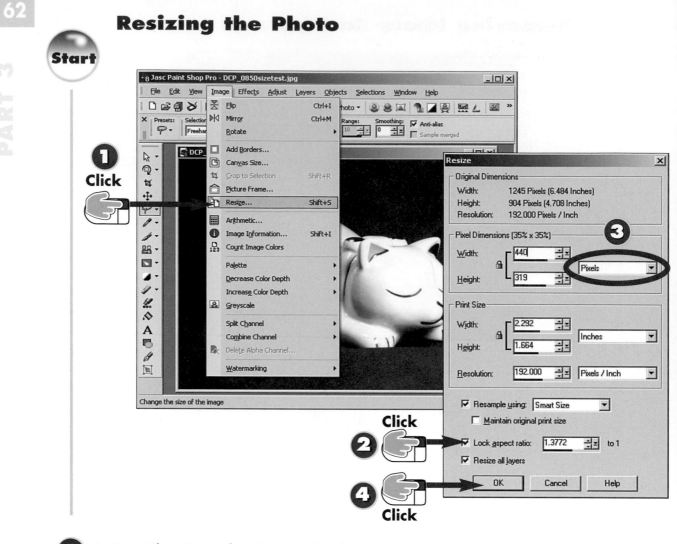

1 **Click**

2 **Click**

3

4 **Click**

① In Paint Shop Pro, select **Image**, **Resize**.

② Make sure **Lock Aspect Ratio** is checked.

③ Set the new height or width and make sure that the units are set to **Pixels**.

④ Click **OK**.

Start

End

Your digital camera puts out very large images, so the first step in cutting them down to something manageable is to resize them to the number of pixels you'll actually be displaying on the page. eBay suggests 440 pixels wide by 330 pixels high, but depending on what you'll use the photo for, you might have other sizes in mind.

Print Size Versus Web Size

Image size on the web is different from image size in print. The browser doesn't care what the pixels per inch setting on the image is; it just displays every pixel.

Web Resolution

The actual size your photo appears on a user's screen depends on how big her monitor is and the resolution she has set. A good rule of thumb is to assume your photos will appear at 96 pixels/inch.

Balancing Image Quality and File Size: JPEG Files

Start

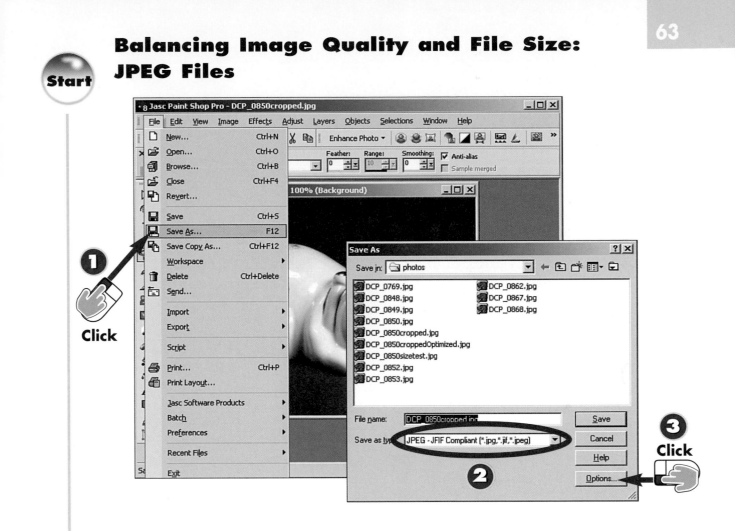

① Click

Click

②

③ Click

① With the JPEG file open, select **File**, **Save As**.

② In the **Save As Type** menu, select **JPEG**.

③ Click **Options**.

See next page

INTRODUCTION

Saving a picture for the Web isn't as simple as it seems. In addition to making your photos look good, you need to ensure they are in the smallest file possible because the larger your file, the longer it takes your auctions to load. You can make your files smaller without sacrificing (too much) quality.

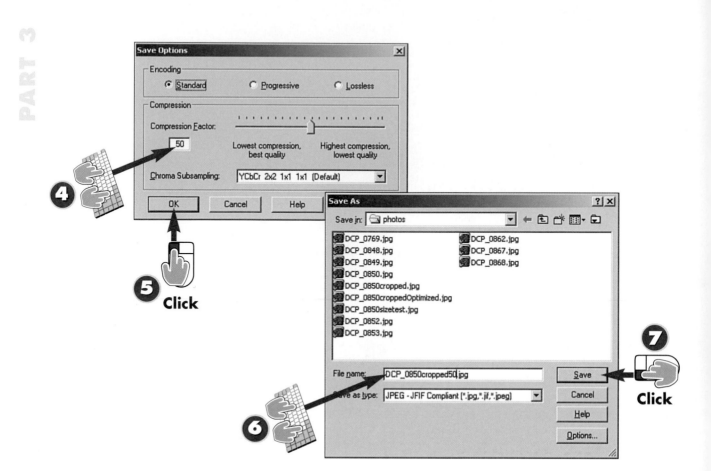

Click

4 Set the **Compression Factor** to **50**.

5 Click **OK**.

6 Type in a new filename to save your photo as a new file while keeping the original. This step is crucial.

7 Click **Save**.

Optimizing Your Images
Paint Shop Pro also includes an optimizer that finds the smallest undistorted image. To use it, click **Options**, **Run Optimizer**, **OK**.

Lossless Versus Lossy
JPEG is what's known as a *lossy* format. Every time you open the file and resave it, information is lost, even if you don't make any changes. You can choose the lossless option when you save, but that increases the file size. The better option is to always work from the original file, so you're never more than one generation away.

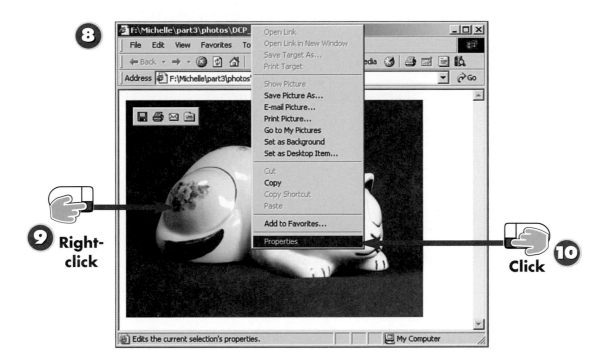

8

9 Right-click

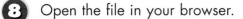

Click 10

8 Open the file in your browser.

9 Right-click the image.

10 Click **Properties** to check the file size. Your goal is an image that looks good but isn't too large.

End

How Large Is Too Large?
A single image shouldn't be more than 100KB. Ideally, the total of all the images on the page should be less than that, but if you have a number of photos, that's a difficult goal.

Finding the Right Balance
If the image quality isn't good enough, reopen the original image and resave with a lower compression factor (or higher save quality). If the image size is too large, try a higher compression factor (or lower save quality).

Uploading Pictures to eBay

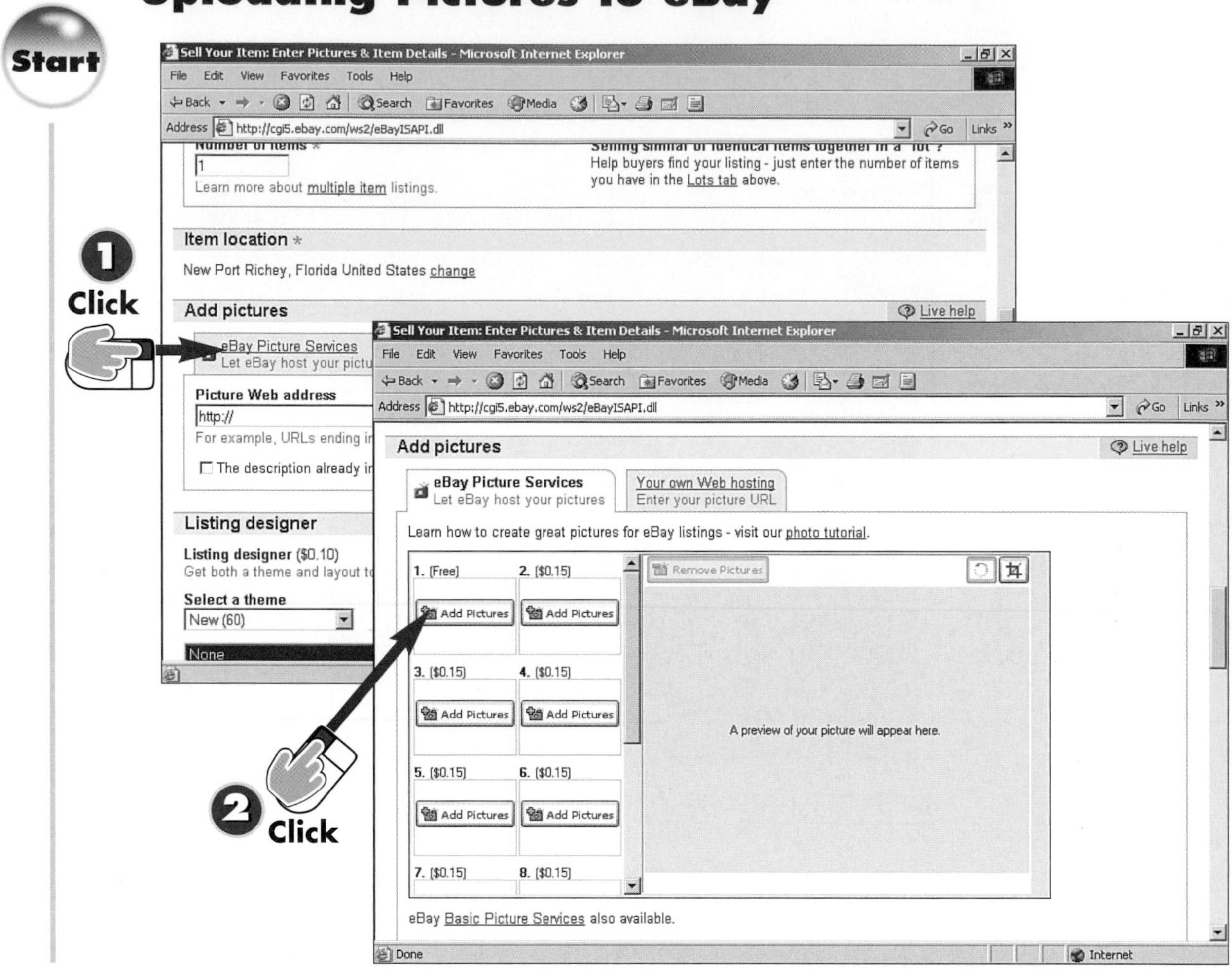

① Set up your listing. On the **Sell Your Item: Enter Pictures & Item Details page, click eBay Picture Services**.

② Click the first **Add Pictures** button.

You can add photos to your eBay listing by simply uploading them to eBay's servers when you create your listing. This way you don't have to host them yourself and can use super-size photos and slideshows. It also carries the disadvantage of taking control of the compression out of your hands. In addition, only the first photo is free; eBay charges for additional photos.

Basic eBay Services
If you're not using Internet Explorer, you might see a screen slightly different from the one shown here, with a column of fields and **Browse** buttons. The process is the same. Just click the **Browse** button instead of **Add Pictures**.

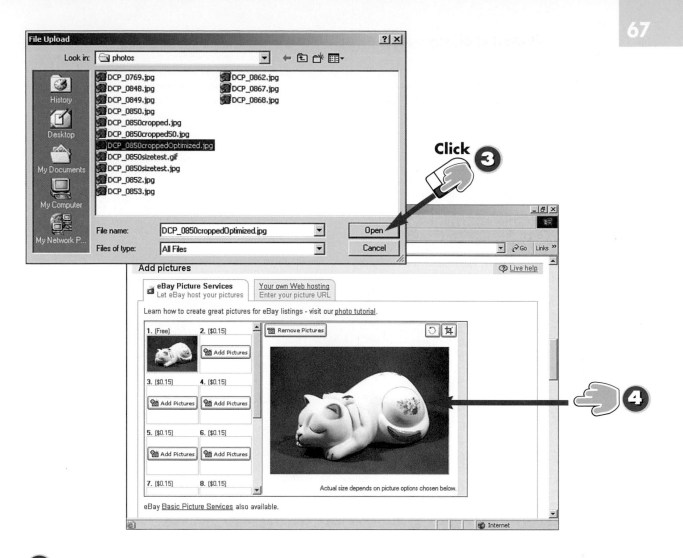

Click 3

4

③ Navigate to your first picture file and click **Open**.

④ Notice that the photo appears to the right, where you can crop or adjust it.

End

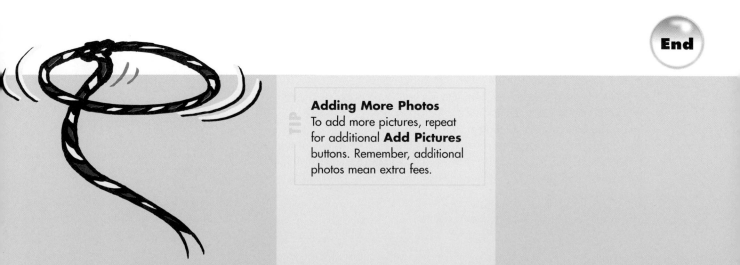

Adding More Photos
To add more pictures, repeat for additional **Add Pictures** buttons. Remember, additional photos mean extra fees.

Adding Images to Your Description

Start

Click

At the Describe Your Item page, add an image tag to the description by typing **1** **<img src= "http://www.nicholaschase.com/roadnick/DCP_0850croppedOptimized.jpg" />
**.

2 Click **Preview Description** to see the added image.

3 You now have an image within your product description.

If you've decided to host your own images, you've probably discovered that eBay allows you to enter only one URL. Fortunately, this doesn't mean you can only include one picture with your auction. In fact, you can add as many images as you like to your description without incurring a penny of extra listing fees. As a bonus, you have complete control over where they go and what they look like.

Where's My Image?
When you're adding images to your description, you need to make sure they're available on the web. You can host them yourself, or you can use an image hosting service such as SpareDollar or Verio.

Click

4 Add the height and width to the **img** tag by adding **width="440" height="319"**.

5 Add alternate text to the image by adding **alt="Formalities cat"**.

6 Click **Preview Description** to see the results.

End

What's This Alternate Text Thing?
Although it's less common on eBay, some users do surf without images on, and many users still have slower connections, particularly in other countries. Because of this, it's best to have alternate text, which shows up in the browser until the image has been downloaded.

Size Does Matter
Be careful when setting the height and width of your images. The browser does what you tell it to, even if you're wrong, so incorrect sizes can lead to distorted images.

Adding Watermarks to Your Images

Start

① In your graphics program, create an image to use as a watermark. Remember that the image will be almost transparent.

② Select **File**, **Save** to save the image as a JPEG file.

③ Go to **http://www.picture-shark.com** to download free watermarking software.

④ Click **Download Now** and then install the program.

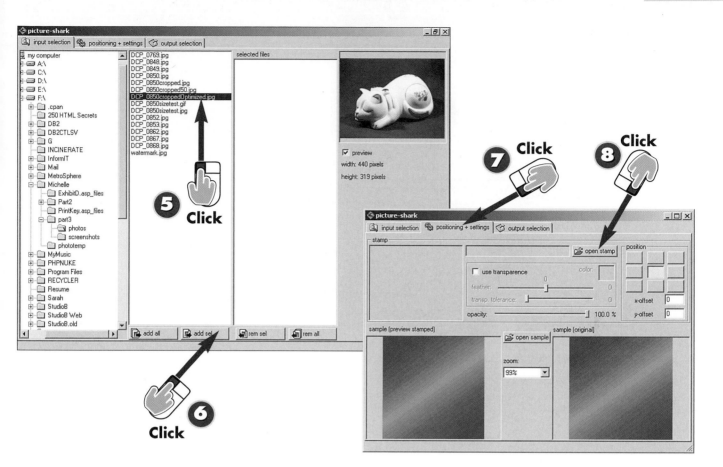

5 Select the file you want to watermark.

6 Click **Add Sel** to add it to the list to be processed. In an online watermarker, click **Browse** and select the image.

7 Click the **Positioning + Settings** tab in Picture Shark.

8 Click **Open Stamp** (at the top of the window) to find the watermark image.

See
next
page

Position the Stamp
You can decide where on the image you want the watermark by clicking one of the position tiles in the upper-right corner.

Using Transparency
You can tell Picture Shark to ignore a particular color by clicking the **Use Transparence** box. Click the **Color:** box and select the color to ignore.

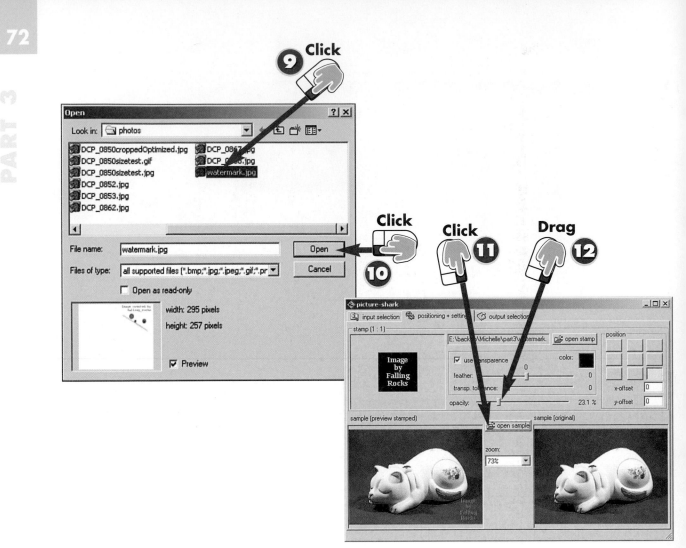

9 Select the image to use as a watermark.

10 Click **Open**.

11 Click **Open Sample** to choose the image you want to watermark.

12 Set the opacity of the watermark.

How Faint Should It Be?

In most cases, you will want it to be faint enough so it doesn't distract (much) from the image, but not so faint that it disappears altogether. In Picture Shark, slide the **Opacity** slider to the left to make the watermark more translucent. In the online watermarker, select a transparency level of 80 or so.

Click 13

Click 14

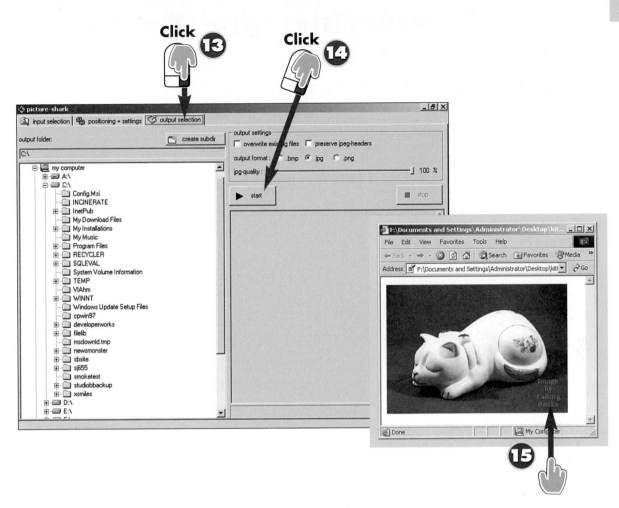

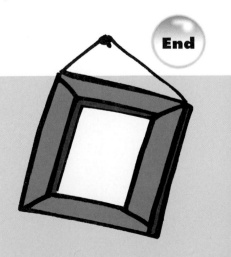

13 Add the watermark to the image. In Picture Shark, click the **Output Selection** tab.

14 Click **Start**.

15 View the resulting image and adjust the transparency accordingly.

End

Digital Watermarking
In addition to visual watermarking, you can also do digital watermarking. Digital watermarking doesn't affect the image itself; it encodes information into the file so you can search for "stolen" images on the Web.

Arranging the Page

So far in this book, we've talked about the basics of creating an eBay auction description. We've covered the basics of adding text and adding pictures. Now we'll start really manipulating the page or, more specifically, where items appear on the page.

HTML is designed to be flexible. In most cases, that's an advantage; your page should look good no matter what size the user's browser window is or what fonts he has installed. On the other hand, this flexibility can be frustrating. HTML isn't like a word processor; you can't always control where objects end up. For example, if you want to line text up in a column, you can't do so by simply adding spaces because the browser collapses all those spaces into one.

Fortunately, we do have some control over where items appear on the page. In this part, we look at arranging the page using tables. Tables enable you to create rows and columns of information. You can use them for something as simple as lining up technical information, but you can also use them for general page layout tasks. For example, many sellers use tables when they are building their About Me pages because they enable the seller to create a column of information, such as menu items, categories, or links, that runs along the left side of the page, with the normal page content beside it.

From there, we look at gaining even more control over where your content ends up by abandoning tables and moving to sections and positioning styles. These styles enable you to set your content in a specific location—even if it's outside the description.

Controlling the Layout of Your Description

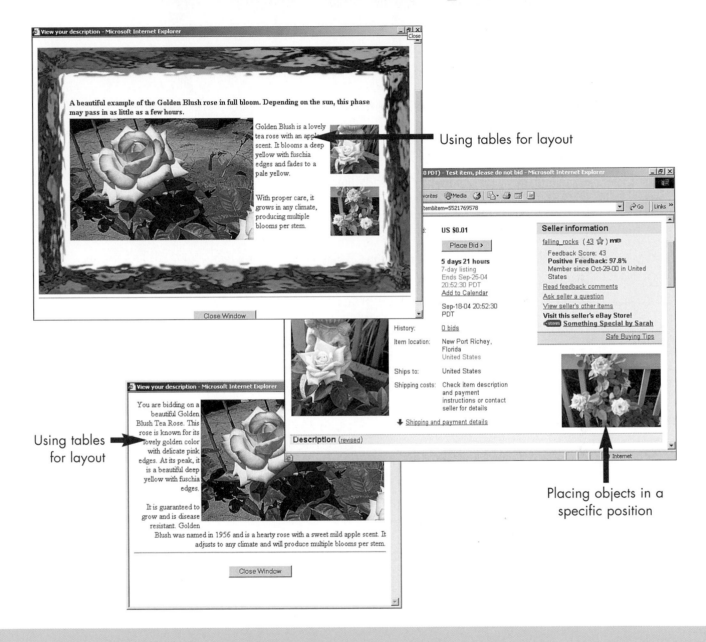

Using tables for layout

Using tables for layout

Placing objects in a specific position

Creating a Table of Text

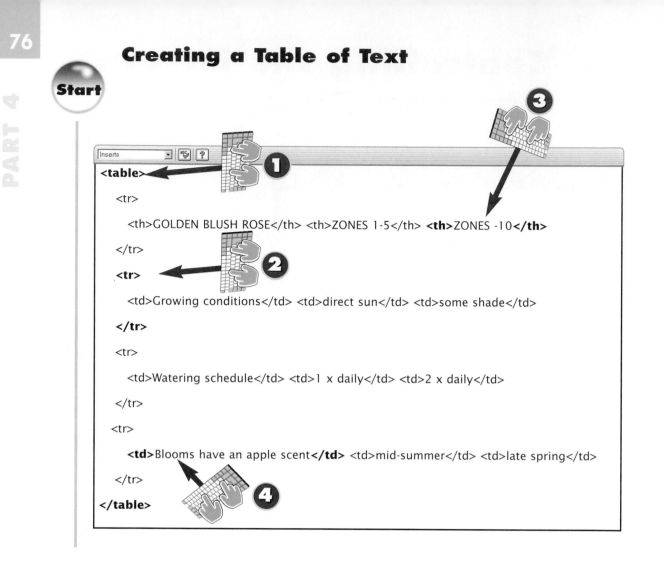

Start

```
Inserts
<table>

   <tr>

      <th>GOLDEN BLUSH ROSE</th> <th>ZONES 1-5</th> <th>ZONES -10</th>

   </tr>

   <tr>

      <td>Growing conditions</td> <td>direct sun</td> <td>some shade</td>

   </tr>

   <tr>

      <td>Watering schedule</td> <td>1 x daily</td> <td>2 x daily</td>

   </tr>

   <tr>

      <td>Blooms have an apple scent</td> <td>mid-summer</td> <td>late spring</td>

   </tr>

</table>
```

1 Add the actual table to the description by typing the table tags **<table>** and **</table>**.

2 Create four rows in the table by typing the table row tags **<tr>** and **</tr>**.

3 Create three column headers in the first row by adding three table header tags: **<th>** and **</th>**.

4 Add data to each row using table data cells or the **<td>** and **</td>** tags.

For most people, the first time they realize that HTML is a little more unpredictable than they expected is when they attempt to line up information on the page. Fortunately, HTML provides tables. Tables consist of rows and columns that help you line things up. Before starting this task, create a new auction and edit the description. (See Part 1, "Creating an Auction Listing," for help.)

Arranging Your HTML Code

TIP

You don't have to put all your table data cells on one line, like I've done here. The browser knows that everything in a single table row **<tr></tr>** goes on one line.

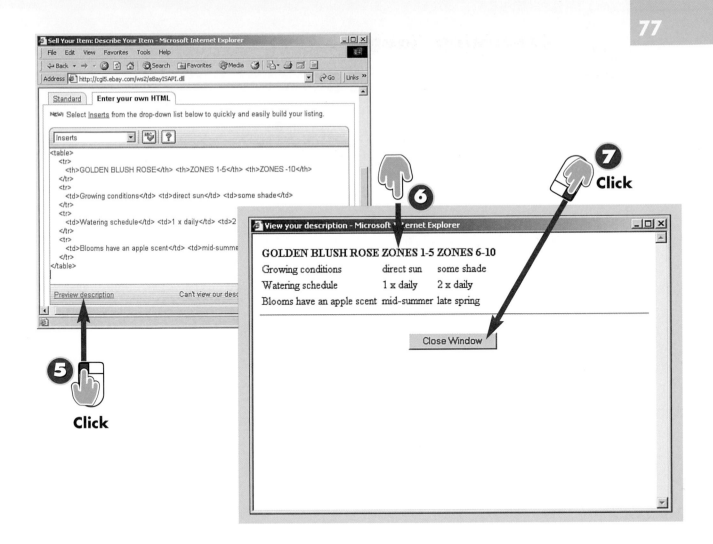

5 Click **Preview Description** to see what you have so far.

6 Your description is now in a simple table format.

7 Click **Close Window** to close the preview.

End

Seeing the Table
If you want to see the lines that make up the actual table, add a border by typing **<table border="1">**. Strictly speaking, this is an outdated way of doing things—we look at a better way in Part 6, "Styling the Text"—but it'll do for getting a quick look.

Tables Are Flexible
A table automatically adjusts to fit its content. A column will be as wide as its widest cell, and a row will be as high as its tallest cell.

Arranging Images with a Table

Start

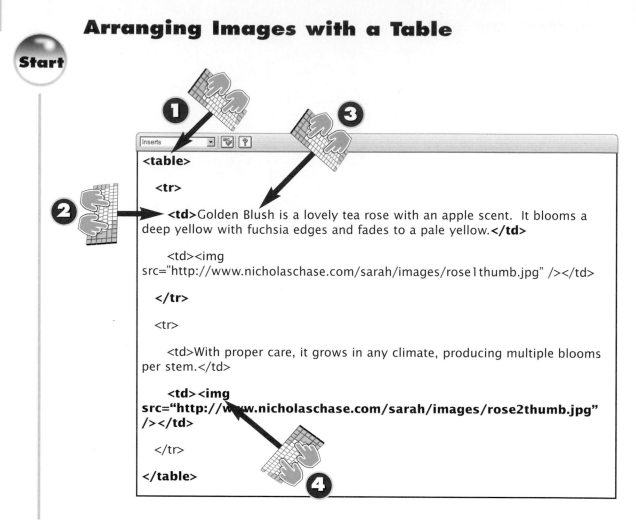

1

3

2

4

```
Inserts

<table>

  <tr>

    <td>Golden Blush is a lovely tea rose with an apple scent.  It blooms a
deep yellow with fuchsia edges and fades to a pale yellow.</td>

    <td><img
src="http://www.nicholaschase.com/sarah/images/rose1thumb.jpg" /></td>

  </tr>

  <tr>

    <td>With proper care, it grows in any climate, producing multiple blooms
per stem.</td>

    <td><img
src="http://www.nicholaschase.com/sarah/images/rose2thumb.jpg"
/></td>

  </tr>

</table>
```

1 After the end of your first table, add an empty table to the description with two rows and two columns by placing the **<table>** and **</table>** tags. (You might want to add a couple of line breaks before it using the **
** tag.)

2 Add table row and table data tags by inserting **<tr>** and **</tr>** and then the **<td>** and **</td>** tags.

3 Add descriptive text to the first column in each row. Remember that columns are located between the **<td>** tags.

4 Add images to the second column in each row by placing the **<img />** tag within the second table data tag (**<td></td>**) in each row.

INTRODUCTION

Often in an auction you have information about various parts of an item, with accompanying photos. One challenge is to add these photos in such a way that they line up with their respective descriptions. Fortunately, tables aren't limited to just text.

TIP

What's an img Tag Again?
The **<img />** tag contains the location of the source image and usually size and supplemental information, as in **<img src= "http://myserver.com/ myimage.jpg" height= "200" width="100" alt= "Photo of a hot rod" />**.

TIP

Why the Slash?
In the most recent versions of HTML (or XHTML, for the particular), all tags must have an open and close tag. Adding the slash to single tags such as **
** and **<img />** is an abbreviation that lets them work with both older and newer browsers.

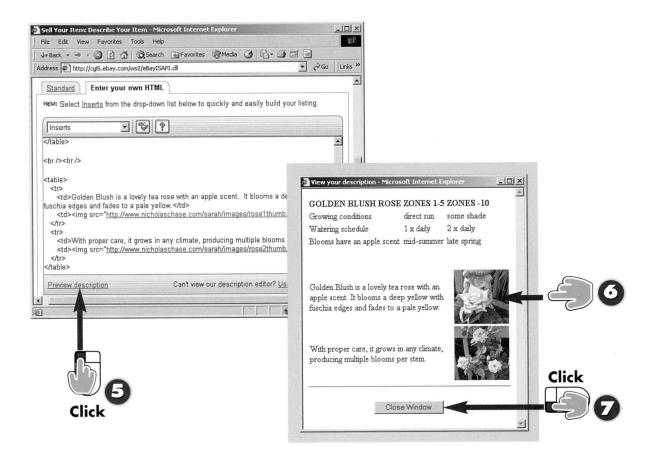

5 Click **Preview Description** to see the results.

6 You now have images on your page with their descriptive text nearby.

7 Click **Close Window** to close the preview screen.

End

Mixing It Up

You're not limited in how you lay out a table of photos. You could, say, alternate, first photo on the right, then photo on the left, then the right, and so on. The important thing is that, because of the table, the text always lines up with the correct photo.

TIP

Using Irregular Tables

Start

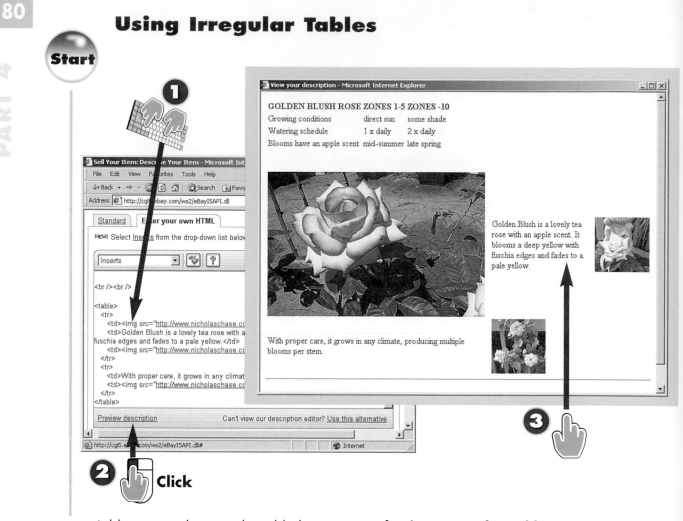

Click

① Add a new column to the table by typing **<td><img src="http://www.nicholaschase.com/sarah/images/rose1medium.jpg" /></td>** into the first row.

② Click **Preview Description** to see the changes.

③ Notice how the new column has broken the layout we already had.

Tables are obviously perfect for a grid, but what if your layout isn't quite a regular grid? For example, many eBayers like to put a banner at the top of their About Me page, with a column of links down the left side. We cover links later, in Part 7, "Creating Links," so we can't do exactly that here. But let's look at spanning rows or columns, making that kind of layout possible.

INTRODUCTION

Hosting Issues
Some web hosting companies are fussy about hosting images that are displayed on pages from other sites. If your web host has a problem with this, try http://www.andale.com.

TIP

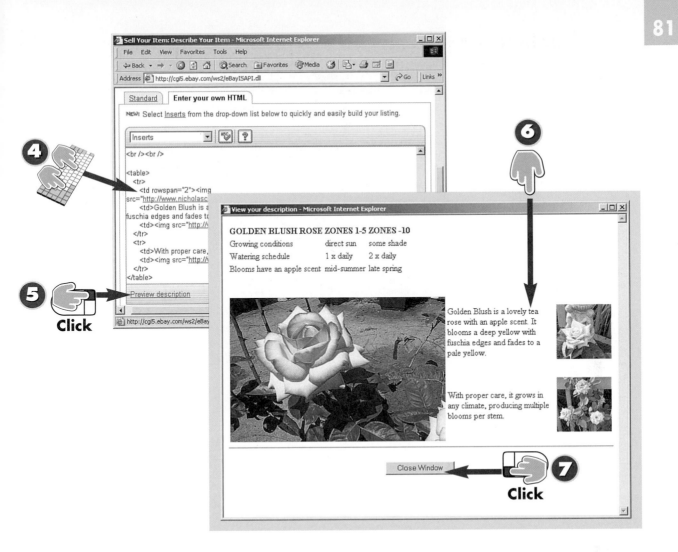

Click

Click

4 Using the **rowspan** attribute, specify that the new table data cell should span both rows of the table by replacing the first **<td>** with **<td rowspan="2">**.

5 Click **Preview Description** to see the effect.

6 Notice that the first cell now occupies, or *spans*, two rows. Notice also that the text and thumbnails once again line up.

7 Click **Close Window** to exit the preview screen.

See next page

What Is Spanning?
In a table, each cell of information takes up a specific spot in the table's grid. In some cases, however, you want one cell to take up more than one spot. A cell can span two or more rows or columns. In this case, we've told one cell to span two rows.

Starting Off the Row
Notice that because the first cell spanned the remaining rows, the first cell in the second row of the table just naturally starts in the second column. You don't need to add an empty cell for the first column because the first column in the row (in this case, the text) always drops into the first available position (in this case, the second column).

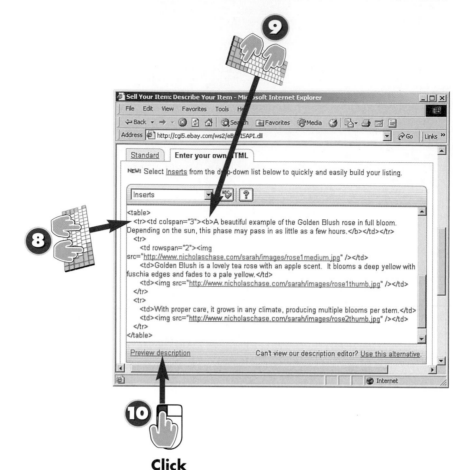

Click

8 Add a new row and cell. It should span all three columns of the table so add **<tr><td colspan="3">A beautiful example of the Golden Blush rose in full bloom</td></tr>** immediately after the opening **<table>** tag.

9 To make this text bold, add a **** before the text and a **** after the text.

10 Click **Preview Description** to see the effect.

Using rowspans and colspans
By using the **colspan** and **rowspan** attributes, you can individually control how many rows and columns a single cell occupies. Here I've used a **rowspan** for one cell and a **colspan** for another, but you can also combine them on a single cell if necessary. For example, a table data cell that starts with **<td rowspan="4" colspan="2">** is four rows high and two columns wide, and adjacent cells will adjust their positions to accommodate it.

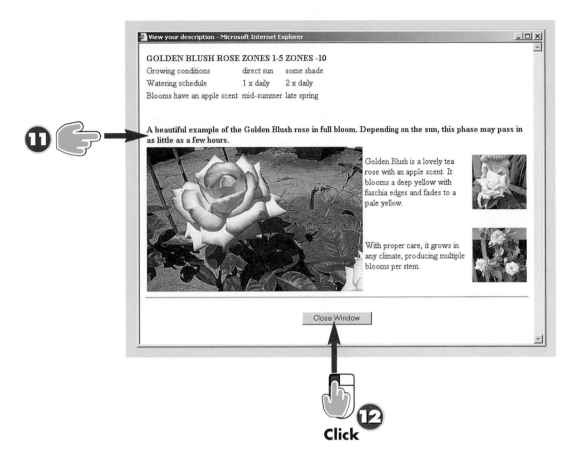

Click 12

11 Notice that even though the description starts in the first cell of the table, because of the **colspan**, it occupies all three columns.

12 Click **Close Window** to leave the preview screen.

End

A Span Too Far

TIP

You don't actually have to span all the rows or columns of a table, as we're doing here. Instead, you can specify only as many as you want to use.

Framing the Description

Start

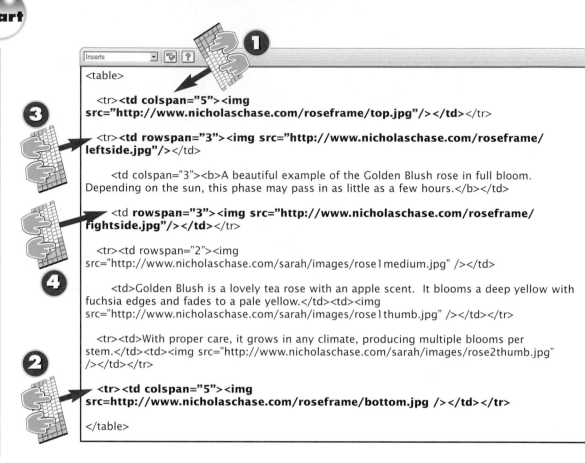

1

```
<table>

  <tr><td colspan="5"><img
src="http://www.nicholaschase.com/roseframe/top.jpg"/></td></tr>

  <tr><td rowspan="3"><img src="http://www.nicholaschase.com/roseframe/
leftside.jpg"/></td>

     <td colspan="3"><b>A beautiful example of the Golden Blush rose in full bloom.
Depending on the sun, this phase may pass in as little as a few hours.</b></td>

     <td rowspan="3"><img src="http://www.nicholaschase.com/roseframe/
rightside.jpg"/></td></tr>

  <tr><td rowspan="2"><img
src="http://www.nicholaschase.com/sarah/images/rose1medium.jpg" /></td>

     <td>Golden Blush is a lovely tea rose with an apple scent.  It blooms a deep yellow with
fuchsia edges and fades to a pale yellow.</td><td><img
src="http://www.nicholaschase.com/sarah/images/rose1thumb.jpg" /></td></tr>

  <tr><td>With proper care, it grows in any climate, producing multiple blooms per
stem.</td><td><img src="http://www.nicholaschase.com/sarah/images/rose2thumb.jpg"
/></td></tr>

  <tr><td colspan="5"><img
src=http://www.nicholaschase.com/roseframe/bottom.jpg /></td></tr>

</table>
```

1 Add a new row to the top of the table and include the appropriate image by typing **<tr><td colspan="5"><img src="http://www.nicholaschase.com/ roseframe/top.jpg"/></td></tr>**.

2 Add a new row to the bottom of the table and include the appropriate image by typing **<tr><td colspan="5"><img src="http://www.nicholaschase.com/ roseframe/bottom.jpg"/></td></tr>**.

3 Add a new column to the table for the left image by adding **<td rowspan="3"><img src="http://www.nicholaschase.com/roseframe/leftside.jpg"/></td>**.

4 Add a new column to the table for the right image by adding **<td rowspan="3"><img src="http://www.nicholaschase.com/roseframe/rightside.jpg"/></td>**.

The ability to put images into a table and have irregular rows and columns lets you create a frame for your descriptions. You create top and bottom rows and left and right columns that contain your frame; then place your content in the middle.

TIP

colspan and rowspan
The **colspan** attribute tells a table data cell to occupy, or *span*, more than one column, and the **rowspan** attribute tells it to occupy more than one row. Here the top and bottom graphics span five columns (but only one row each), but the left and right graphics span three rows (but only one column each).

Click

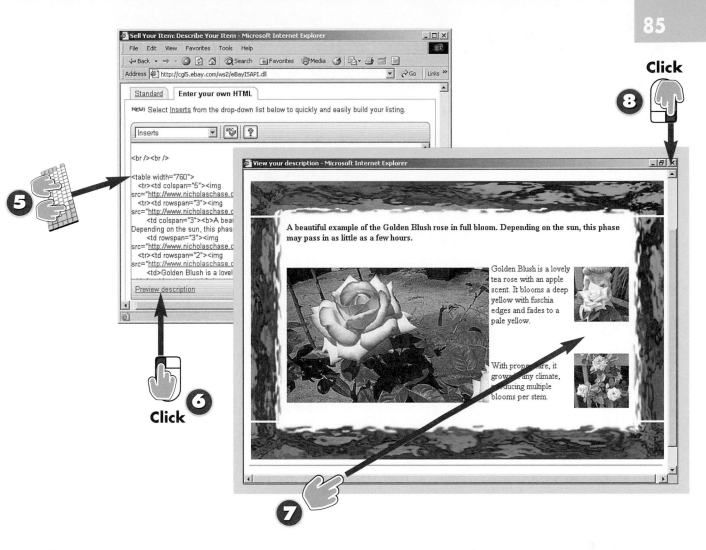

Click

Click

5. To prevent the browser from spreading the table across the whole page, set the width by typing **<table width="760">**.

6. Click **Preview Description** to see what you've done.

7. Notice that the graphics now surround the text, but there are still spaces between them.

8. Click the **x** to close the preview screen.

See next page

Where Things Are
Sometimes it's hard to tell how things are lining up in a table. You can see things more clearly if you turn on the table border by adding a border attribute to the table tag, as in **<table border="1">**.

Setting the Width
Some people have their monitors and browsers set to wider than the 800 pixels we're using here, so to keep the browser from spreading the table over the entire window, we're telling it to limit the size of the table to 760 pixels.

```
Inserts

<table cellpadding="0" cellspacing="0" width="760px">

  <tr><td colspan="5"><img src="http://www.nicholaschase.com/roseframe/top.jpg"/></td></tr>

  <tr><td rowspan="3"><img src="http://www.nicholaschase.com/roseframe/leftside.jpg"/></td>

    <td colspan="3"><b>A beautiful example of the Golden Blush rose in full bloom. Depending on the sun, this phase may pass in as little as a few hours.</b></td>

    <td rowspan="3"><img src="http://www.nicholaschase.com/roseframe/rightside.jpg"/></td></tr>

  <tr><td rowspan="2"><img src="http://www.nicholaschase.com/sarah/images/rose1medium.jpg" /></td>

    <td>Golden Blush is a lovely tea rose with an apple scent.  It blooms a deep yellow with fuchsia edges and fades to a pale yellow.</td><td><img src="http://www.nicholaschase.com/sarah/images/rose1thumb.jpg" /></td></tr>

  <tr><td>With proper care, it grows in any climate, producing multiple blooms per stem.</td><td><img src="http://www.nicholaschase.com/sarah/images/rose2thumb.jpg" /></td></tr>

  <tr><td colspan="5"><img src="http://www.nicholaschase.com/roseframe/bottom.jpg" /></td></tr>

</table>
```

9 Remove the space inside each cell by adding **cellpadding="0"** inside the opening **<table>** tag.

10 Remove the space between cells by adding **cellspacing="0"** inside the opening **<table>** tag.

Space Inside a Table

TIP

Tables are designed to be ready to use. You should be able to add data to them without having to worry about all the data running together as a jumbled mess. To that end, by default (meaning, unless you tell it differently) the browser adds some space, or padding, around the content inside the cell and between cells. When you're trying to make different cells run into each other—as we are here—that's a problem. Fortunately, you can control how much space the browser uses. **cellpadding** represents the space inside the cell; **cellspacing** represents the space between them. Set both to **0** to eliminate space between table cells.

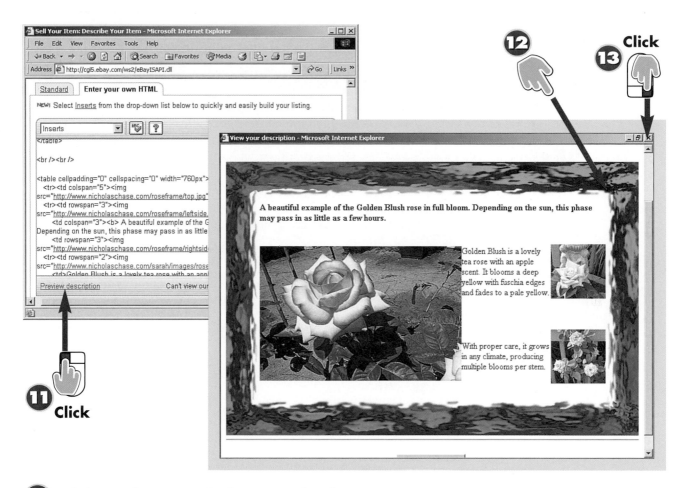

11 Click **Preview Description** to see the changes.

12 Notice that there's no longer any space within or between the cells that hold each graphic, so they all butt up against each other.

13 Click the **x** to close the preview screen.

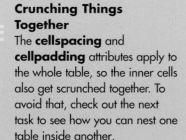

End

Crunching Things Together
The **cellspacing** and **cellpadding** attributes apply to the whole table, so the inner cells also get scrunched together. To avoid that, check out the next task to see how you can nest one table inside another.

Nesting Tables

Start

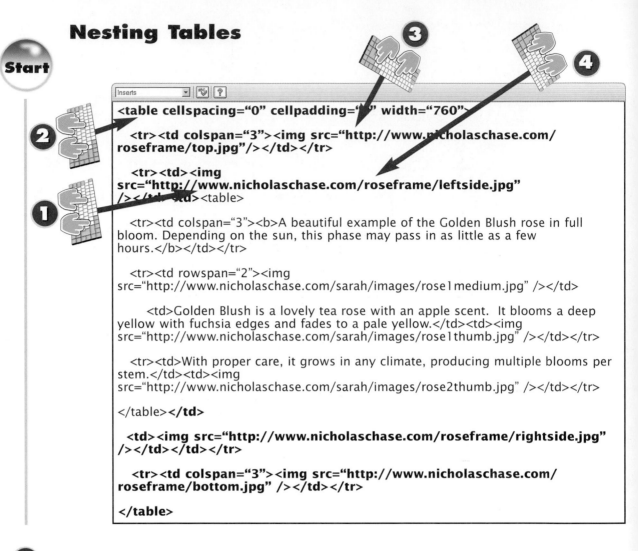

```
Inserts

<table cellspacing="0" cellpadding="0" width="760">

   <tr><td colspan="3"><img src="http://www.nicholaschase.com/
roseframe/top.jpg"/></td></tr>

   <tr><td><img
src="http://www.nicholaschase.com/roseframe/leftside.jpg"
/></td><td><table>

    <tr><td colspan="3"><b>A beautiful example of the Golden Blush rose in full
bloom. Depending on the sun, this phase may pass in as little as a few
hours.</b></td></tr>

    <tr><td rowspan="2"><img
src="http://www.nicholaschase.com/sarah/images/rose1medium.jpg" /></td>

      <td>Golden Blush is a lovely tea rose with an apple scent.  It blooms a deep
yellow with fuchsia edges and fades to a pale yellow.</td><td><img
src="http://www.nicholaschase.com/sarah/images/rose1thumb.jpg" /></td></tr>

    <tr><td>With proper care, it grows in any climate, producing multiple blooms per
stem.</td><td><img
src="http://www.nicholaschase.com/sarah/images/rose2thumb.jpg" /></td></tr>

</table></td>

   <td><img src="http://www.nicholaschase.com/roseframe/rightside.jpg"
/></td></td></tr>

   <tr><td colspan="3"><img src="http://www.nicholaschase.com/
roseframe/bottom.jpg" /></td></tr>

</table>
```

1 Create a table of information.

2 Create a table around the original table, so the original table is in a data cell of the new table.

3 Add the top and bottom rows to the outer table.

4 Add the left and right columns to the outer table.

If you're selling on eBay, you've already been working with tables, whether you know it or not. The eBay auction page is one big table, with your description placed in one of the cells. You can use this to create a layered look with one table nested inside another. You can create tables with different characteristics.

TIP

Closing Tables
Very few things mess up the formatting of an HTML page like leaving out the close table tag (**</table>**). If your page looks funny, that's the first place to check. (Some older browsers don't even display the table if it's not closed.)

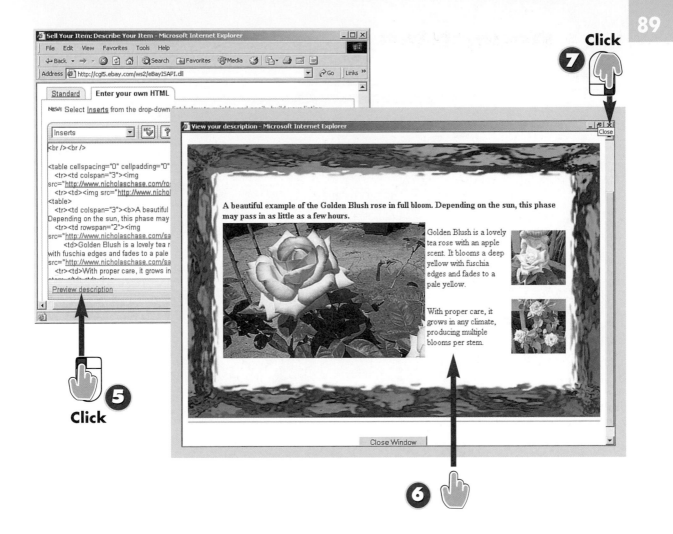

5 Click **Preview Description** to see the changes.

6 Notice that the first table, with the content, is now included in the second with the graphics but with different spacing applied.

7 Click the **x** to close the preview window.

End

I Don't See Any Changes!

At first glance, it might seem as though there's no difference between what we did here and what we did in the previous task, but that's not quite true. In the previous task, to remove the spacing between the images, we had to affect the whole table, so the text was mashed up against the photos. Now, the inner table has its own **cellpadding** and **cellspacing** values, so its spacing is preserved. See http://www.nicholaschase.com/easyhtml4ebay/ sidebyside.html for a side-by-side comparison of the two results.

Wrapping Text Around Images

Start

Revise Your Item: Title & Description - Microsoft Internet Explorer

File   Edit   View   Favorites   Tools   Help

Back | Search   Favorites   Media |

Address http://cgi5.ebay.com/ws/ebayISAPI.dll?ReviseItem&SessionId=467626672&ItemId=5   Go   Links

Standard   **Enter your own HTML**

NEW! Select Inserts from the drop-down list below to quickly and easily build your listing.

Inserts

```
<img src="http://www.nicholaschase.com/sarah/images/rose1medium.jpg" />
<p>You are bidding on a beautiful Golden Blush Tea Rose.  This rose is
known for its lovely golden color with delicate pink edges.  At its peak,
it is a beautiful deep yellow with fuschia edges.</p>

<p>It is guaranteed to grow and is disease resistant.  Golden Blush was
named in 1956 and is a hearty rose with a sw
It adjusts to any climate and will produce mul
stem.</p>
```

Preview description   Can

View your description - Microsoft Internet Explorer

You are bidding on a beautiful Golden Blush Tea Rose. This rose is known for its lovely golden color with delicate pink edges. At its peak, it is a beautiful deep yellow with fuschia edges.

It is guaranteed to grow and is disease resistant. Golden Blush was named in 1956 and is a hearty rose with a sweet mild apple scent. It adjusts to any climate and will produce multiple blooms per stem.

Click

 1 Add an image to your description by typing **<img src="http://www. nicholaschase.com/sarah/images/rose1medium.jpg" width="300" />**.

 2 Add descriptive text to your listing.

 3 Click **Preview Description** to see the changes.

 4 Notice that the image and text are both present, but because of the paragraph tags, not on the same line.

One way you can make your auctions look a little nicer is to integrate the images with the text. By default, only a single line of text appears next to an image—no matter how big the image is—but by floating an image to the left or right, you can make the text flow around it.

Where Can I Float Images?

You can float an image to the left or right. Floating the image moves it in the specified direction until it hits something, such as the side of table data cell or another floated image.

Can I Float Anything Else?

You can float any object, such as an image or a table, this way.

Click

5 Using the style attribute, set the image to float to the right side of the window by adding **style="float: right"** to the **img** tag.

6 Click **Preview Description** to see the changes.

7 Notice that the image now sits at the right side of the window and that the text wraps around it.

End

What Is This "style"?
The **style** attribute lets you add properties to an object on the page. For example, here we're floating the image, but we can use styles to, say, change the appearance of text or even place an object in a certain position. You'll use the **style** attribute a lot.

Unwrapping Text
Floating an object such as an image makes everything next to it wrap around it. To move down under the floated object, use the **clear** attribute. For example, if you floated an image to the right, start a new paragraph with **<p style="clear: right" >** to get underneath it.

Creating a Section on the Page

Start

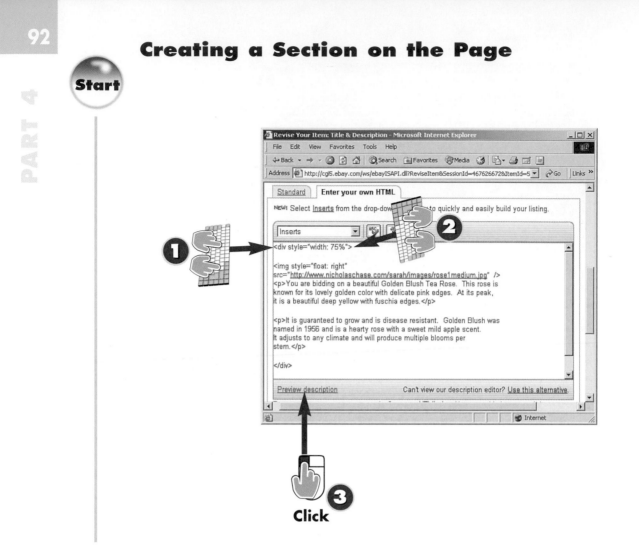

Click

 Add **div** tags around the section you created in the previous task by placing **<div>** before it and **</div>** after it.

 Apply a style, setting the width to 75% by adding **style="width: 75%"** to the opening **<div>** tag.

3 Click **Preview Description** to see the new section.

INTRODUCTION

Another way to arrange your page is to use sections, or divisions. A division, or **<div> </div>** tag, lets you apply a style to a particular block of the page. In this task, we'll make the section of the page narrower than the page and center it.

TIP

Setting Widths
When you set any kind of a size, such as a width or height, you can set it as a specific number of pixels (such as **750px**), inches (such as **7.5in**), centimeters (such as **200cm**), or a percentage of the available area (such as **75%**).

Click

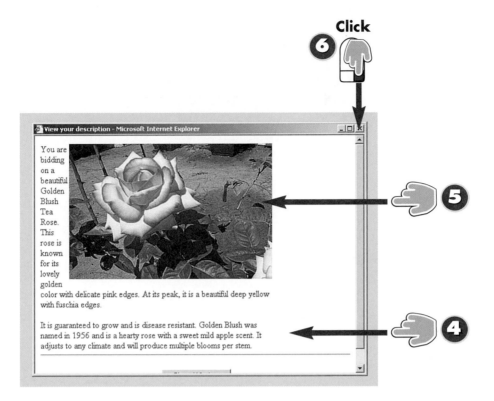

4 Notice that the entire section now takes up only 75% of the window.

5 Notice that the image is still floating to the right of the text.

6 Click the **x** to close the preview screen.

End

Aligning Objects to the Left or Right

Start

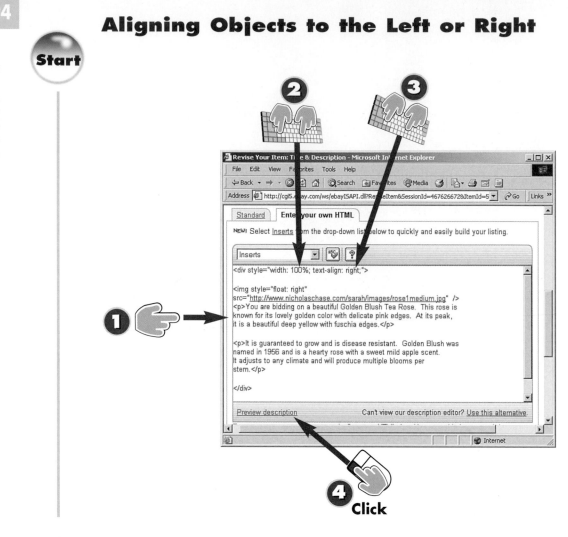

1

Click

---

1 Create a new section of text and images.

2 Set the width of the section to 100% by adding **style="width: 100%;"** to the opening **<div>** tag.

3 Use the **text-align** property to align the section to the right by adding **text-align: right** to the **<div style>** tag.

4 Click **Preview Description** to see the changes.

One advantage of creating sections as we did in the last task is the ability to align text, images, and other objects by using the text-align style.

TIP

What Alignments Can I Use?

You can align text to the **right** or **left**, **center** it, or use **justify** to space out the text from edge to edge.

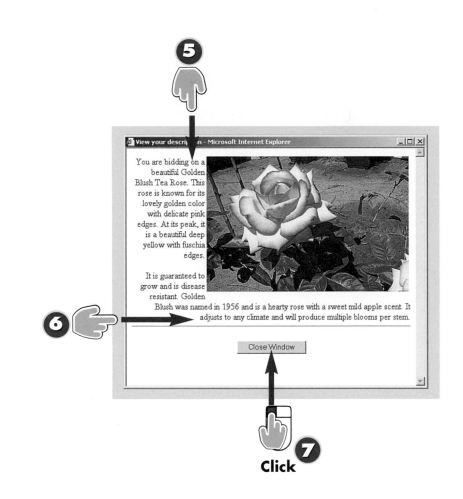

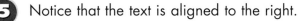

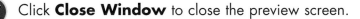

Click

5 Notice that the text is aligned to the right.

6 Notice that the overall alignment of the section is unchanged; the text is still wrapped around the image.

7 Click **Close Window** to close the preview screen.

End

Why Didn't It Work?

When you use the **text-align** style, you align the content inside the **div**. If you don't explicitly set the size of a section. It's only as large as necessary to hold the text, so even if it is aligned one way or the other, it won't look it. Be sure to set the width of the section to the full width to see the alignment effect.

What Gets Aligned?

All objects in an aligned section are aligned, including text, images, tables, and other objects.

Placing Objects in a Specific Location

Start

1 Place an image in the description by typing **<img src="http://www. nicholaschase.com/sarah/images/rose1small.jpg" width="200" />**.

2 Add a style specifying the absolute position of the item relative to its bounding box by adding **style="position: absolute; top: 375;"** to the **img** tag.

3 Click **Preview Description** to see the results.

4 Notice that the image is no longer displayed in the description area.

Click

By now, you might have wondered whether you'd ever be able to decide where you want something to appear and put it there, like you can in a painting or word processing program. The answer is "yes." In this task we place two photos at the top of the page, where we normally wouldn't have any control.

Why Bother?
This technique puts a second image under the one eBay displays at the top of the page. You can see it at http://www.nicholaschase.com/easyhtml4ebay/shiftingobjects.html.

Shifting Objects
In this step, we're stating we want to move the image from a reference point (the upper-left corner of the window). We want to move it 375 pixels from the top. If we didn't move it, it'd be the first item on the line. Thus, when we do move it, it still is.

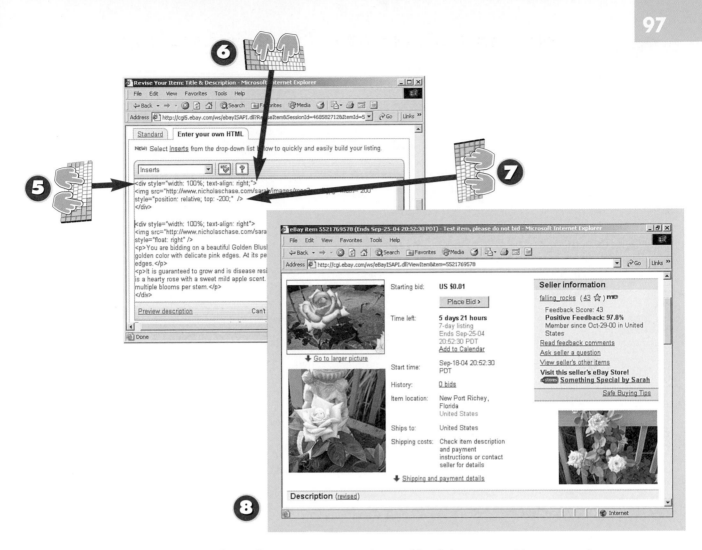

5 Create an image inside a **div** section set to the width of the page. Place it at the top of the description.

6 Align the section to the right by typing **text-align: right** in the **div** style tag.

7 Set the position to be 200 pixels higher than normal by specifying a negative **top** value by typing **position: relative; top: -200px** in the **div** style attribute.

8 Previewing the description won't show the image, but the final page is shown above.

End

Understanding Positioning Values
Sometimes positioning can be confusing. For example, to move something to the right, you specify the left value. This is because you're actually specifying a margin on the left side.

Proceed with Caution
Be very careful when you start shifting objects on the page because the effect can depend on issues outside your control, such as the size of the browser window. This is particularly true with relative positioning, which also leaves a big hole where the object *should* be.

PART 5

Decorating the Page

So far we've moved a lot of items around on the page, but we haven't done much to alter their appearance. For example, sellers often want to enhance their listings through the use of borders, colors, backgrounds, and other attributes.

In this part of the book, we look at decorating both individual items within the description of your item and the overall description itself. For example, you can create backgrounds and apply them to just a section of the page, or you can choose a background color for the entire description. (Recent changes by eBay make it difficult, if not impossible, to control the background of the overall page.)

Before we start, I want to remind you that the purpose of extra touches such as borders or backgrounds is to enhance the look of your listing and not to distract someone from actually reading it. If you're wondering whether your listing is too busy, it probably is. I demonstrate several techniques in the same auction purely for reasons of space; your best bet is to keep your auctions simple and straightforward.

In this part, we discuss borders, backgrounds, and colors and how to make them work for you rather than distracting the user from your item.

Using Backgrounds, Borders, and Colors

Create borders

Create backgrounds

Specify background colors

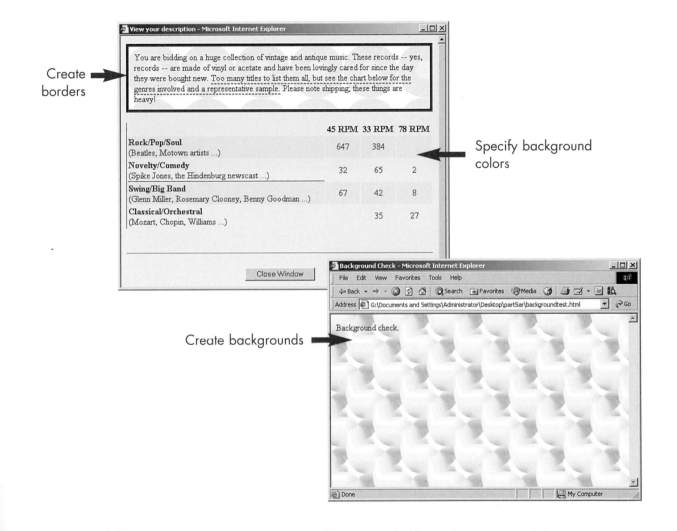

Adding Borders to a Table

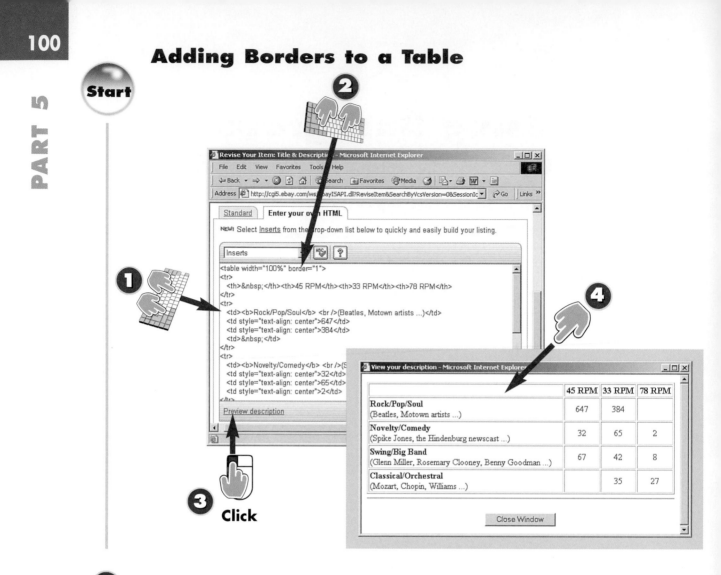

1. Add a table of information to the description.

2. Turn the border on by adding **border="1"** to the opening **<table>** tag.

3. Click **Preview Description** to see the results.

4. Notice that the table now has a border showing each table data cell.

INTRODUCTION

Table borders have been around longer than any of the other styles we'll use in this book, but they have changed slightly. It used to be the default to show the border on a table. Nowadays, if you want to show the table border, you have to say so.

The Nonbreaking Space

TIP

I've taken a necessary shortcut on this page with the use of the nonbreaking space, ** **. The nonbreaking space is invisible, but the browser doesn't collapse it the way it does a normal space.

Borders Are Your Friend

TIP

It can be difficult to see what the problem is with a table with borders off. Turn them on to help see which row or column actually holds the item you're trying to place.

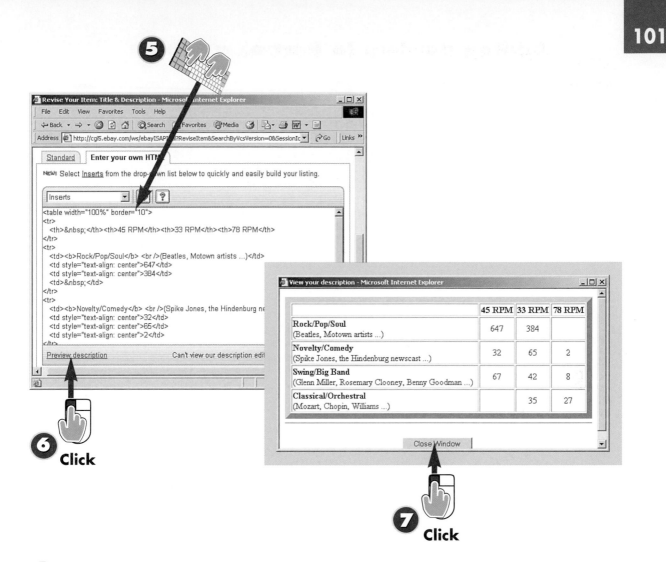

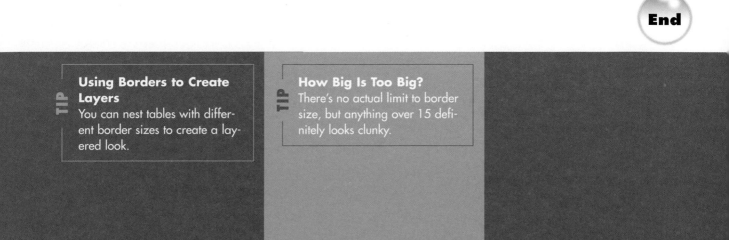

5 Increase the border size to give a raised look to the table by typing **border="10"**.

6 Click **Preview Description** to see the change.

7 Notice how the table now has a thick, raised border. Click **Close Window** to close the preview window.

End

TIP

Using Borders to Create Layers
You can nest tables with different border sizes to create a layered look.

TIP

How Big Is Too Big?
There's no actual limit to border size, but anything over 15 definitely looks clunky.

Adding Borders to Part of a Table

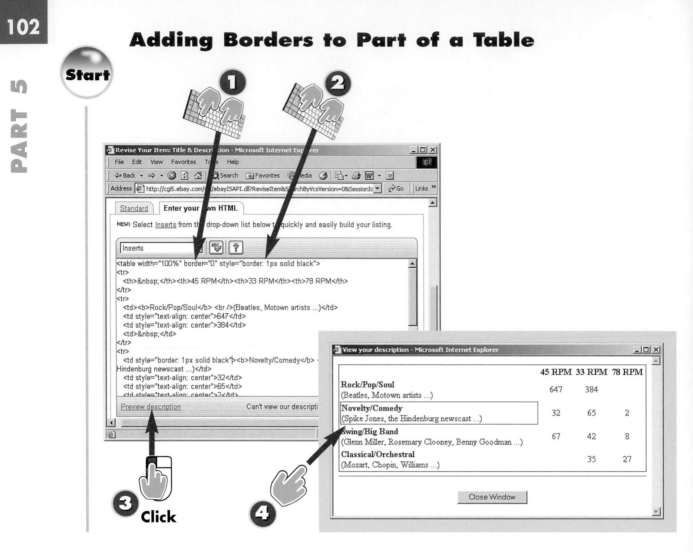

1. Turn off the border for the table by typing **border="0"**.

2. Add a border style to the table by adding **style="border: 1px solid black"** to the opening table tag and to a cell by adding it to the **td** element.

3. Click **Preview Description** to see the results.

4. Notice there are now two borders—one around the table and one around an individual data cell.

End

The table's border attribute works, but it's a bit…inelegant. Using styles, you can add more pleasant borders with much greater control. In this task, we add borders to part of a table.

Just Plain Borders?
Cascading style sheets, as we're using here, give you a lot of control over the appearance of the border.

Where Can I Add a Border?
Technically, you can add a border to any individual part of a table, such as a row or table data cell, but you'll find that adding borders to table rows doesn't always work in practice.

Setting Partial Borders

Start

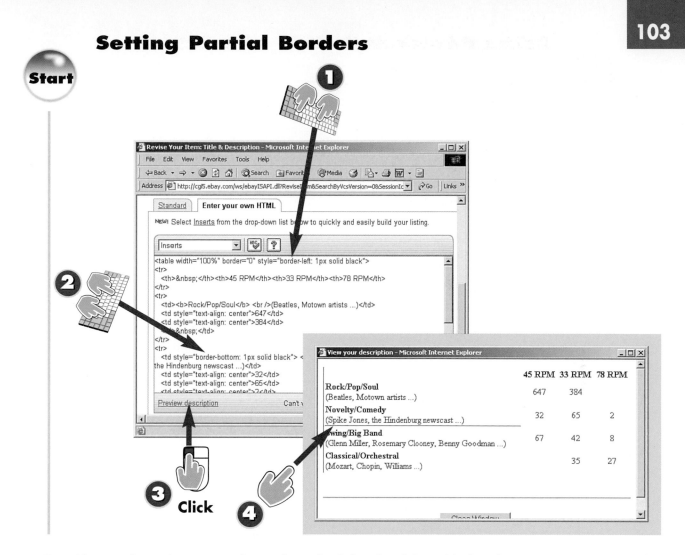

3 Click

4

① Change the style so it applies only to the left side of the table by changing **style="border:** to **style="border-left:**.

② Adjust the style to apply to only the bottom of the table data cell by typing **style="border-bottom:**.

③ Click **Preview Description** to see the changes.

④ Notice that only part of the table and cell now have a border.

End

INTRODUCTION

So far, you've set borders for an entire object, such as a table or a data cell, but you can actually control each side of a border individually. You can also set the general border for an object and then override that setting for one part of the border.

TIP

What Borders Can I Set?
You can individually set the **border-left**, **border-right**, **border-bottom**, and **border-top** properties for an object. You can even use them to combine styles.

TIP

Freedom to Choose
You don't have to use a table to set up a border. You can add borders to virtually any object, such as a **div** section, as you can see on page 104.

Using Border Styles

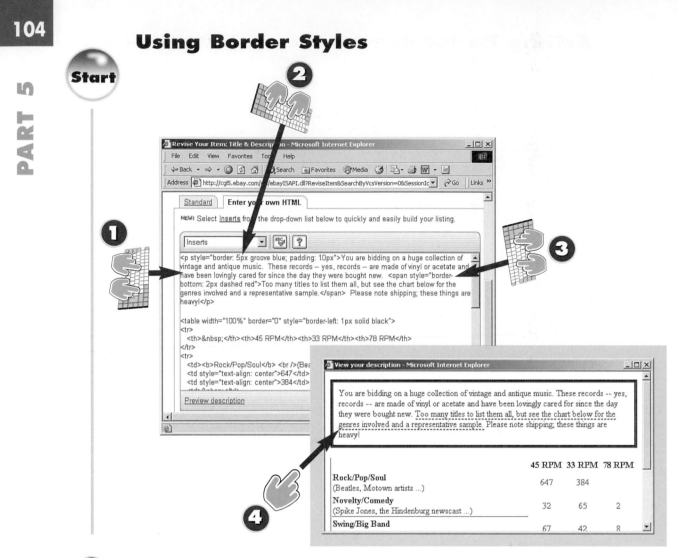

1. Add content to the description.

2. Add a thick blue border groove to the section by typing **border: 5px groove blue;** in the opening **<p>** tag's **style** attribute.

3. Add a dotted line to the bottom of a sentence to act as an underline by typing **** and adding **** after the sentence.

4. Preview the description and notice the new border around the paragraph and underneath the sentence.

End

INTRODUCTION

One of the advantages of border styles is that you have several to choose from. Another is that you can set them just about anywhere. If you set a border on a block element, such as a **p** or **div**, the border runs around the outside of the block. If you set it on an inline object, such as a **span**, the border runs around each line.

TIP

What Styles Are Available?
You can set the **border** style to **none**, **hidden**, **dotted**, **dashed**, **solid**, **double**, **groove**, **ridge**, **inset**, or **outset**. Keep in mind, however, that some browsers don't support all these styles.

TIP

What Sizes and Colors Are Available?
You can make borders virtually any size, but it's best to keep them fairly thin—say, less than 10px. You can use any available color for a border.

Adding Background Colors to Objects

Start

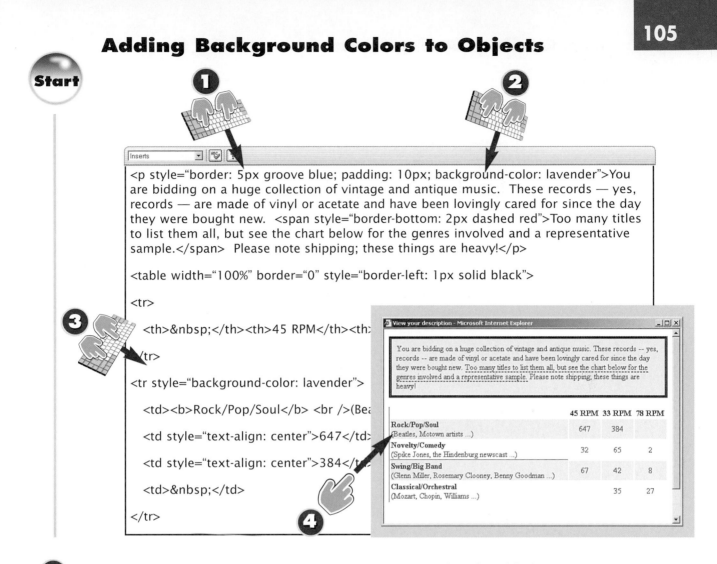

```
<p style="border: 5px groove blue; padding: 10px; background-color: lavender">You
are bidding on a huge collection of vintage and antique music.  These records — yes,
records — are made of vinyl or acetate and have been lovingly cared for since the day
they were bought new.  <span style="border-bottom: 2px dashed red">Too many titles
to list them all, but see the chart below for the genres involved and a representative
sample.</span>  Please note shipping; these things are heavy!</p>

<table width="100%" border="0" style="border-left: 1px solid black">

<tr>

  <th> </th><th>45 RPM</th><th

</tr>

<tr style="background-color: lavender">

  <td><b>Rock/Pop/Soul</b> <br />(Bea

  <td style="text-align: center">647</td>

  <td style="text-align: center">384</t

  <td> </td>

</tr>
```

1. Add a section of content to the page or use one you've already added.

2. Set the background color of the section by typing **background-color: lavender"** in the opening **<p>** tag.

3. Set the background color for alternating rows of the table by adding **style= "background-color: lavender"** to every other opening **<tr>** tag.

4. Preview the description, noting the changes.

End

INTRODUCTION

One easy way to add visual interest to your description is through the use of background colors. You can add a background color to virtually any object using the **background-color** style.

TIP

What Colors Can I Use?

Colors can be set by name, number, or hex code. Names are, of course, convenient, but using the number or hex code of a color gives you more control. There are only a few dozen color names; the hex code gives you complete control over the red, green, and blue values of a color. See http://www.nicholaschase.com/easyhtml4ebay/colors.html for more information.

Adding Background Images to Objects

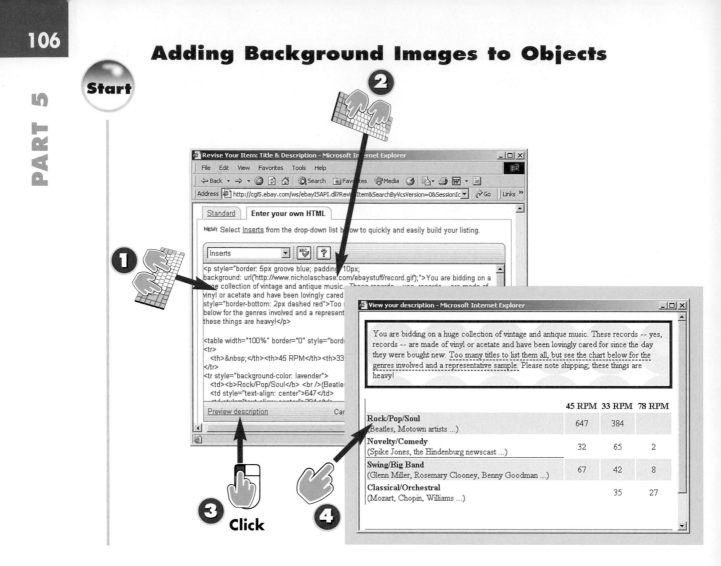

1 Add content to the description.

2 Add the background URL to the style for the object by typing **background: url('http:// www.nicholaschase.com/ebaystuff/record.gif')** within the **style** attribute.

3 Click **Preview Description**.

4 Notice that the image fills the area behind the text, repeating as necessary.

End

TIP

Similar to the Page
Adding a background to a section gives you many of the same capabilities as adding one to the page. See page 107 for more information.

TIP

Keeping It Readable
It's easy to obscure your text with a distracting background. What's more, even if people can read the text, a distracting background makes them leave your ad more quickly, so be sure to keep your backgrounds subtle.

Adding a Background Color to the Overall Description

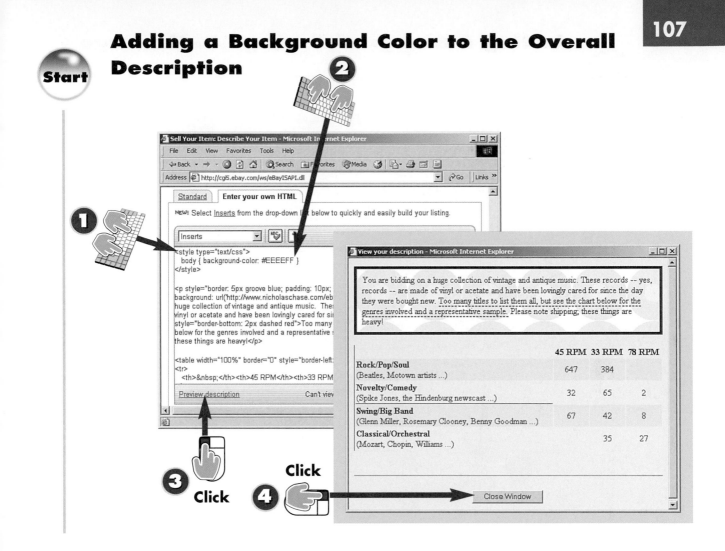

1 Create a style section by typing **<style type="text/css">** and **</style>**.

2 Type **body { background-color: #EEEEFF }** between the opening and closing **<style>** tags to create a style rule for the body and to set the background color.

3 Click **Preview Description**.

4 Note the changes; then click **Close Window** when you are finished.

End

TIP

I Don't See It!
In some browsers you might not be able to see the results of your handiwork until after the auction is submitted because you're working on the body tag and it's not present in the preview window.

TIP

What Colors Can I Use?
You can use the same colors that are available for other objects. Remember to keep your text legible!

Adding a Background Image to the Page

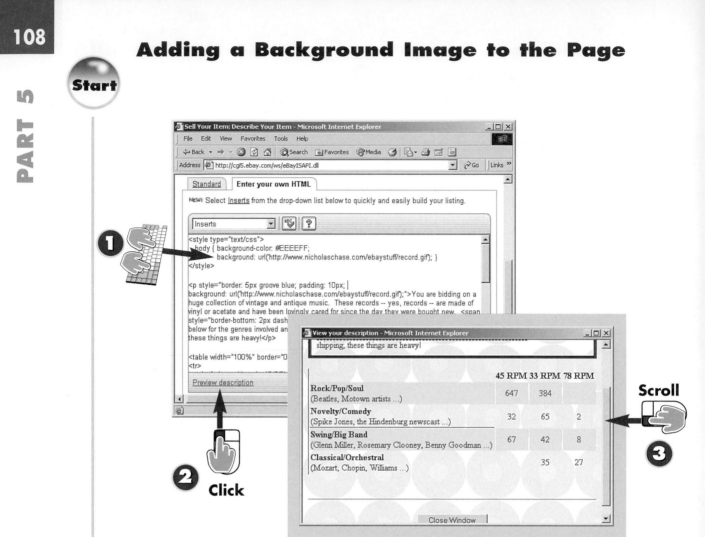

Start

Scroll

Click

1. Add the background style to the body with a reference to a background image by typing **background: url(http://www.nicholaschase.com/ebaystuff/record.gif**.

2. Click **Preview Description** to see the results.

3. Scroll the page and notice how the background moves.

Just as you can add a background image to a section, you can add one to the actual page. You can also control whether the background moves when the user scrolls the page by using the **background-attachment** style.

4 Set the background to stay fixed to the browser window using the **background-attachment** property. Type **background-attachment: fixed;**.

5 Click **Preview Description** to see the results.

6 Scroll the page and notice that the background doesn't move.

End

Match Colors

TIP

If the user has problems downloading the background image, the browser doesn't show an error—it just doesn't show the background. You can maintain your color scheme by also setting a background color that matches the dominant color in the image, just in case.

Creating a Tiling Background

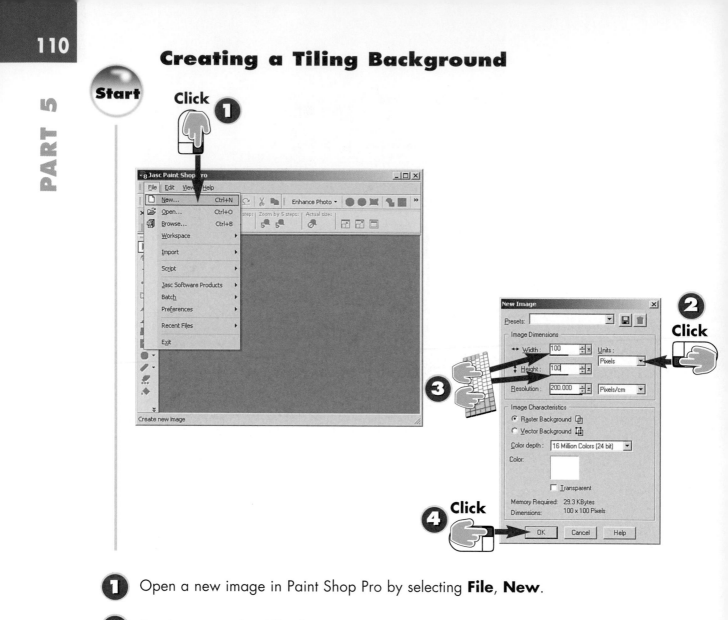

Start

Click 1

Click 2

3

Click 4

1. Open a new image in Paint Shop Pro by selecting **File**, **New**.

2. For the units, select **Pixels**.

3. Set the width and height to **100** pixels.

4. Click **OK**.

INTRODUCTION
Many designers use small tiled images that repeat behind content because they can fill a large space. Because the edges of these tiles must match, a lot of techniques involve slicing up an image and blending edges and so on, but Paint Shop Pro actually provides a fairly simple process.

TIP
How Big Should I Make the Tile?
There's no set size for a background image, but 100 × 100 is generally large enough to create a pattern that's not maddeningly distracting.

TIP
Reinventing the Wheel
You don't have to create your own backgrounds. There are plenty of sites where you can download free or nearly free backgrounds that others have created, such as http://www.grsites.com/textures/.

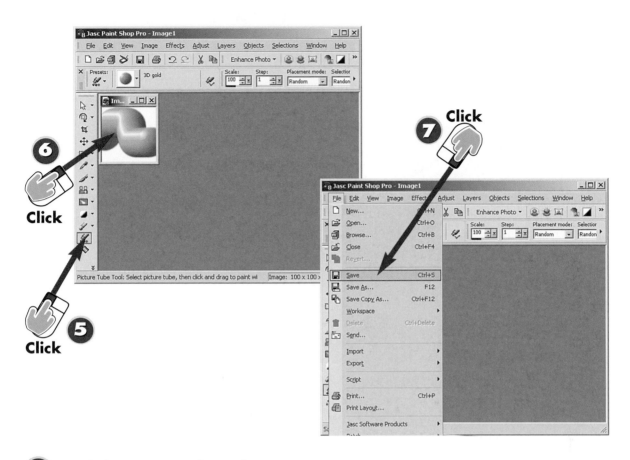

5 Click the **Picture Tube** tool.

6 Click in the image and start drawing.

7 Select **File**, **Save** to begin saving the image.

See next page

What Can I Draw?
You can make a background tile out of just about anything. Usually, people choose geometric shapes or textures. I've chosen something obviously irregular so you can see a definite effect.

TIP

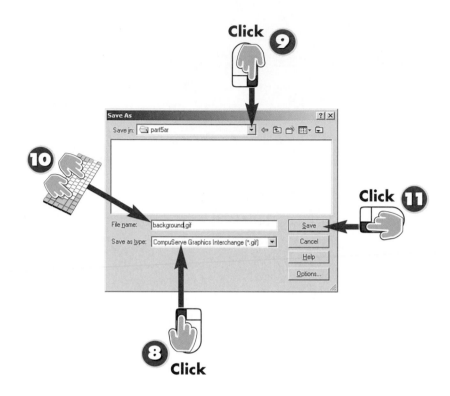

Click **9**

Click **11**

8 Click

8 Set the **Save As** type to **CompuServe Graphics Interchange (*.gif)**.

9 Choose a location for the file.

10 Name the file.

11 Click **Save**.

Which File Format Should I Use?

Photographs and images with gradients save better as JPEG files, whereas line art and other graphics with solid colors save better as GIF files.

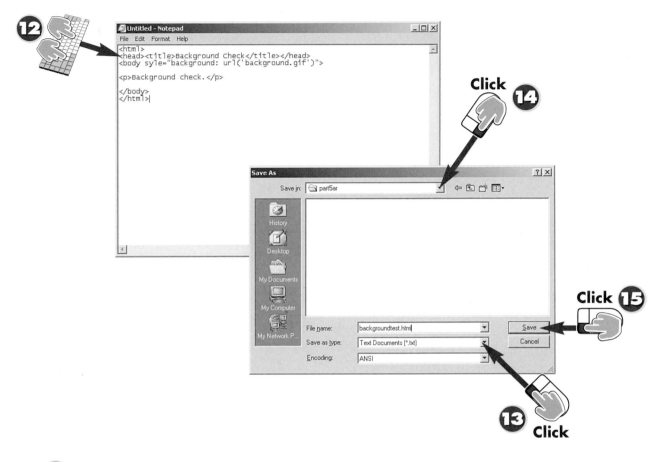

12 Open Notepad and add the HTML for a plain page with a background.

13 Save the file; make sure the **Save As** type is set to **Text Documents (*.txt)**.

14 Choose the directory where you saved the test background.

15 Name the file and click **Save**.

See next page

Do I Have to Use Notepad?
No, you can use any text editor, such as WordPad, that lets you save a plain text file. You can also add the background directly into an auction to see how it will look.

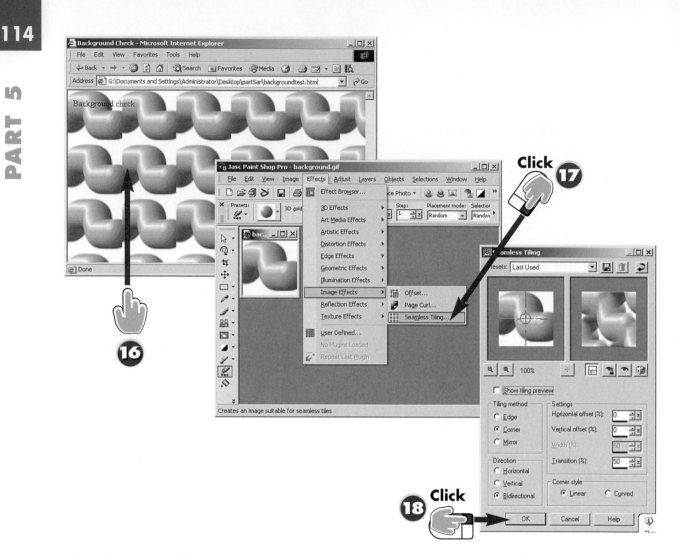

16 Open your file in your browser, notice that the background tiles don't mesh together and that the text is hard to read..

17 Back in Paint Shop Pro, select **Effects**, **Image Effects**, **Seamless Tiling**.

18 Click **OK**.

What Is Happening Here?

TIP

The secret to creating a tiling image is in ensuring that the edges match. The Seamless Tiling function creates, overlaps, and shifts copies of the original image to make that happen. Paint Shop Pro also enables you to control aspects of the conversion, such as the center point.

Why a Separate HTML Page?

TIP

To see a background image on an eBay auction, you need to upload it to a server every time you make a change. Here you are creating a simple HTML page that uses a local image file as a background so you can quickly see changes.

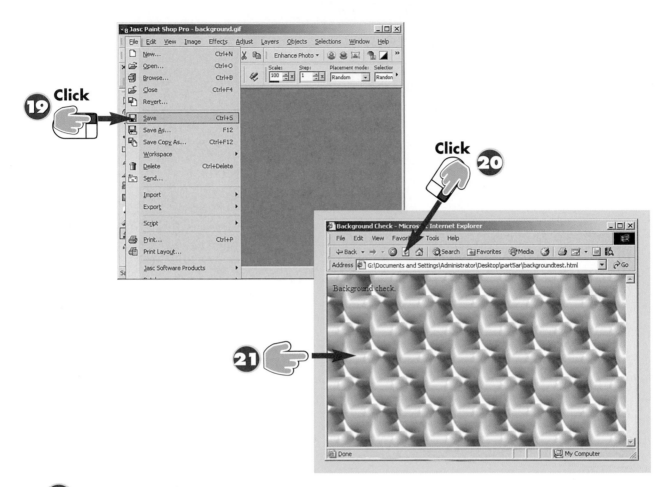

19 Select **File**, **Save**.

20 Back in the browser, click **Refresh**.

21 Notice that the tiles now flow seamlessly into one another but that the image is still too dark and obscures the text.

See next page

Only 256 Colors?
The GIF format allows only 256 colors. In most cases, that's plenty, but if you're saving as a GIF file, the program might warn you of this limitation. Just click OK.

TIP

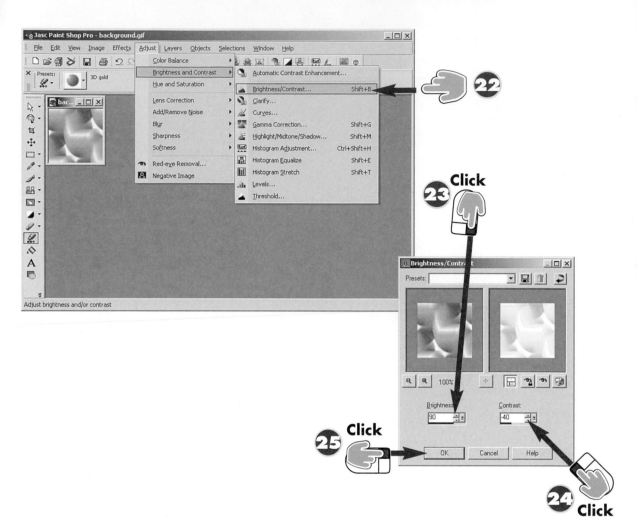

 Back in Paint Shop Pro, select **Adjust**, **Brightness and Contrast**, **Brightness/Contrast**.

 Adjust the brightness up to lighten the image.

24 Adjust the contrast down to soften it.

25 Click **OK**.

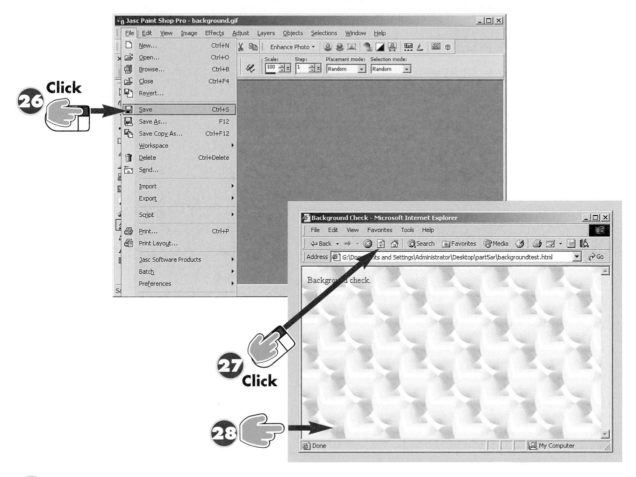

26 Click **File**, **Save**.

27 Back in the browser, click **Refresh**.

28 Notice that although this image could probably stand a little more work, the page is much more readable. Be sure to keep your background images as subtle as possible.

End

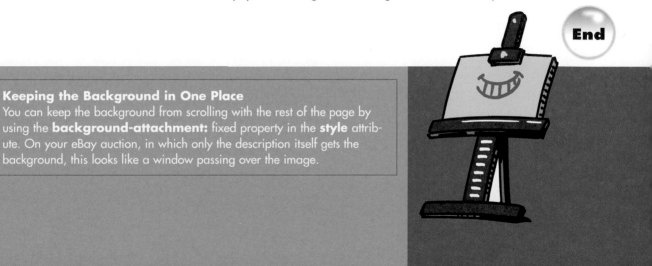

Keeping the Background in One Place
You can keep the background from scrolling with the rest of the page by using the **background-attachment:** fixed property in the **style** attribute. On your eBay auction, in which only the description itself gets the background, this looks like a window passing over the image.

TIP

Styling the Text

By now you might be wondering whether there is any way of enabling web pages to duplicate some of the functions available in a word processing program, such as controlling the appearance of your text. Maybe you want to make your headings stand out by changing their color. Maybe you want to change the typeface, or font, of your text. Maybe you want to create a bulleted list of features or a numbered list of steps. In this part, we look at all those things.

To make those changes, you need to use styles. Styles are collections of properties that apply to a particular object, such as a block of text, on the page. For example, a headline style might include the color (black), size (24-point), and font (Times New Roman). Changing any of those properties changes the style, and thus the appearance, of your text.

The key in effective text styling (besides good design sense, which I can't teach you in this book) is to know which properties—such as font, size, and so on—you can change and how to change them.

In this part, we look at the various properties and the values you can use. We also look at font issues and how you can create an "arbitrary" style that takes effect for the whole page so you don't have to set the style for each paragraph, for example.

Styling Text

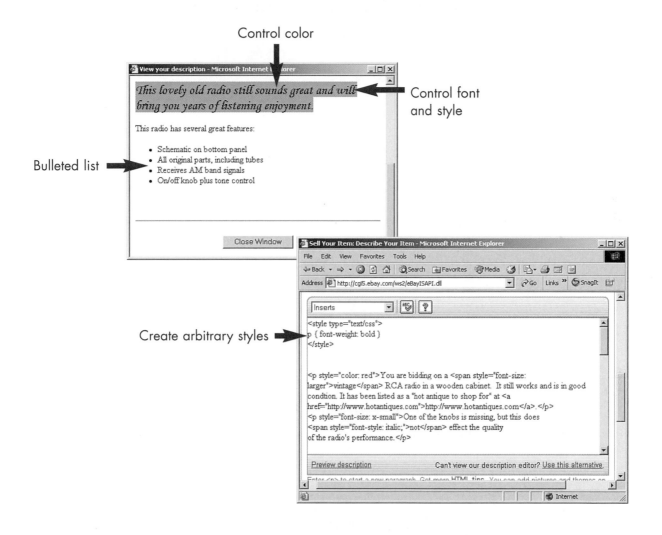

Changing the Size of Your Text

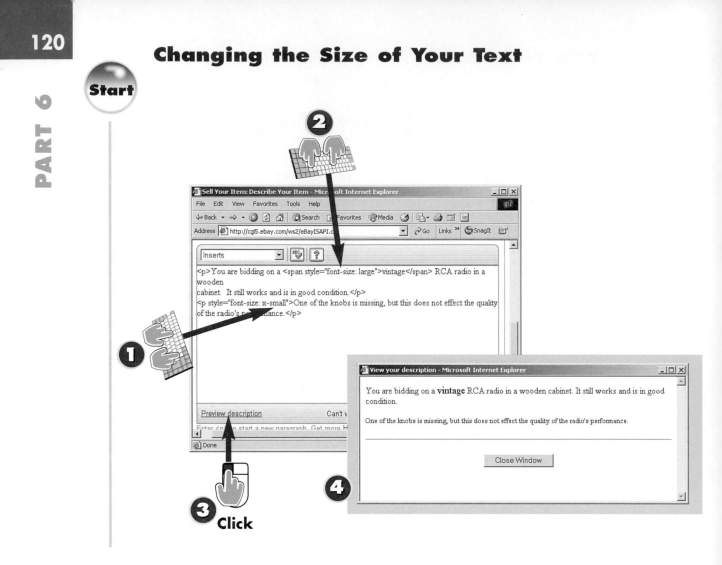

Start

Click

End

1. Edit your item description and set the size of one paragraph to be the fine print by adding **style="font-size: x-small"** to the second **<p>** tag.

2. Set the word **vintage** to be larger than normal by creating a span and setting the size of the text to be larger by typing **vintage**.

3. Click **Preview Description** to see the results.

4. Note the size changes. The **vintage** text is now larger than the surrounding text and the second paragraph is smaller.

INTRODUCTION

Perhaps the most common thing you'll want to do to your text is to make it bigger or smaller. Using styles, you can make the text larger or smaller than the sur-rounding text, or you can set a specific size.

TIP

Style Is No Substitute for Substance!
Just because you can create a large heading with styles rather than tags, such as **<h1>** or **<h2>**, doesn't mean you should. These tags give structure to the page, and you should use them whenever possible.

TIP

Measurements
You can set text using relative sizes, such as **xx-small**, **x-small**, **small**, **medium**, **large**, **x-large**, and **xx-large**. You can even use **larger** or **smaller** or set spe-cific sizes, such as **75px** or **8pt**.

Changing Text Colors

Start

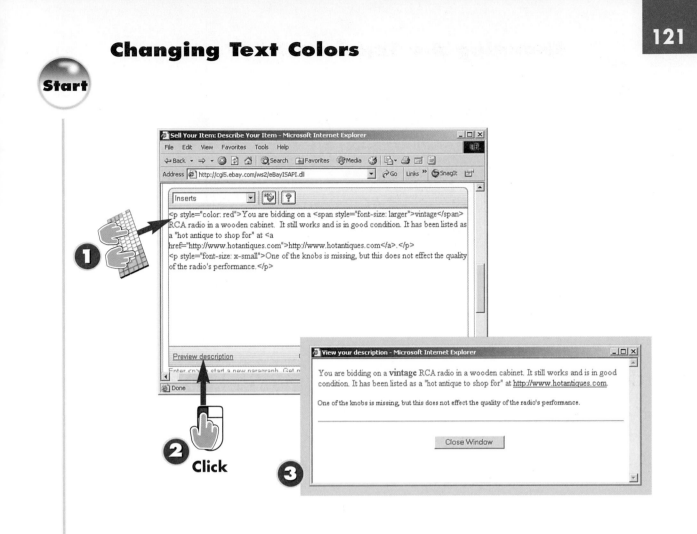

2 Click

1 Edit a description that has a link in it and set the color on a paragraph by typing **style="color: red"** in the opening tag.

2 Click **Preview Description** to see the results.

3 Note that the first paragraph is now red.

End

INTRODUCTION

Just as you can set the color for a section of the page, you can set it for areas of text. It works because the color style affects everything in the element.

TIP

But It Didn't All Change!
In general, setting the color style affects all the contents within an element, but sometimes—as in the case of the link—it is overridden by a higher-priority style. You can overcome this by placing the color style directly on the affected element, such as the **<a></a>** tag, in this case.

Changing the Typeface

Start

Sell Your Item: Describe Your Item - Microsoft Internet Explorer

File Edit View Favorites Tools Help

Back ▾ → ▾ ⊗ ⊗ ⊗ | ⊗Search ⊗Favorites ⊗Media ⊗ | ⊗▾ ⊗ ⊗ ⊗

Address ⊗ http://cgi5.ebay.com/ws2/eBayISAPI.dll ▾ ⊗Go | Links » ⊗SnagIt ⊗

Inserts ▾ ⊗ ⊗

\ You are bidding on a \vintage\ RCA radio in a wooden cabinet. It still works and is in good condition. It has been listed as a "hot antique to shop for" at \<a href="http://www.hotantiques.com">http://www.hotantiques.com\</a>.\

\ One of the knobs is missing, but this does not effect the quality of the radio's performance.\

①

\ This lovely old radio still sounds great and will bring you years of listening enjoyment.\

Preview description

Enter \<p> to start a new paragraph. Get

Done

② **Click**

③

View your description - Microsoft Internet Explorer

You are bidding on a **vintage** RCA radio in a wooden cabinet. It still works and is in good condition. It has been listed as a "hot antique to shop for" at http://www.hotantiques.com.

One of the knobs is missing, but this does not effect the quality of the radio's performance.

This lovely old radio still sounds great and will bring you years of listening enjoyment.

Close Window

① Edit an item description and use the **font-family** style to change the font and size for the first paragraph by adding **style="font-family: 'Monotype Corsiva'; font-size: large "** to the **\<p>** tag.

② Click **Preview Description** to see the results.

③ Notice that the last paragraph is now displayed in the new font.

End

If you don't like the plain, serif font that is the default for an eBay description, you can change it for your item description. Keep in mind, though, that the browser can use only fonts that are installed on the user's computer. Just because you have some fancy font and can see it, doesn't mean everybody else can.

What Fonts Can I Use?

You can use any font you want. You can probably get a list by looking at the formatting options in your word processing program, but remember to use the more common fonts wherever possible.

Allowing for Missing Fonts

Start

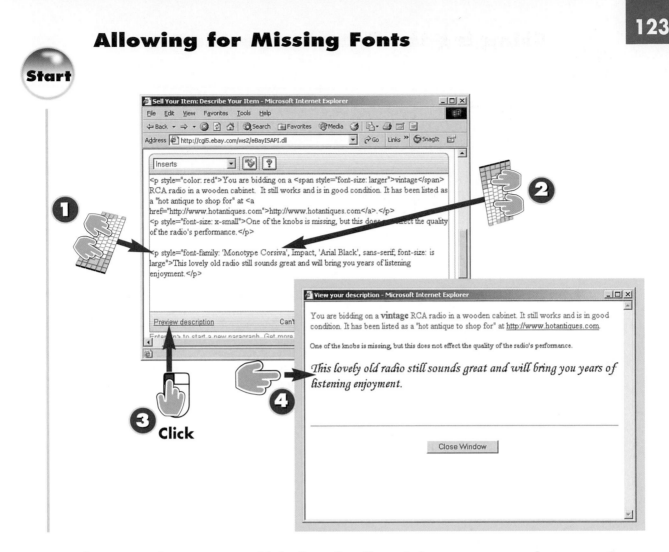

1 Edit an item description to add the **font-family** style by typing **<p style= "font-family: ; font-size: large ">**.

2 Add the preferred font, then a similar, more common font, and then the general font family by adding **'Monotype Corsiva', Impact, 'Arial Black', sans-serif**.

3 Click **Preview Description** to see the results.

4 Now, if your font is not available on the user's computer, a more common replacement font appears instead.

End

INTRODUCTION
Many web designers create a beautiful page with a lovely, fancy font—only to discover that nobody sees the page as he does because that great font isn't available on others' machines. To avoid this, you can provide more common alternatives in case your preferred font isn't available.

TIP
How Does the Browser Decide?
The browser starts at the front of the list and keeps going until it finds something it can use. If it gets to the general font family, it chooses among the installed fonts that belong to that family.

TIP
What's a Font Family?
A *font family* is a group of fonts, such as all sizes and styles of Palatino. In this case, however, I'm referring to general font families, such as serif and sans serif.

Using a Span to Style Specific Text

Start

Add small print to your description by adding **<p style="font-size: x-small">**
One of the knobs is missing, but this does not effect the quality of the
radio's performance.</p>.

Add a span tag with styling information to the word **not** by typing **<span**
style="font-style: italic;"> before **not**, and **</span>** after **not**.

Click **Preview Description** to see the results.

Notice that the word **not** is now in italics.

End

INTRODUCTION

Earlier in the book I introduced you to the **div** element, which is to simply provide a container to which styles can be applied. The only trouble with a **div** tag is that it must appear on its own line, so you can't use it to add style to a single word in the middle of a line. That's where the **<span></span>** tag comes in.

TIP

Why Not Use a div?
A **div** is called a *block* element because it forces the browser to create a line just for it. A **span** is called an *inline* element because it doesn't affect the lines the browser creates.

TIP

What Values Can I Use for font-style?
The **font-style** property is a little odd. All you can really do with it is make your text italic. The three permissible values are **none**, **italic**, and **oblique**. (**oblique** is similar to italic.)

Using Strikethrough

Start

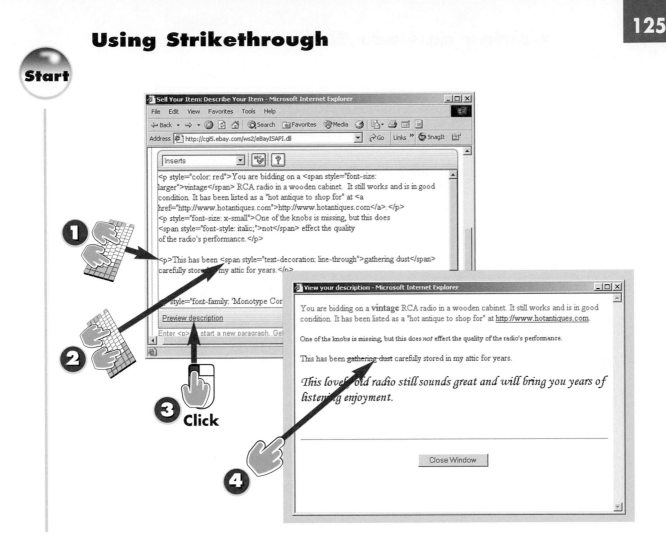

3 Click

1 Add text to the description by typing **\<p>This has been gathering dust carefully stored in my attic for years.\</p>**.

2 Add a **span** tag with the **text-decoration** property to add a line through the text by adding **** before **gathering dust** and adding **** after it.

3 Click **Preview Description** to see the results.

4 Notice that the strikethrough style has been applied to the text in the **** tag.

End

TIP

What About the \<del> Tag?
HTML defines a tag, **\<del>**, that represents content that has been deleted. I don't recommend that you use it, though, because even though some browsers show it with a strikethrough, others simply don't display the text at all.

TIP

What text-decorations Can I Use?
Possible values for the **text-decoration** property include **none**, **underline**, **overline**, and **line-through**.

Adding an Underline

Start

Sell Your Item: Describe Your Item - Microsoft Internet Explorer

File   Edit   View   Favorites   Tools   Help

Back   •   →   •   ⊗   ⊉   ⚙   ⚲Search   ⊛Favorites   ⚙Media   ⚙   ⚲•   ⚲   ⚲   ⚲

Address http://cgi5.ebay.com/ws2/eBayISAPI.dll   ⚲Go   Links   ⚲   SnagIt

Inserts

1

```
<p>This has been <span style="text-decoration: line-through">gathering dust</span>
carefully stored in my attic for years.</p>

<p>This radio might be vintage, but to the right person,
<span style="text-decoration: underline">the memories are priceless</span>.</p>

<p style="font-family: 'Monotype Corsiva', Impact, 'Arial Black', sans-serif; font-size:
large">This lovely old radio still sounds great and will bring you years of listening
enjoyment.</p>
```

2

Preview description

Done

3 **Click**

View your description - Microsoft Internet Explorer

You are bidding on a **vintage** RCA radio in a wooden cabinet. It still works and is in good condition. It has been listed as a "hot antique to shop for" at http://www.hotantiques.com.

One of the knobs is missing, but this does *not* effect the quality of the radio's performance.

This has been ~~gathering dust~~ carefully stored in my attic for years.

This radio might be vintage, but to the right person, <u>the memories are priceless</u>.

This lovely old radio still sounds great and will bring you years of listening enjoyment.

Close Window

4

---

1 Add text to the page by typing **<p>This radio might be vintage, but to the right person, the memories are priceless.</p>**.

2 Add an underline style by adding **<span style="text-decoration: underline">** before **the memories are priceless** and adding **</span>** after it.

3 Click **Preview Description** to see the results.

4 The affected text is now underlined.

End

Another style you typically see only in advertising is the underline. There's a good reason for this on the Web: People are used to underlines representing links. When something is underlined but they can't click it, users get frustrated. So in case you have a very good reason, I'll show you how to do this, but I'm asking you, please don't.

TIP

What Should I Use Instead?
Most people use underlines to emphasize something, so why not use the emphasis (**<em></em>**) or strong (**<strong></strong>**) tags? You can also use bold (**<b></b>**) or italics (**<i></i>**).

TIP

Turning Things Around
You can actually remove the underline from a link. Common practice is to replace the underline with a different color and to have something flash, light up, or change when the user rolls the mouse over it.

Controlling the Space Between Letters

Start

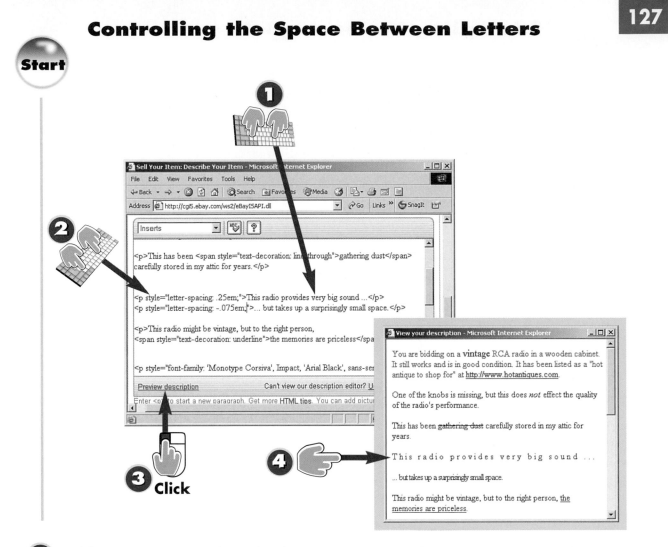

Click

1 Add two new paragraphs to the description.

2 Spread out the letters in the first line by adding **<p style="letter-spacing: .25em">** and scrunch the text in the second line with **<p style="letter-spacing: -.075em">**.

3 Click **Preview Description** to see the results.

4 Notice the changes in spacing in the text.

End

INTRODUCTION

One form of text manipulation graphic designers often try to employ is adjusting the spacing between letters, or *kerning*. Often they're relieved to find that they can also do this kind of adjustment in HTML.

TIP

What Values Can I Use for Kerning?
You can specify that the **letter-spacing** should be normal or based on ems and ens, pixels (px), or centimeters (cm). Internet Explorer treats the en unit like the px unit.

TIP

Word Spacing
You can use the **word-spacing** property to keep the distance between letters normal but spread out the words instead. The same measurements apply.

Controlling the Space Between Lines

Start

<p>This has been <span style="text-decoration: line-through">gathering dust</span> carefully stored in my attic for years.</p>

<p style="letter-spacing: .25em; line-height: 175%">This radio provides very big sound ...</p>
<p style="letter-spacing: -.075em; line-height: .75em">... but takes up a surprisingly small space.</p>

<p>This radio might be vintage, but to the right person,
<span style="text-decoration: underline">the memories are priceless</span>.</p>

Preview description   Can't view our description editor? Use this alternative

Click

carefully stored in my attic for years.

This radio provides
very big sound ...

... but takes up a surprisingly small space.

This radio might be vintage, but to the right person, the memories are priceless.

① Use the **line-height** property to spread out the lines of text in the first paragraph by typing **<p style="letter-spacing: .25em;line-height: 175%">**.

② Move the lines of the second paragraph closer together by typing **<p style= "letter-spacing: -.075em;line-height: .75em">**.

③ Click **Preview Description** to see the results.

④ Notice how the first part of the sentence has a larger gap between lines but the second part has a smaller gap.

End

What Values Can I Use for the Line Height?
You can set a specific height of the line based on its "normal" value. You can provide a percentage, a number to multiply by the normal value, or a length value.

How Can I Move Them Closer?
Line heights (and letter spacings, for that matter) can also be negative values, which move the text closer together.

Changing the Text Background

Start

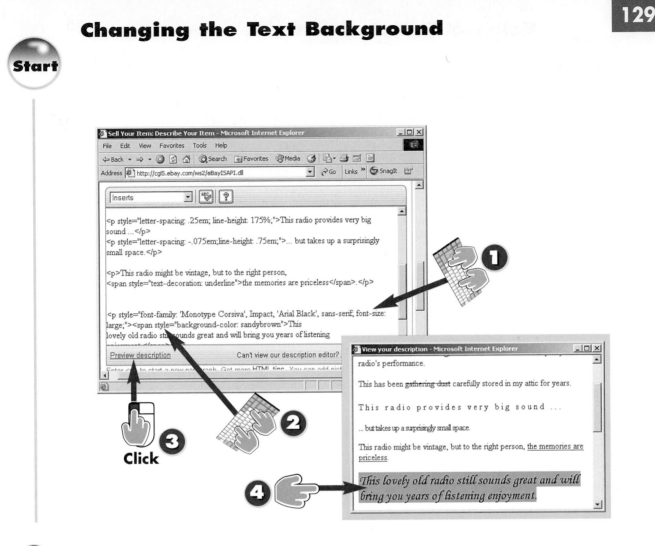

Click

1 Add text to the description, or use text you already have.

2 Add a span with a **background-color** style that surrounds the text to color by adding **<span style="background-color: sandybrown">**.

3 Click **Preview Description** to see the results.

4 Notice that the text within the span now has a background color.

End

INTRODUCTION

Just because you're dealing with text doesn't mean you can't control the background.

TIP

Can I Add a Background Image?
Yes, you can add a background image to text just as you would add it to a section. See page 106 for details.

TIP

What Are Those Spaces?
In some browsers, only the area behind the actual text has the background color. If you want the whole block to be filled, you need to add the color to the paragraph tag or another block enclosing the text.

Using a Bulleted List

Start

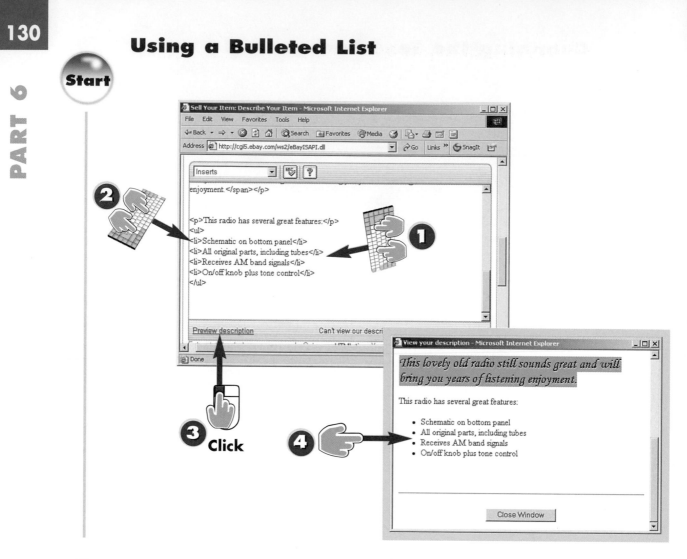

 Add a list of items to the description.

 Create an unordered list by adding **<ul>** tags; then designate each entry by adding an **<li>** tag to it.

 Click **Preview Description** to see the results.

 You now have a bulleted list of your items.

End

TIP

Do I Have to Use Those Circles?
You can use the **list-style-type** style to change the bullets. Acceptable values for an unordered list are **disc**, **circle**, and **square**. You can also specify the **list-style-image** property to use a small image instead.

TIP

Can I Use a List Within a List?
Yes, you can. Just add your new list as the content of a list item.

Using a Numbered List

Start

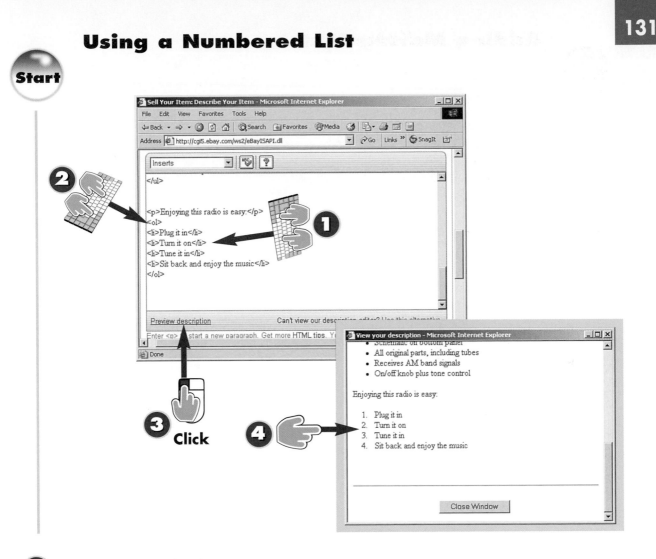

Click

1. Add list items to the description.

2. Create an ordered list by adding **<ol>** tags; then make each item into a list item by adding an **<li>** tag to each.

3. Click **Preview Description** to see the results.

4. You now have a numbered list.

End

INTRODUCTION

Sometimes there's a definite order to items you want to include in a list. In that case, you should use a numbered list.

TIP

Do I Have to Start with 1?
No. You can set a new starting number for the list by adding the **start** attribute to the list itself, as in **<ol start="10">**. You can also specify a value for a specific list item, as in **<li value="10">**, and the list will continue on from there.

TIP

Do I Have to Use Plain Numbers?
You can change the numbering style by setting the **list-style-type** property. Values include **decimal-leading-zero**, **decimal**, **upper-** and **lower-roman**, **upper-** and **lower-latin**, and **none**.

Adding Moving Text

Start

Inserts

`<p>This radio might be vintage, but to the right person,`
`<span style="text-decoration: underline">the memories are priceless</span>.</p>`

`<marquee behavior="scroll" width="75%"><p style="font-family: 'Monotype Corsiva', Impact, 'Arial Black', sans-serif; font-size: large;"><span style="background-color: sandybrown">This lovely old radio still sounds great and will bring you years of listening enjoyment.</span></p></marquee>`

`<p>This radio has several great features:</p>`
`<ul>`
`<li>Schematic on bottom panel</li>`

Preview description   Can't view our desc

Click

View your description - Microsoft Internet Explorer

performance.

This has been gathering dust carefully stored in my attic for years.

This radio provides very big sound ...

... but takes up a surprisingly small space.

This radio might be vintage, but to the right person, the memories are priceless.

o still sounds great and will bring you y

This radio has several great features:

- Schematic on bottom panel
- All original parts, including tubes

1 Find text in your description you want to move and add the marquee by typing **<marquee behavior="scroll" width="75%" >** before and **</marquee>** after the text.

2 Click **Preview Description** to see the results.

3 Your text now moves across the screen like a marquee.

End

Images and the <marquee> Tag

The **<marquee>** tag adds motion to anything inside it. Here I've used text, but the most common use of a **<marquee>** on eBay is to create a series of moving images. Typically, sellers create a marquee of thumbnails that link to their other auctions. Simply create the links (see Part 7 for information about links) and place the **<marquee>** tag around them.

Applying General Styles

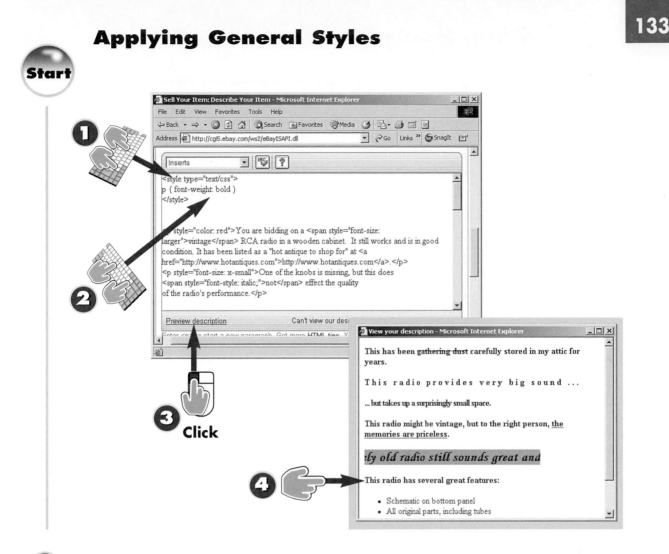

1 Add a style section by typing **<style type="text/css"></style>**.

2 Make all paragraphs bold by adding a **font-weight** style for all **p** elements. Type **p { font-weight: bold }**.

3 Click **Preview Description** to see the results.

4 Notice that all the text in a **<p>** element is now bold but that the list items, which are in a **<li>** element instead, are not.

End

INTRODUCTION

You don't have to set your styles individually. You can create a *style rule* that applies to a certain element or a certain type of element. For example, you can specify that all bold text should be blue or that all links should be green.

TIP

What's Going On Here?
When you create a style rule, first tell the browser to which elements the rule applies. In this example, we've specified all the **<p>** elements. Next, specify the property to change (such as **font-weight**) and the value to change it to (such as **bold**).

TIP

Style More Than One Element with One Rule
You can add a style to more than one element (as in **p, li { font-weight: bold }**) or to a specific type of element (such as **ol>li**, which applies only to list items that are part of an ordered list).

Creating Links

In many ways, links are the foundation of the World Wide Web. Without links, which let you move from page to page, send emails, start chat sessions, and perform other actions, there wouldn't be much web in the World Wide Web. In fact, the Web was originally designed specifically for linking from resource to resource. All the HTML we've used so far has just been window dressing added on afterward.

Still, you could conceivably sell on eBay for years without ever creating a link of your own because the overall eBay page takes care of most of the things you'd want to let people link to, such as sending you an email or looking at your other auctions. It would be nice, though, if you could control those things yourself so you could integrate them into your presentation. Besides, there's so much more you can do with links, such as popping up a window with more information.

In short, being able to control your own links in an eBay auction means you have the ability to completely control the user's view of your auction. It's almost like creating your own site, in which you can decide which links you want to emphasize; thus, you can steer the user in the direction in which you want her to go.

In this part, we look at what links are, how to create them, and how to control what they do and how they look.

Creating Links

Create an email link →

Link to your other auctions

Pop up a new window →

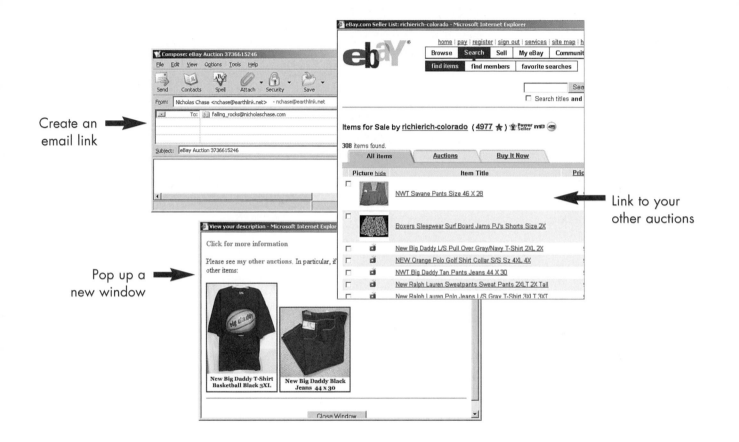

Creating a "Send Me Email" Link

Start

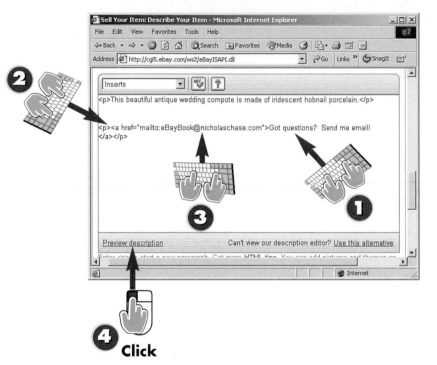

4 Click

1 Add the text you want to link to your description by typing **<p>Got questions? Send me email!</p>**.

2 Add the link, or anchor tag by adding the opening **<a>** and closing **</a>** tags to the text.

3 Add the text **mailto:** and your email address to the **href** attribute.

4 Click **Preview Description** to see your progress.

By far the most common question I get asked is, "How do I make a link so people can send me email?" It's no wonder; fast, receptive customer service is one key to having a successful eBay business. A buyer who can't immediately resolve any questions usually just moves on. Fortunately, creating an obvious email link is easy.

What's This mailto: Stuff?
Links usually just send email or go to another page, but they can tell the browser to do just about anything. That bit before the colon is called the *protocol*. Common protocols include **http** for linking to other pages, **ftp** for downloading files, and **mailto** for creating an email message.

Click 5

This beautiful antique w...ng compote is made of iridescent hobnail porcelain.

Got questions? Send me email!

Close Window

8

6

Compose (no subject)

File   View   Options   Tools   Help

Send   Contacts   Spell   Attach   Sec...   Save

From: Nicholas Chase <nick@nicholaschase.com> - *nick@nicholaschase.com*

To: eBayBook@nicholaschase.com

Subject:

7

---

5 Click the link. The window that pops up depends on what email program you have installed.

6 Notice that your email address is already in the **To:** box because it was part of the link.

7 To test it, type text in the subject line.

8 Click **Send**.

End

What About Setting the Subject?
You can actually set any of the information for this message. See page 138 for information on how to set the subject line.

What About Webmail?
The browser can pop up an email window only if the user has an email client (such as Microsoft Outlook or Mozilla Firefox) installed. Users who exclusively use webmail have to enter the address manually—just as they do with any other email link they encounter.

Setting the Subject Line on an Email

Start

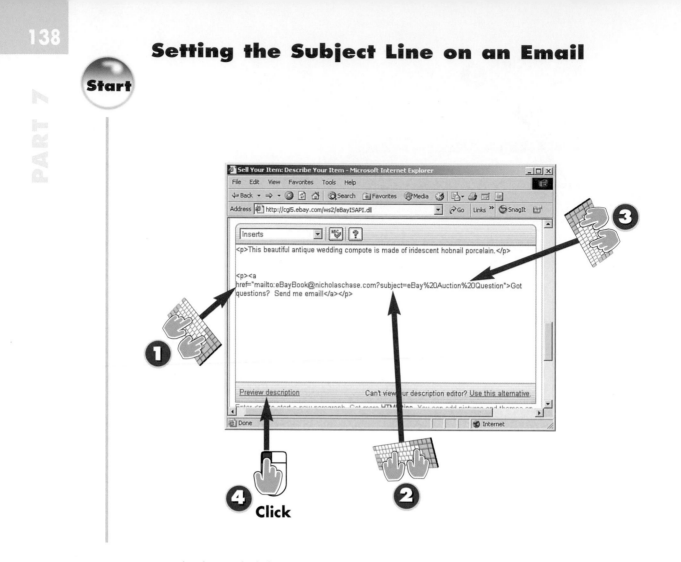

Click

1. Create the basic link by typing **<p><a href="mailto:eBayBook@ nicholaschase.com">Got questions? Send me email!</a></p>**.

2. When you want to add more information to a URL, you put it after a question mark by adding **?subject=eBay Auction Question** directly after your email address.

3. Some browsers don't like spaces in a URL, so replace spaces with **%20**. It's turned back into spaces later, when it's safe.

4. Click **Preview Description** to see your changes.

If you receive a lot of email regarding your auctions, you'll find life a lot easier if they all have the same format so they're easy to pick out from the spam. This task shows you how to automatically set the subject line when the buyer clicks the link.

TIP

Freedom of Expression
Just because you're setting the subject line doesn't mean you can count on it arriving intact. All you're doing is setting it for the user's convenience. When the message window pops up, the user is free to change the subject to anything she wants.

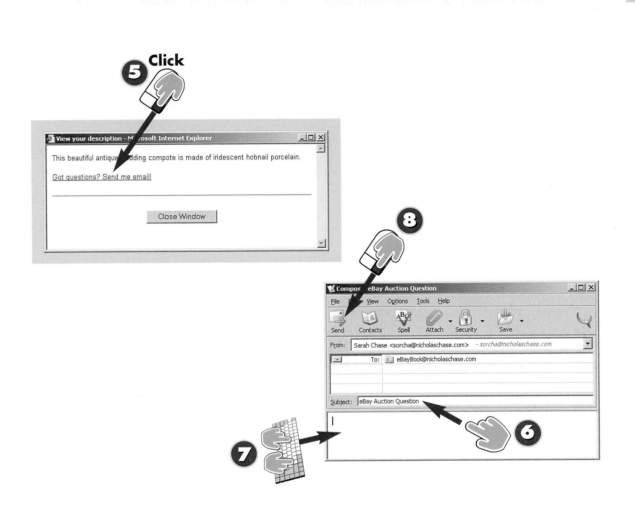

5 Click the email link.

6 Notice that the subject line has been set.

7 Type a sample message.

8 Click **Send**.

End

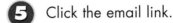

Including the Auction Number

One common use for setting subject lines is to include the auction number, but when you're building the auction you don't have that information yet. You can add the auction number by revising the description after saving it, or you can set it automatically. See page 140 for details.

Including the Auction Number in an Email Link Automatically

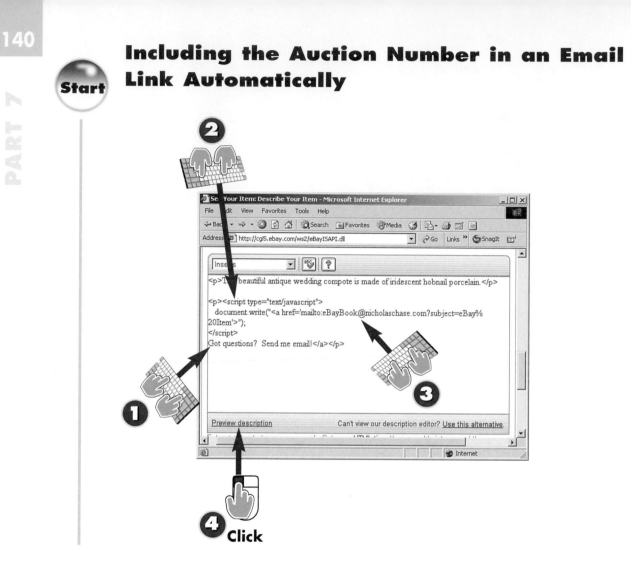

Click

 Add the text you want to turn into an email link by typing **<p>Got questions? Send me email!</a></p>**.

 Create a script section by typing **<script type="text/javascript"></script>**.

 Add the link tag around the text by typing **document.write("<a href='mailto: eBayBook@nicholaschase.com?subject=eBay%20Item'>");**.

4 Click **Preview Description** to see the changes.

To add the auction number to an email link using the techniques in the previous task, you have to submit the auction and then revise the description to add it. Fortunately, you can use a script to pull the auction number automatically and drop it into the link.

What Am I Doing Here?
Don't worry about how the script does what it does; you don't have to understand it to make it work. In this case, we're using JavaScript to write the first part of the link tag. The **document.write()** command outputs the content to the page.

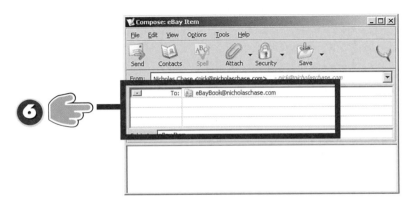

5 Click the link.

6 Because the mail window pops up, you know the script is working. Now you just need to make it add the item number to the subject.

See next page

TIP

What Is JavaScript?
JavaScript is a way of including a tiny (or even not-so-tiny) program for the user's browser to run. We'll use JavaScript a lot more in Part 10, "Making Your Listings Stand Out."

<p>This beautiful antique wedding compote is made of iridescent hobnail porcelain.</p>

<p><script type="text/javascript">
  var itemnumber = 'none';
  document.write("<a href='mailto:eBayBook@nich...echase.com?subject=eBay%
20Item%20"+ itemnumber + "'>");
</script>
Got questions? Send me email!</a></p>

Inserts

Preview description   Can't view our description editor? Use this alternative.

Done   Internet

Click

7 Create a variable, or placeholder, called **itemnumber** by typing **var itemnumber = 'none';**.

8 Add the variable to the URL by typing **+ itemnumber + "** at the end of the URL.

9 Click **Preview Description** to see the description.

What Is a Variable?

A *variable* is a kind of placeholder for data. For example, here we're creating a variable called **itemnumber** and assigning it a value of **none**. Anywhere we put the **itemnumber** variable, the browser uses the **none** value instead. Variables are useful because you can change the result just by changing the value. For example, right now **"eBay%20;Item%20"+itemnumber** outputs **eBay%20;Item%20none**. If we set **itemnumber** to **123456789**, it would output **eBay%20;Item%20123456789**.

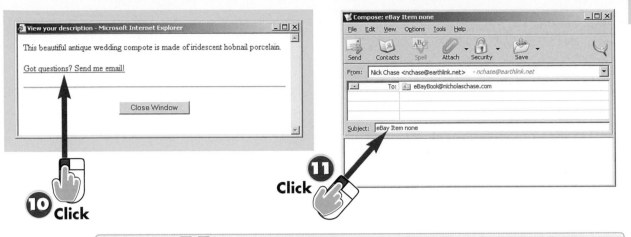

10 Click

11 Click

```
<p><script type="text/javascript">
  var itemnumber = '';
  var querystring = document["location"].toString();
  if (querystring) {
    myArray = querystring.split(/&/);
    x = 0;
    while (myArray[x]) {
        values = myArray[x].split(/=/);
        if (values[0] == "item") {
            itemnumber = values[1];
        }
        x = x + 1;
    }
  }
  document.write("<a
href='mailto:eBayBook@nicholaschase.com?subject=eBay%20Item%20"+ itemnumber + "'>");
</script>

Got questions?  Send me email!</a></p>
```

10 Click the link.

11 The script adds the value of the **itemnumber** variable to the subject line.

12 Add the bold text above to your listing verbatim; then check your entire listing to ensure that it matches.

See next page

Do I Have to Learn This JavaScript Thing?
JavaScript can be very useful in creating effects in your page, but in this case you don't necessarily need to understand it; just copying it will do.

What Does This Mean?
For those who are interested, the part of the URL that comes after the question mark is called the *querystring*. Here you're grabbing that querystring and breaking it up into pairs at the ampersands. Next, look at each pair and, when you find the one that corresponds to the item, use that value for the **itemnumber**.

```
Sell Your Item: Describe Your Item - Microsoft Internet Explorer
File   Edit   View   Favorites   Tools   Help
Back                 Search    Favorites   Media
Address  http://cgi5.ebay.com/ws2/eBayISAPI.dll        Go   Links    SnagIt

Inserts

<p><script type="text/javascript">
  var itemnumber = '';
  var querystring = document["location"].toString();
  if (querystring) {
    myArray = querystring.split(/&/);
    x = 0;
    while (myArray[x]) {
        values = myArray[x].split(/=/);
        if (values[0] == "item") {
            itemnumber = values[1];
        }
        x = x + 1;
    }
  }
  document.write("<a href='mailto:eBayBook@nicholaschase.com?subject=eBay%
20Item%20"+ itemnumber + "'>");
</script>

Got questions?  Send me email!</a></p>
Preview description                    Can't view our description editor? Use this alternative.

Done                                                      Internet
```

Click **14**

```
View your description - Microsoft Internet Explorer
This beautiful antique w...ng compote is made of iridescent hobnail porcelain.
Got questions? Send me email!
_____
             Close Window
```

13 Click

13 Click **Preview Description** to see the results.

14 Click the link.

Click

16

```
Compose: eBay Item                                    _ □ ×
File   Edit   View   Options   Tools   Help

  Send    Contacts   Spell   Attach   Security   Save

From:  Sarah Chase <sorcha@nicholaschase.com>  - sorcha@nicholaschase.com    ▼
       To:    eBayBook@nicholaschase.com


Subject:  eBay Item
```

15

15 Notice that no auction number appears in the subject line. It will when you save the auction.

16 Click the **x** to close the email window.

End

Why Doesn't the Item Number Appear?
The script pulls the item number from the URL, but until you save the auction, there is no item number to pull. The preview is just a temporary URL to show temporary data. After you save the auction and view it, the item number shows up.

Testing, Testing...
You can test this for yourself without creating a new auction. Save the description as a text file ending in **.html**, such as **mail.html**. Open the file in your browser and test the email link; then add an item number to the URL, as in **file:///F:/projects/ testclicking.html?other=bogus&item=23424**.

Linking to More Information

Start

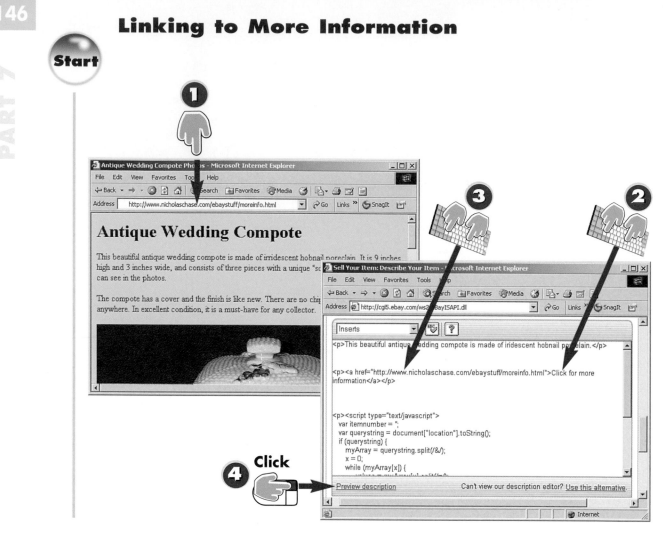

 Make note of the URL to which you want to link. (If you need to, point your browser to the page and copy the URL from the location box.)

 Add the text you want to make into a link to your item description by typing **<p>Click for more information</p>**.

 Add the **link** tag by typing **<a href="http://www.nicholaschase.com/ebaystuff/moreinfo.html">** before **Click for more information** and typing **</a>** after it.

 Click **Preview Description**.

INTRODUCTION

eBay frowns on links to other pages within an auction because they don't want potential buyers to leave the site and buy somewhere else. You can, however, link to other eBay pages, such as your About Me page or eBay store, or to a page with more information on the specific item you're selling.

When to Use It

A great use for this technique is size charts, condition grading code charts, and so on. Although technically allowed, eBay frowns on descriptions outside of the auction itself because of potential fraud.

Link to an Image

You can actually link to anything that has a URL. So, rather than linking to an actual HTML page, you can link to a plain image, but used this way, it could be a bit awkward for a user because the auction goes away and there's no information to replace it.

⑤ Click

View your description – Microsoft Internet Explorer

This beautiful antique wedding compote is made of iridescent hobnail porcelain.

Click for more information

Got questions? Send me email!

Close Window

Antique Wedding Compote Photos – Microsoft Internet Explorer

Antique Wedding Compote

This beautiful antique wedding compote is made of iridescent hobnail porcelain. It is 9 inches high and 3 inches wide, and consists of three pieces with a unique "screw type" base, as you can see in the photos.

The compote has a cover and the finish is like new. There are no chips or scratches anywhere. In excellent condition, it is a must-have for any collector.

 ⑥

⑤ Click the link.

⑥ Notice that the description preview is replaced by the new page.

End

Does My Auction Have to Go Away?

Presented just like this, the new content replaces your auction, and that's not necessarily what you want. Check out page 148 for a way to keep the auction in place but pop up the content in a new window when the user clicks your link.

Opening a New Window

Start

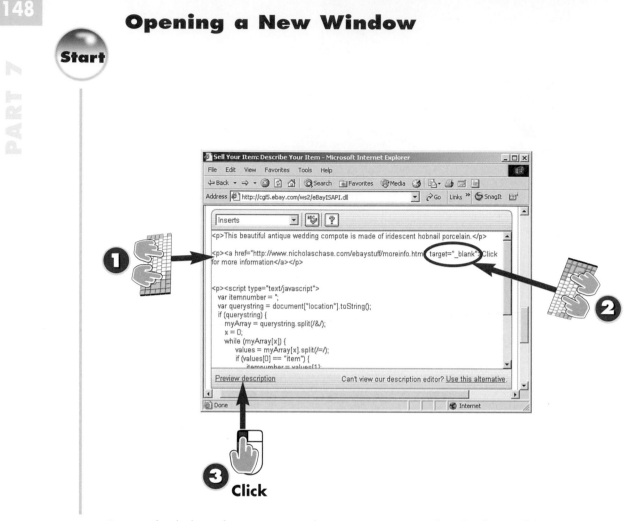

3 Click

1 Create the link to the new page by typing **\<p>\<a href="http://www.nicholaschase.com/ebaystuff/moreinfo.html">Click for more information\</a>\</p>**.

2 Add the **target** attribute and give it a value of **_blank** by adding **target="_blank"** to the link. This causes the browser to open a new window.

3 Click **Preview Description** to see the description.

Normally, when you click a link, the browser moves to the new page as the current content disappears, replaced by the new content. The trouble with that approach is that when users leave the eBay page, they can't bid on your item. Fortunately, you don't have to do it that way. Instead, you can pop up a new window with the information.

Why Not a Pop-up?
Other websites often open windows using JavaScript, but these pop-ups can be a problem on eBay because users often have pop-up blocking software. Besides, eBay tends to discourage the use of JavaScript, blocking certain commands.

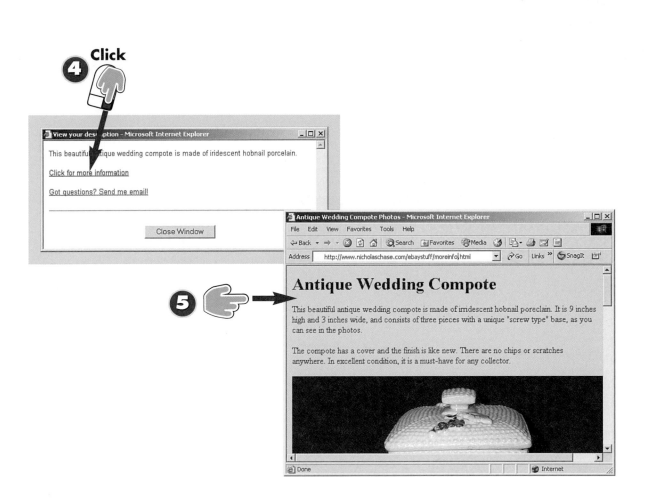

Click

(4) Click the new link.

(5) Notice that a new window opens for the content and your description preview stays where it is.

End

Multiple Pages, One Window

TIP

If you have multiple links you want to open in a single, separate window—such as enlarged photos of one item—give them all the same **target** name (other than **_blank**, which always opens a new window). When the user clicks subsequent links, the browser sees that the target already exists and uses it rather than opening a new window.

Cross-promoting with Images

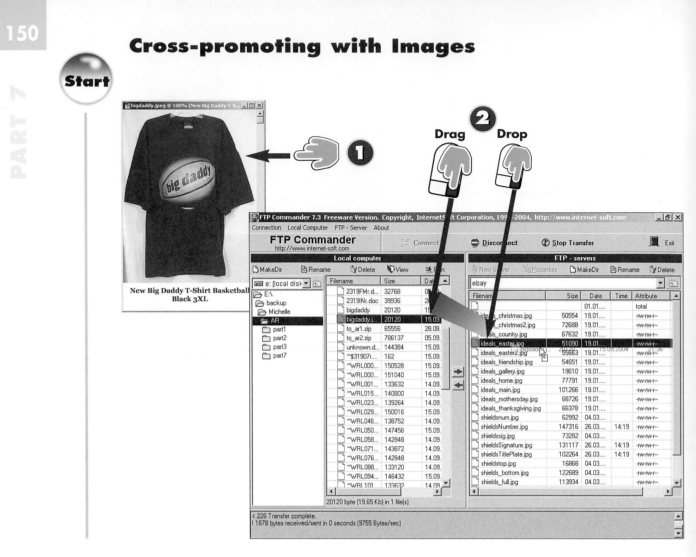

Start

① Drag ② Drop

1. Create an image that includes any information about the item you want to cross-promote, including the title, if desired.

2. Upload the image to your server or hosting service just as you would any other image.

Linking to your other auctions is an excellent way to drum up more business, but eBay forbids you to mention other auctions in your item description. This is because it causes your item to come up for searches that don't apply, so it's considered keyword spamming. You can get around this by including images that reference your items, rather than text.

One Picture Versus Many
For every photo on the page, the browser has to make a new connection to the web server, and that takes time. If you have several items to promote, consider creating a single image file that has all your items.

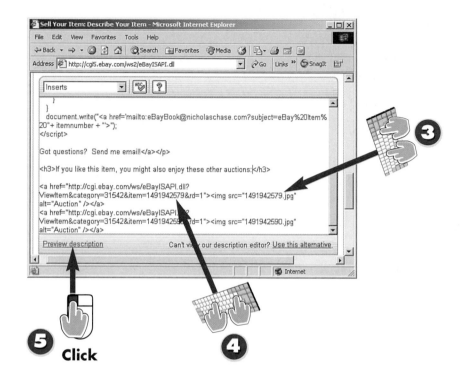

5 Click

4

3 Add the images to the description with the **<img>** tag by typing **<img src="1491942579.jpg" alt="Auction" />**.

4 Add links to the other auctions by adding **<a href="http://cgi.ebay.com/ws/ eBayISAPI.dll?ViewItem&category=31542&item=1491942579&rd=1">**.

5 Click **Preview Description** to see the changes.

See next page

Click

6

View your description - Microsoft Internet Explorer

If you like this item, you might also enjoy these other auctions:

New Big Daddy T-Shirt Basketball Black 3XL

New Big Daddy Black Jeans 44 x 30

Close Window

eBay item 3926964119 (Ends Sep-22-04 01:04:20 PDT) - NWT Big Daddy Black Jeans 44 X 30 ...

eb**a**y®

home | pay | register | sign out | services | site map | hel

Browse | Search | Sell | My eBay | Community

← Back to home page

Listed in category:

Clothing, Shoes & Accessories > Men's Clothing > Jeans

NWT Big Daddy Black Jeans 44 X 30

Item number: 3926964119

You are signed in

• **Watch this item** in My eBay

Buy It Now Price: US $21.00

Buy It Now >

Item location: www.FilthyRichFashions.com
Denver, Colorado
United States /Denver

Ships to: Worldwide

Sell
rich
(49

Fe
Po
99
Me
99

 7

6 Click one of the new links.

7 Notice that the browser goes to the other auction.

 End

Using the alt Attribute

As far as accessibility goes, I've committed a small sin here because the **alt** attribute has only the word **Auction**. For visitors without images, such as the blind or users with slow connections who've turned off images, the **alt** attribute should have a short description of the pictured item. However, because eBay considers this text when performing a search, this could be considered keyword spamming, and is not permitted.

Controlling the Link Appearance

Start

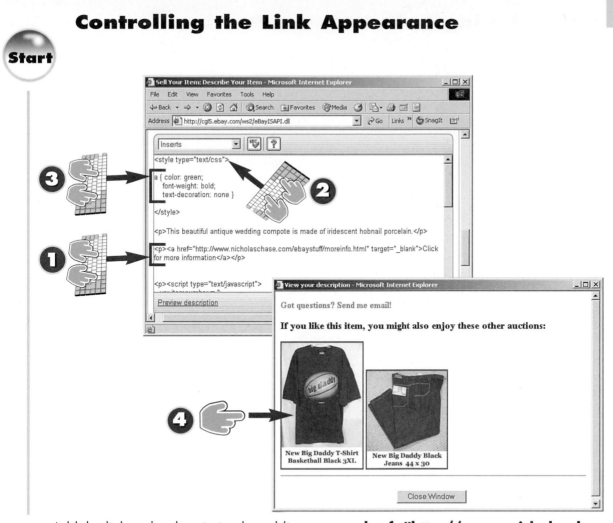

1. Add the link to the description by adding **<p><a href="http://www.nicholaschase.com/ebaystuff/moreinfo.html" target="_blank">Click for more information</a></p>**.

2. Add a **style** section to the page by adding these tags: **<style type="text/css"></style>**.

3. Add the style rule by typing: **a { color: green;   font-weight: bold;   text-decoration: none }**.

4. If you click **Preview Description**, you can see the changes.

 End

Linking to Your Other Auctions

Start

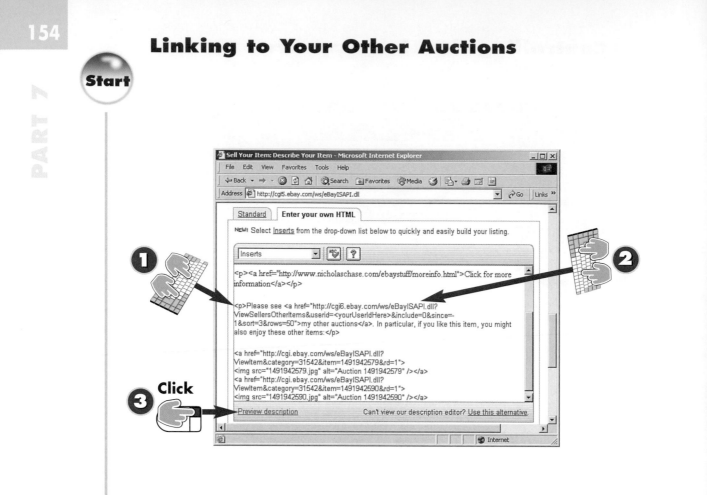

1 Create link text by typing **<p>Please see my other auctions. In particular, if you like this item, you might also enjoy these other items:</p>**.

2 Add the URL to the link. It will likely be in a form similar to **<a href="http://cgi6. ebay.com/ws/eBayISAPI.dll?ViewSellersOtherItems&userid=<yourUser IdHere>&include=0&since=-1&sort=3&rows=50">**, with your eBay user ID replacing **<yourUserIdHere>**.

3 Click **Preview Description**.

INTRODUCTION

If nobody sees your auctions, nobody's going to bid on them. One way to get traffic is to bring in users who've already found one of your auctions and lead them to your other auctions by linking to a page that lists them all. eBay provides that page. You just have to link to it.

Click 4

View your description - Microsoft Internet Explorer

Click for more information

Please see my other auctions. In particular, if you like this item, you might also enjoy these other items:

New Big Daddy T-Shirt Basketball Black 3XL

New Big Daddy Black Jeans 44 x 30

Close Window

eBay.com Seller List: richierich-colorado - Microsoft Internet Explorer

home | pay | register | sign out | services | site map | help

Browse   Search   Sell   My eBay   Community   Powered By IBM

find items   find members   favorite searches

Search   tips
☐ Search titles **and** descriptions

Find more great stuff at my eBay store

Items for Sale by richierich-colorado (4977 ★) Power Seller me

View text-only format

308 items found.

| | All items | Auctions | Buy It Now |

Picture hide		Item Title	Price	Bids	Time (Ends PDT)
☐		NWT Savane Pants Size 46 X 28	$12.50 Buy It Now		46 mins, 10 secs
☐		Boxers Sleepwear Surf Board Jams PJ's Shorts Size 2X	$9.99	-	4 hours, 38 mins +
☐		New Big Daddy L/S Pull Over Gray/Navy T-Shirt 2XL 2X	$17.99	-	4 hours, 42 mins +
☐		NEW Orange Polo Golf Shirt Collar S/S Sz 4XL 4X	$12.99	-	4 hours, 42 mins +
☐		NWT Big Daddy Tan Pants Jeans 44 X 30	$16.99	-	4 hours, 43 mins +
☐		New Ralph Lauren Sweatpants Sweat Pants 2XLT 2X Tall	$24.99	-	4 hours, 43 mins +
☐		New Ralph Lauren Polo Jeans L/S Gray T-Shirt 3XL T 3XT	$13.99	1	4 hours, 43 mins +

5

④ Click the link to see your other auctions.

⑤ Notice that your page of auctions appears.

End

Controlling the List

You can control what the "other auctions" page looks like to some extent by changing the number of rows that appear on a single page or the column by which it's sorted. All you have to do is change the values that are part of the URL.

Ch-ch-ch-changes...

The previous URL is what currently works on eBay, but it could just as easily change at a moment's notice. To get the current URL, go to one of your auctions and click View Seller's Other Items. The location in your browser will be the URL you need. Use the same technique to direct users to your eBay store.

Adding Sound, Video, and Animation

Before you even think about adding sound or video to your auctions, ask yourself one question: Is this trip really necessary? Sure, you can load your auctions with all kinds of things flying around, and music playing in the background and video downloading, but most of the time all that does is brand you as an amateur (or at the very least, design-challenged).

Worse than that, it's irritating to users. Experienced eBayers know that an eBay auction needs to be clean, fast, and straightforward. In most cases, all the bells and whistles work against that goal, cluttering up the page and annoying potential buyers.

But note that I said "in most cases." Sometimes sound, video, or animation can come in handy in an auction. For example, as in this part, a snippet of sound can remind buyers of the song your sheet music represents or an animation can explain how something works.

In this part, I'll spend a little time on how to create these files and explain how to add them to your auction in a way that helps bidders instead of driving them away.

Adding Sound, Video, and Animation

Create sound, video, and animation files

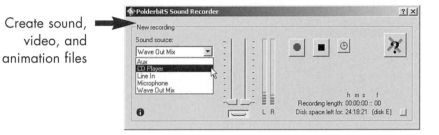

Add sound, video, or animation to your pages

Creating a Sound Recording

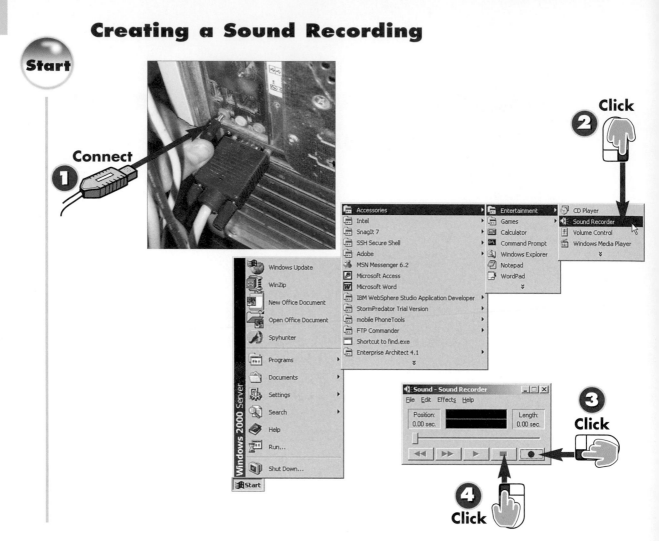

To record a live sound, start by plugging a microphone into the microphone jack of your computer.

Start your sound recording program by selecting **Start**, **Programs**, **Accessories**, **Entertainment**, **Sound Recorder**.

Click **Record** to record the sound you want to capture.

Click **Stop** to stop recording.

The three major "types" of sound files are recordings, which use a microphone to capture a real-life sound; ripped files, which use a file from another source, such as a CD; and MIDI files, created by a program. In this task, we'll take a brief look at recordings. Specifics depend on which operating system and program you're using, but the concepts are the same.

In a Pinch

If your computer doesn't have a built-in microphone and you just need something quickly, you can use the microphone from a computer headset. Just plug it into the microphone jack as usual.

Click **5**

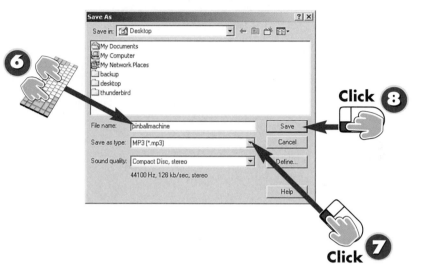

6

Click **8**

Click **7**

5 In Windows SoundRecorder, select **File**, **Save As**.

6 Name the file.

7 Select **MP3 (*.mp3)**.

8 Click **Save**.

End

Recording to Tape First

Recording the sound to tape and then digitizing the sound might be easier (and safer). The process is much the same as recording from a microphone, except you use a cable that runs from the headphone jack of the player to the microphone jack on the computer.

Doing It Right

If you're recording a sound, it's probably to enhance your item, so weigh the extra expense of obtaining quality recording equipment against the potential increase in selling price.

Creating a Sound File from a CD

Start

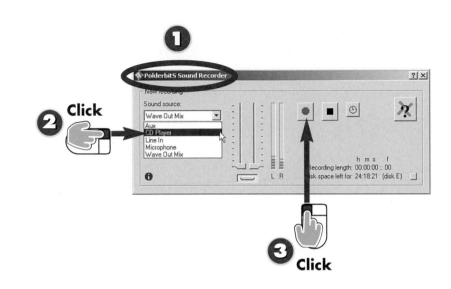

1 Open your sound recorder program and insert a CD into your computer.

2 From the Sound source menu, select **CD Player**.

3 Click the **Record** button.

It should go without saying that it's not legal or ethical to simply copy music off a CD and make it available for others to download. It's generally accepted that a short (less than 30 seconds) representative sample is permissible, but because selling items on eBay is a commercial venture, the fair use defense can be questionable. That said, this task shows you how to record a snippet off a CD.

TIP

Where Can I Get Software?
You can find numerous ripping programs on the Web. This example uses PolderbitS Sound Recorder, available at http://www.polderbits.com/.

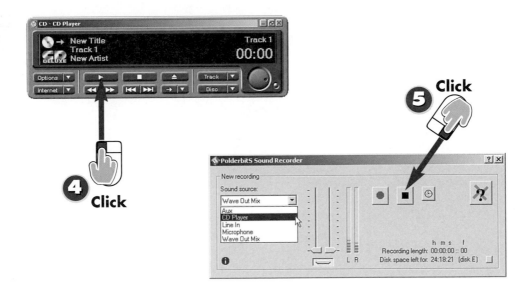

④ Click the **Play** button on your CD player.

⑤ Click the **Stop** button to stop recording.

⑥ If it doesn't start automatically, open your sound editing program.

See next page

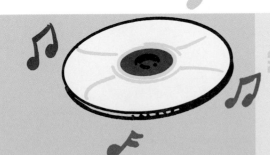

Do I Have to Use a CD?
Ripping software can record
anything that comes through
your computer's speakers,
including streaming audio.

Drag

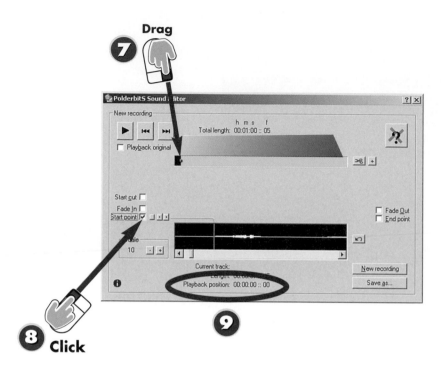

Click

7 Click and drag the blue circle so the green line is at the start of the waveform.

8 Click the **Start Point** check box.

9 Note the playback position.

Do They All Work Like This?

This task uses PolderbitS as an example, but all sound editing programs work differently. Fortunately, though, the concepts are the same for all of them.

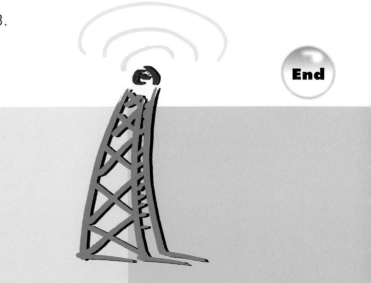

Drop

Drag

10

PolderbitS Sound Editor ? ☐ ✕

New recording

h m s f
Total length: 00:01:00 : 5

☐ Playback original ...d, Compact Disc, stereo

Start cut ☐
Fade In ☐ ☐ Fade Out
Start point ☑ ☑ End point

Scale
10

Current track:
Length: 00:00:29 :: 84 New recording
Playback position: 00:00:29 :: 84 Save as...

Click 11

12 **Click**

10 Drag and drop the blue circle so the playback position is no more than 30 seconds after the start position.

11 Click the **End Point** check box.

12 Click **Save As** and save the file as an MP3.

End

Linking to a Sound

Start

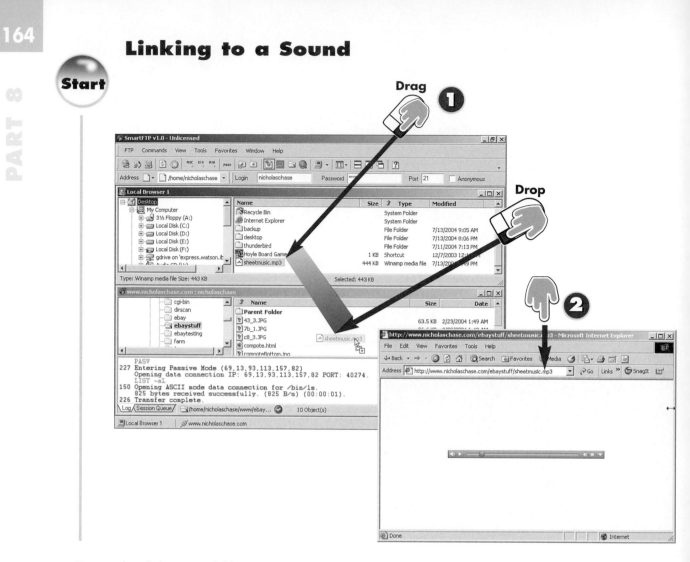

Drag ①

Drop

②

① Upload the sound file to your server or follow instructions from your hosting service to make the file available.

② Get the URL for the sound file from your hosting service or hosting provider. Test it by sending the browser to that URL.

The easiest way to incorporate a sound into your auction is to simply link to it. In this case, the user clicks the link and the browser handles the rest, bringing up the appropriate application to play the sound. To make this happen, you link to the sound just as you'd link to a page.

What Is FTP?
File Transfer Protocol (FTP) is a way to move files from one computer to another over the Internet. You can download a client such as Fetch (http://fetchsoftworks.com/) or FTP Commander (http://www.internet-soft.com/ftpcomm.htm).

Are My Files Safe?
Can others steal your files? Yes. You can make it less convenient for thieves by embedding the sounds or streaming the sounds from a server.

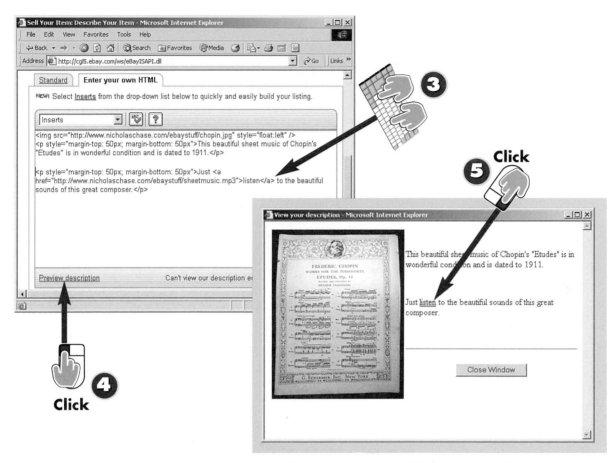

3 Add the link tag to your item's description, including the URL from step 2 by typing **Just <a href="http://www.nicholaschase.com/ebaystuff/sheetmusic.mp3"> listen</a> to the beautiful sounds of this great composer**.

4 Click **Preview Description** to see the results.

5 Click the **Listen** link. The browser should either play the sound automatically or ask you what to do with it.

End

What Do I Do with It?
For some users, clicking the link brings up a window asking what they want to do with the file. For these people, you might want to include text such as "Open this file in a program such as WinAmp to hear a sample."

But This Is Awkward!
This method can be a bit cumbersome for users. In most cases, it's more convenient for buyers to simply click and hear the sound.

Embedding Sound in the Page

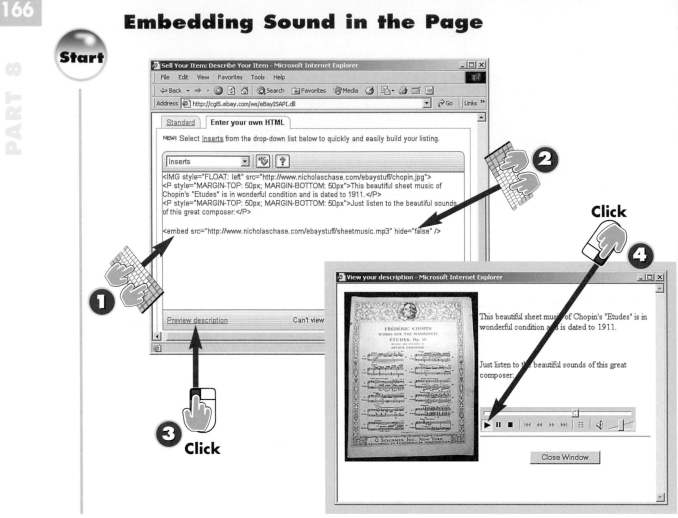

1   Add an **<embed>** tag to the description, with the URL for the sound file in the **src** attribute, by typing **<embed src="http://www.nicholaschase.com/ebaystuff/sheetmusic.mp3" />**.

2   Make sure the controls will appear on the page by specifying the hidden attribute as false by typing **hide="false"** before the closing **/>** you typed in step 1.

3   Click **Preview Description** to see the results.

4   Notice that the sound has been added to the page. If it doesn't start right away, click the **Play** button to hear it.

If a sound is truly integral to an item, embedding the sound right into the page can be the best option. This method also enables you to play the sound when the user loads the page, so it's not overlooked.

Does It Have to Be This Ugly?

You can use JavaScript to create your own controls, but that's beyond the scope of this book. Also, like the rest of the issue of adding sound, it's a browser-compatibility nightmare. For more information, check out http://www.javascripter.net/faq/sound/play.htm.

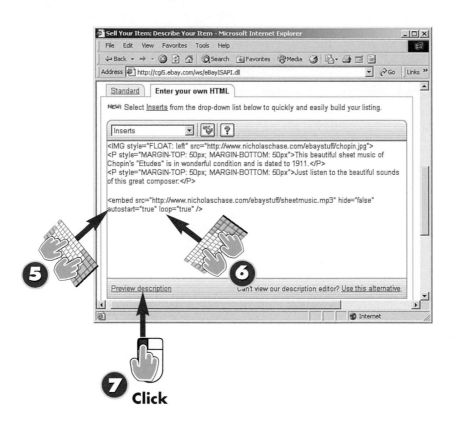

7 **Click**

5 Specify that the sound should start when the page loads by adding the **autostart="true"** attribute.

6 Specify that the sound should loop continuously by adding the **loop="true"** attribute.

7 Click **Preview Description** and note that the sound starts again when it's finished playing.

Control Size
You can control how wide or tall the sound controls appear on the page by using the height and width attributes.

Looping Cleanly
There's a bit of an art to creating a sound that loops without making it obvious. You can find a list of links to free sounds to download at http://www.csuchico.edu/lcmt/dmb2/sndfree.html.

Adding Video

Start

Drag

Drop

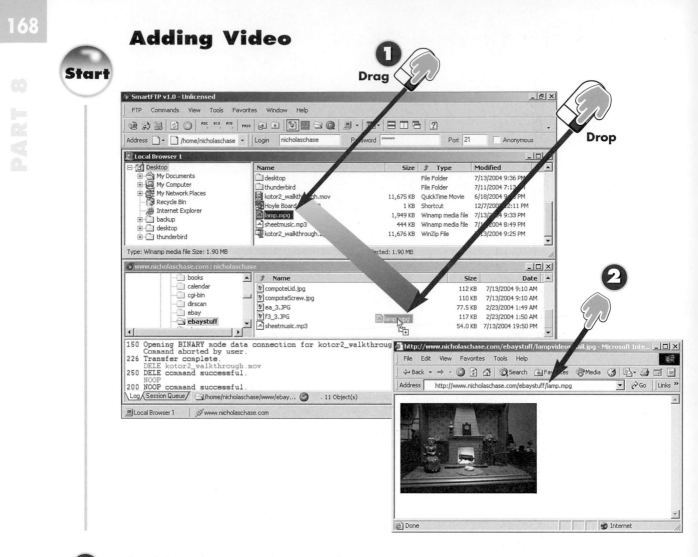

1 Upload the video to your server or hosting service.

2 Note the URL for the video.

INTRODUCTION

You should have a pretty compelling reason to subject potential buyers to the extra bandwidth required for video, and if it's that important, you should use professional-quality video. (In other words, you'll need to know much more than I can teach you here!) When you have the video, however, adding it to the auction is virtually identical to adding sounds.

Getting Small

TIP

If you're going to use video, do whatever you can to make the files as small as possible. You usually won't need full-screen video or millions of colors. Consult your software documentation for more information, including compression options.

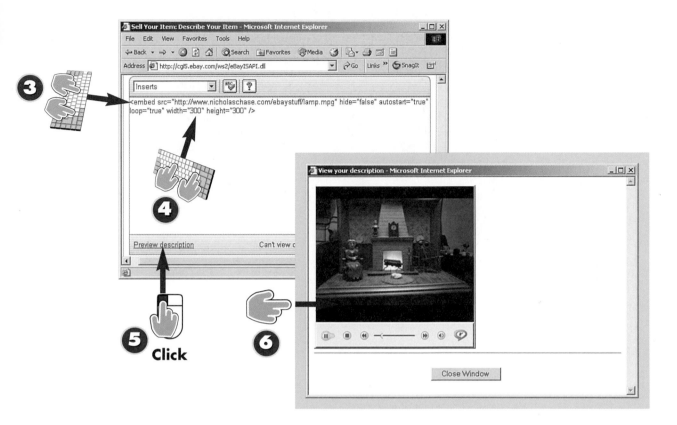

Add the **<embed/>** tag to the description, including the URL from step 2 by typing **<embed src="http://www.nicholaschase.com/ebaystuff/ lamp.mpg" hide="false" autostart="true" loop="true" />**.

Add height and width attributes to determine the size at which you want the video to appear by typing **width="300" height="300"**.

Click **Preview Description** to see the results.

You can now see the video.

Don't Force Video on Buyers

Video can require a huge download, so rather than including it in the main auction page, consider adding it to a separate page and letting buyers see it in a pop-up window (see page 218). They'll still get the benefit of seeing the video, but only if they want it.

Using Animated (Flipbook) Images

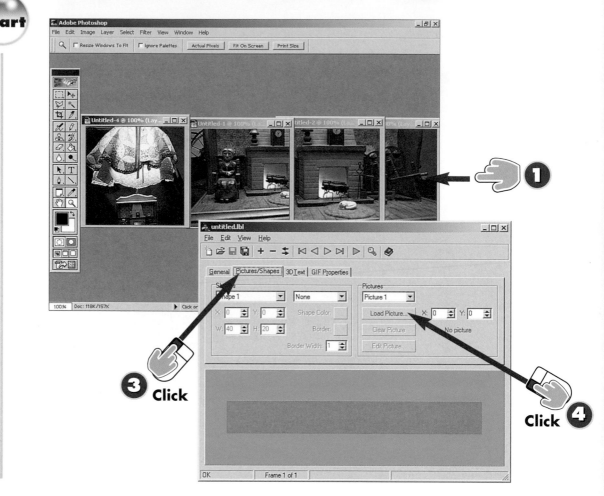

1 Gather the frames for the image. Each of these frames is a single GIF image file.

2 Download an animated GIF maker, such as Aesop Banner Maker, at **http://www.yukudr.com/**; then start the program.

3 Click **Pictures/Shapes**.

4 Click **Load Picture**.

Animated flipbook images were the first animation on the Web, and they're still going strong. They consist of several images (usually GIFs) combined into a single image that flips through each frame in succession.

Good Subjects for Animations
Just because we're calling it an "animation" doesn't mean that each image has to flow into the next like a cartoon. You can use flipbook animations to simply combine a number of images in a single location.

Image Sizes
Before loading your images, click the **General** tab and change the height and width to match those of your images.

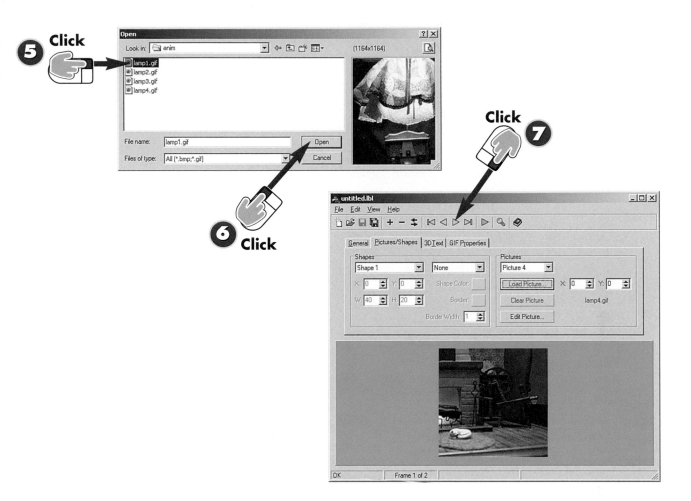

5 Choose the first frame.

6 Click **Open**.

7 Click **Next Frame**.

8 Repeat steps 4–7 for each frame of the animation.

See next page

Watch That Flashing

Animated GIFs can be useful for showing multiple images, but if you're creating a rapid succession of images, be careful not to create a flickering effect because you can actually cause seizures in susceptible viewers—especially if the flicker is in the range of 4–59 flashes per second. The problem peaks at 20 flashes per second.

Click

9

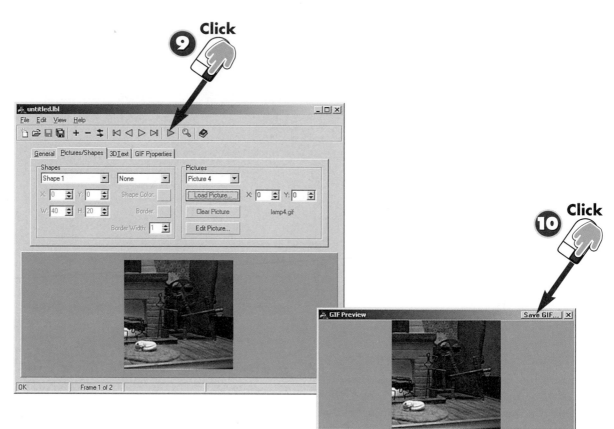

Click

10

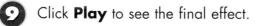

9 Click **Play** to see the final effect.

10 Click **Save GIF** to save the file.

End

Don't Overdo It

It's one thing to have a single image that replaces the bullets on your page; they'll all change in unison. But when you have more than one or two animations bombarding the user, it can become maddeningly distracting, and you'll lose viewers and potential buyers.

TIP

Creating a Flash Image

Start

1 Start Macromedia Flash and click **Create New Flash Document**.

2 Click the **Oval** tool.

3 Click and drag on the stage to create a circle. We'll use that to represent a rock rolling down a hill.

4 Right-click the circle and select **Convert to Symbol**.

See next page

INTRODUCTION

Artistic talent aside, these days it doesn't take much expertise to create an animation. Even an interactive animation can be built fairly easily using Macromedia Flash. There are books full of information showing you how, but here's a crash course. If you don't have Flash installed, download a demo from http://www.macromedia.com/go/tryflash and install it.

TIP

What Can I Draw?
You can draw just about anything in Flash, but remember that it's meant for vector, or line drawing–type art.

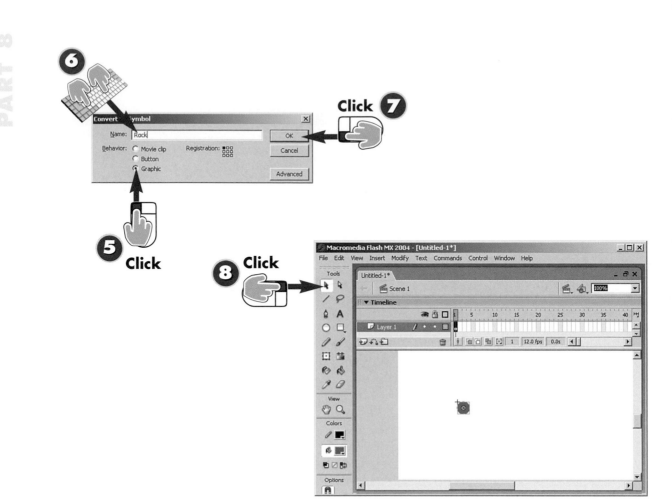

Click 7

5 Click

8 Click

5 Select **Graphic** under **Behavior**.

6 Type **Rock** in the text box.

7 Click **OK**.

8 Click the **Selection** tool.

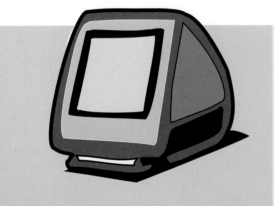

What Are Behaviors?
Flash behaviors provide an easy way to tell Flash what to do with an object. Here we're simply telling it to treat the **Rock** object as a graphic. You can also add behaviors such as playing a movie clip or loading a sound (to the appropriate objects).

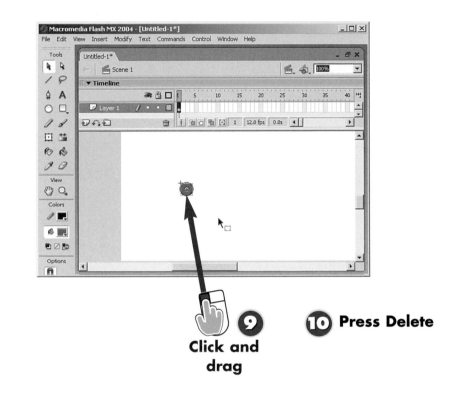

9 Click and drag

10 Press Delete

9 Click and drag to select the circle.

10 Press the **Delete** key.

See next page

Why Convert to a Symbol?
Flash doesn't animate drawings; it animates symbols. You have to create the symbol by drawing and converting it. After you've done that, you don't need the original drawing anymore.

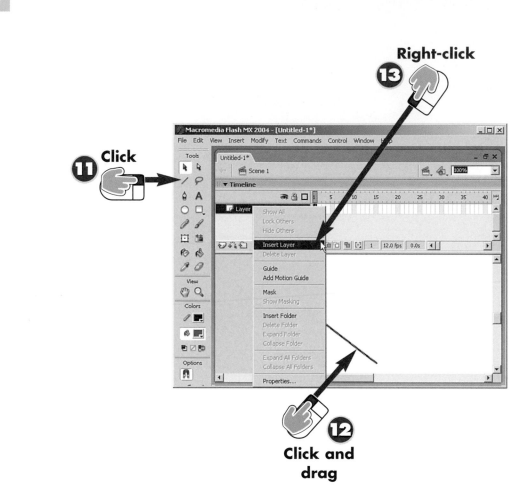

Right-click

Click

Click and
drag

11 Now create the hill by clicking the **Line** tool.

12 Click and drag to create the hill.

13 Right-click **Layer 1** and select **Insert Layer**.

What Are Layers?
Layers are, as the name
implies, different levels of
objects that can be stacked on
top of each other. You can control which objects appear in
front or back by stacking the
relevant layers.

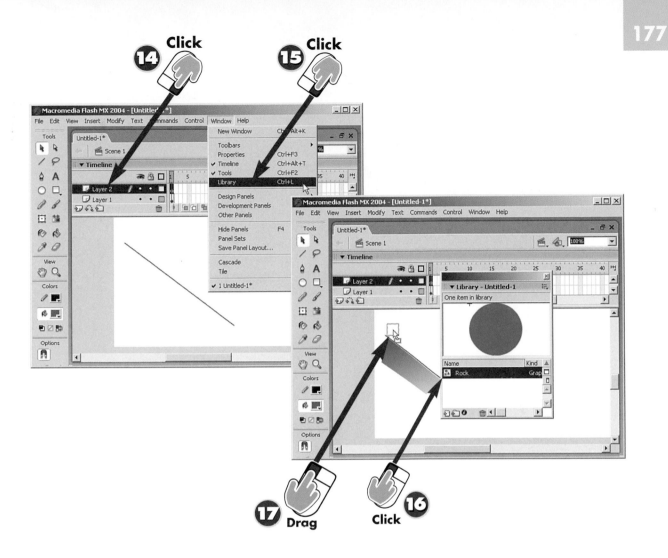

Click 14

Click 15

17 **Drag**

16 **Click**

14 Click **Layer 2** to highlight it.

15 Select **Window**, **Library**.

16 In the Library window, click **Rock**.

17 Drag the circle to the top of the hill.

See next page

Using the Library
You can store all kinds of objects in the library, so that when you need them, they're close at hand.

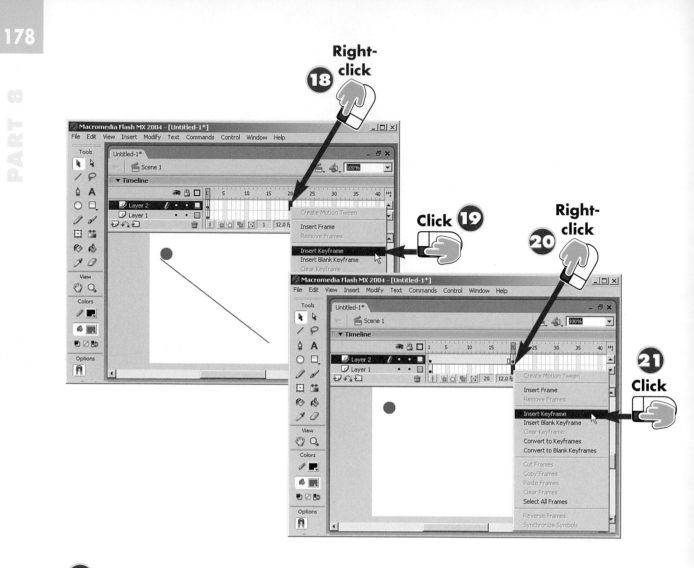

18 Right-click frame **20** in Level 2 of the timeline.

19 Select **Insert Keyframe**.

20 Right-click frame **20** in Level 1 of the timeline.

21 Select **Insert Keyframe**.

What's a Keyframe?

A *keyframe* is a frame on which you specify that something should happen. For example, we're setting frame 20 as a keyframe. We can then specify that the rock (which starts out at the top of the hill in frame 1) should be at the bottom of the hill in that keyframe. Flash then does the work to animate the rock between keyframes so everything appears to move smoothly.

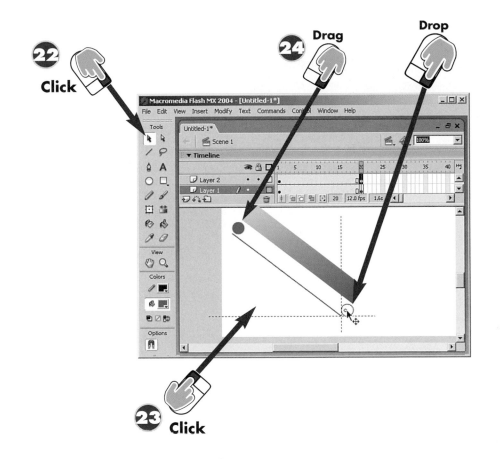

22 Click the **Selection** tool.

23 Click the stage to deselect all objects.

24 Drag the rock to the bottom of the hill.

See next page

Moving Objects

You can move as many objects as you like in a single keyframe. You can also stagger keyframes. For example, we could have created a second rock and specified that it should be at the bottom on frame 15.

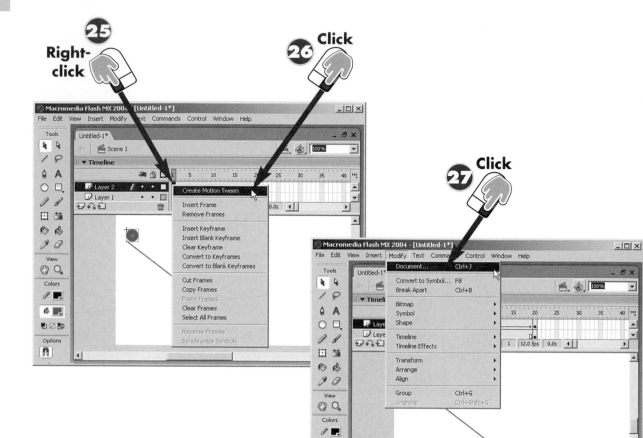

 25 Right-click frame **1** in Level 2 of the timeline.

26 Select **Create Motion Tween**.

27 Select **Modify**, **Document**.

> **TIP**
>
> **What's a Tween?**
> *Tweening* is a term from traditional animation. It refers to the process of creating the frames between keyframes so everything appears to be moving (or changing) smoothly.

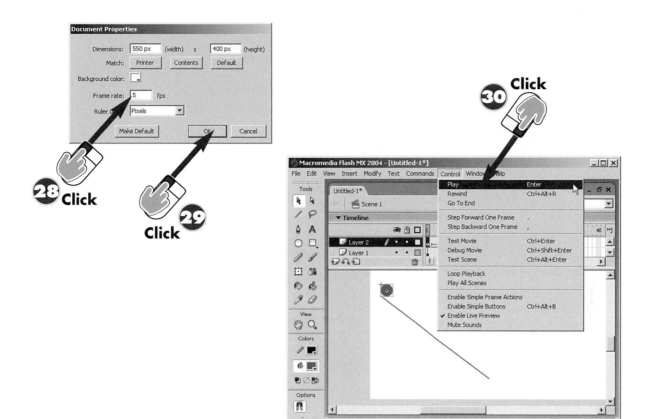

 Click

Click

28 Set the **Frame Rate** to **5** fps.

29 Click **OK**.

30 Select **Control**, **Play**.

See
next
page

Watch Your Speed

The more frames per second you use, the smoother your animation will look. However, there's a limit to how fast you should go because not all computers are created equal. If you set your image to use, say, 60 fps, it might look great on your computer, but 1 second takes 60 images. A user's machine might take 4 or 5 seconds for this same animation.

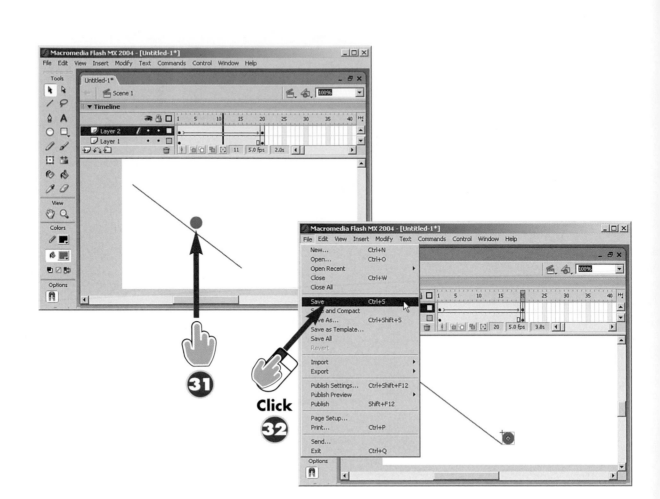

 Watch the rock roll down the hill.

32 Select **File**, **Save** to save the movie.

More Than Just Simple Animation
You can also add sound and interactivity to your Flash movies. Just be sure it's actually warranted!

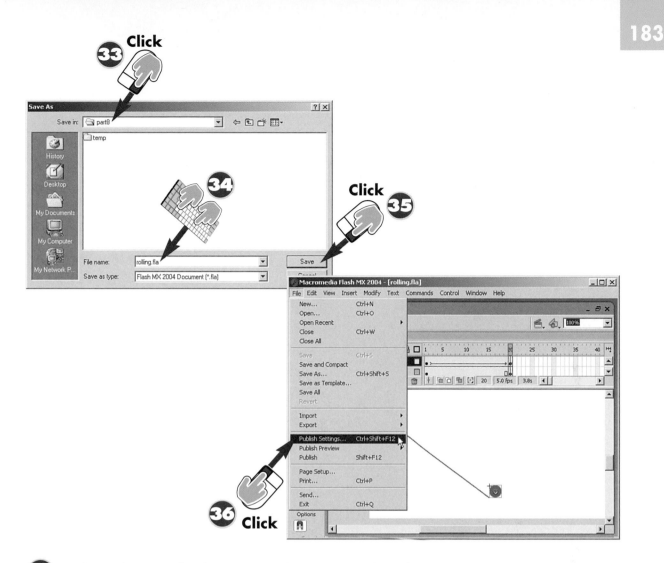

Click 33

34

Click 35

Click 36

33 Select a location for the movie in the **Save in** drop-down.

34 Type the movie's name in the **File Name** box.

35 Click **Save**.

36 Select **File**, **Publish Settings**.

See next page

Using Other Formats
Flash gives you the opportunity to publish your movie in several formats, including an animated GIF file or video.

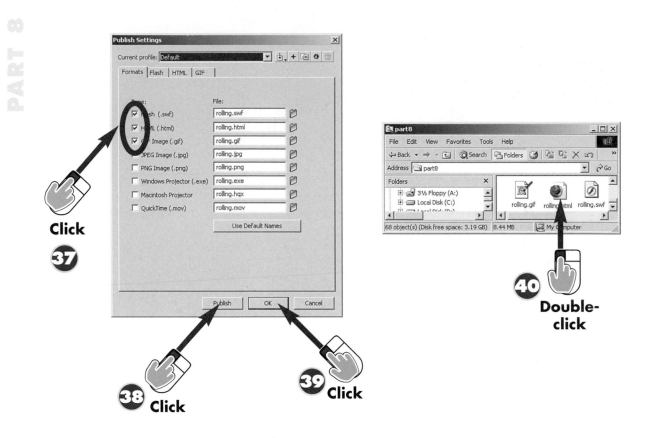

Click

37

38 Click

39 Click

40 Double-click

37 Make sure that **Flash**, **HTML**, and **GIF Image** are selected.

38 Click **Publish**.

39 Click **OK**.

40 In Windows Explorer double-click the HTML file. (You'll find it in the directory where you saved the original Flash movie.) Notice that the movie plays in your browser.

End

Adjusting Position
To get the rock just where you want it, click the **Selection** tool and drag the rock into place.

Is It Worth It?
Before spending all this time, ask yourself whether the additional capabilities Flash gives you are really worth it. After all, you'll still have to find a way to present the information to users without Flash, so this is truly an extra step.

Adding Flash to the Page

Start

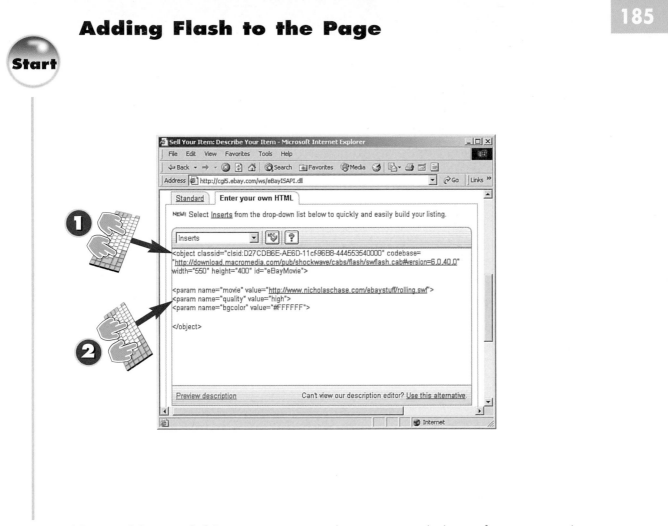

1 Add an **<object></object>** tag to your description, including information such as the **codebase**, which helps the browser obtain the right code to view this file. This tag works with Internet Explorer.

2 Add parameters, including information about the movie itself.

See next page

INTRODUCTION

Now you have your Flash movie ready to add to the page. Although they're commonly referred to as *images*, in this case they act more like audio or video, so I'll call this project a movie to be consistent.

TIP

Setting the Size
When you're planning the size of your Flash movies, you should assume the user's monitor is no bigger than 800 pixels wide by 600 pixels high.

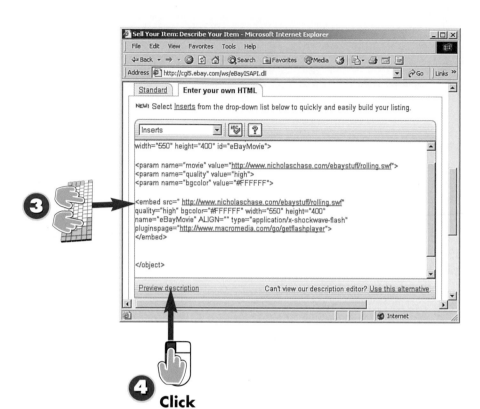

Click

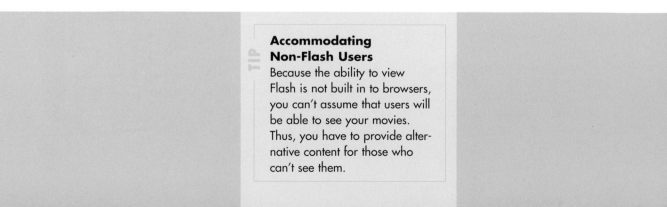

Add the **<embed/>** tag to accommodate the Netscape family of browsers and their cousins, the Mozilla family.

Click **Preview Description**.

Accommodating Non-Flash Users

TIP

Because the ability to view Flash is not built in to browsers, you can't assume that users will be able to see your movies. Thus, you have to provide alternative content for those who can't see them.

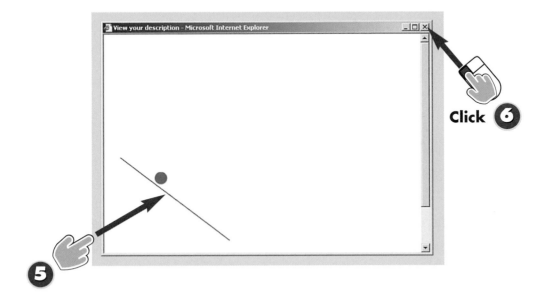

Click **6**

5

5 The Flash movie now appears in your description. The ball will roll down the line.

6 Click the **x** to close the animation.

End

About Me Pages and eBay Stores

By now you might have realized that a web page is a web page is a web page, so why should there be anything special about creating eBay Stores and About Me pages? On the surface, you're right—there is nothing different.

On the surface.

If you dig a little deeper, however, you'll find that eBay has some hidden gems in these sections, which we're going to look at.

The Web is inherently an anonymous place, but deep down inside that makes buyers nervous. The About Me page gives you a place to improve your credibility by dispelling that anonymity. You can talk about yourself or your products or link directly to your products. It also gives potential repeat customers a page to bookmark.

First, we'll look at creating an About Me page. At first, you might think you don't have much flexibility beyond choosing the basic layout for this page, but that's not the case. Not only can you directly edit the HTML for this page, but eBay also provides a set of custom tags you can use to automatically add information such as your current items and feedback to the page. These elements also provide customization, enabling you to do things like display just the items in a particular category.

When it comes to eBay stores, however, they're not quite as flexible. You have to choose one of the predetermined layouts, but I'll show you how to customize colors and such. I'll also show you how to add some arbitrary HTML to the main page and how to add more pages you can (almost) completely control.

About Me Pages
and eBay Stores

Create and customize an eBay Store

Create an About Me page

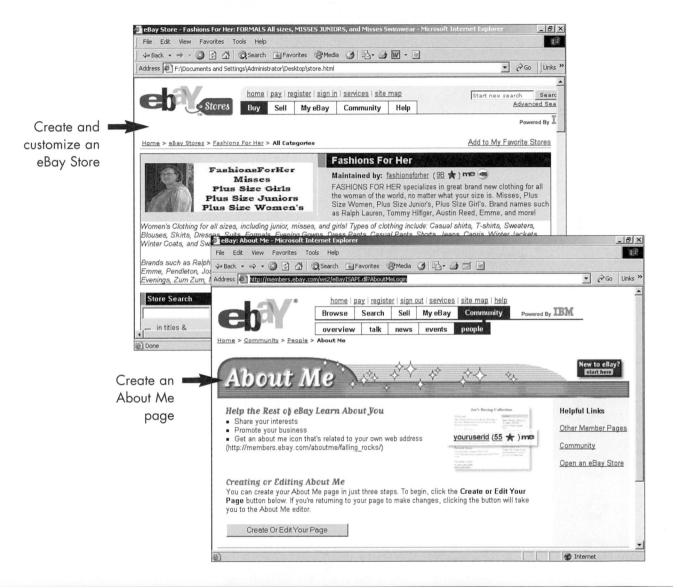

Creating an About Me Page

Start

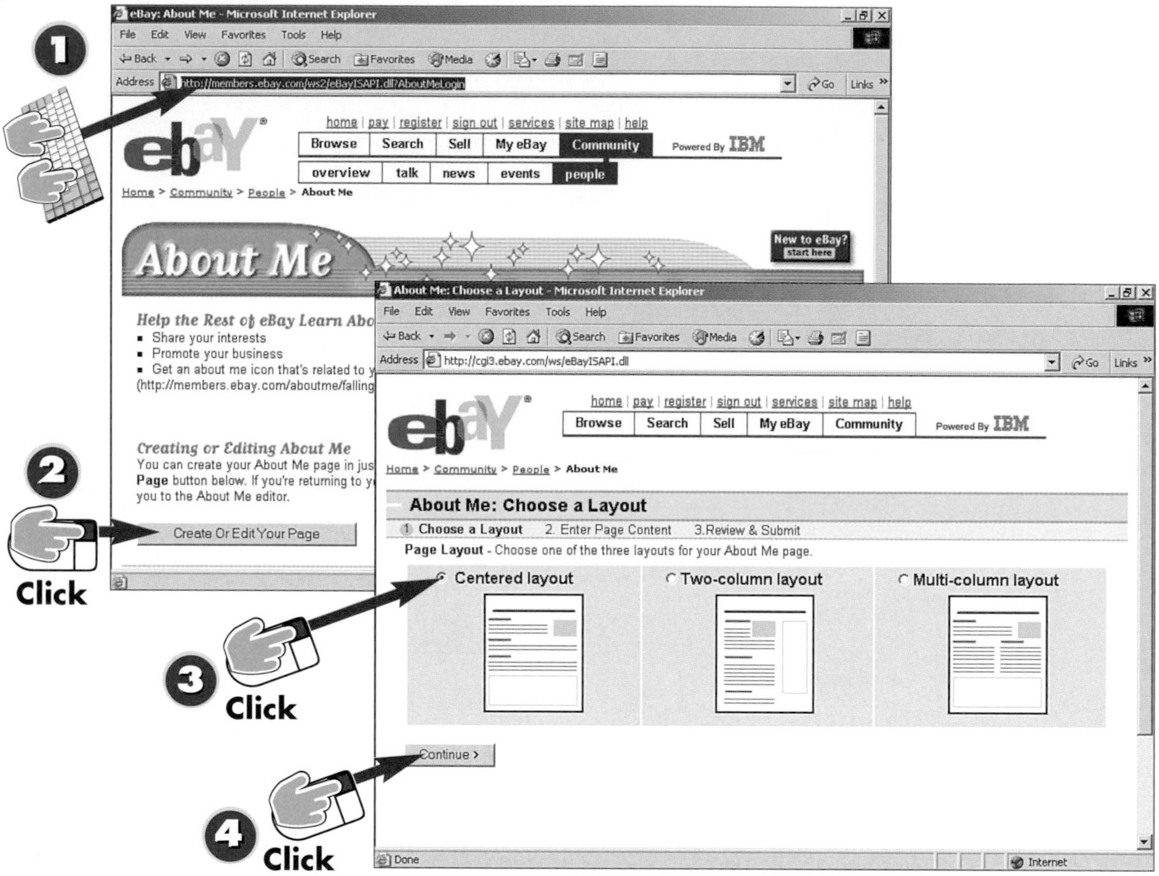

1

2
Click

3
Click

4
Click

1 Point your browser to **http://members.ebay.com/ws2/eBayISAPI.dll? AboutMeLogin**.

2 Click **Create or Edit Your Page**.

3 Choose a layout by clicking **Centered Layout**.

4 Click **Continue**.

INTRODUCTION

In many ways, success on eBay is about repeat business. In an environment with millions of sellers, though, how do you establish an identity? One way is to create an About Me page that enables you to not only promote your items, but also to establish a "brand" for yourself. In this task, we'll create a basic About Me page.

TIP

Can I Get Greater Control?
After you create your basic page, you can go back and edit the actual HTML text of your page.

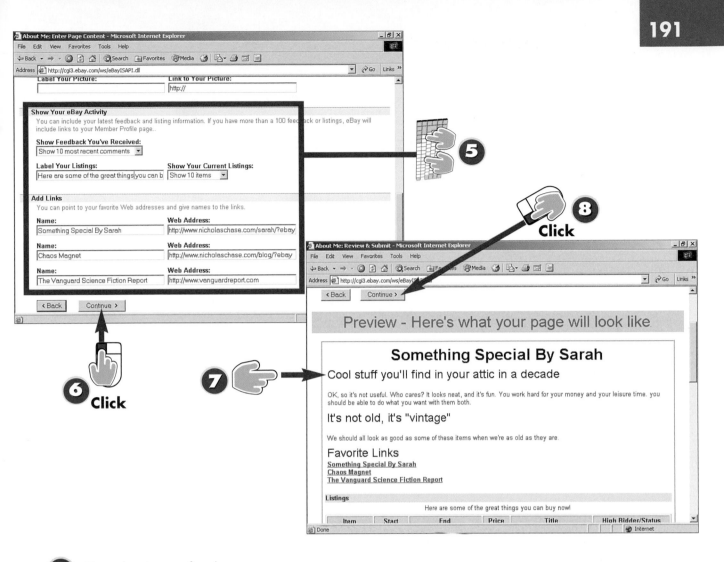

5 Enter basic text for the page.

6 Click **Continue**.

7 Verify that your information is correct.

8 Click **Continue**.

See next page

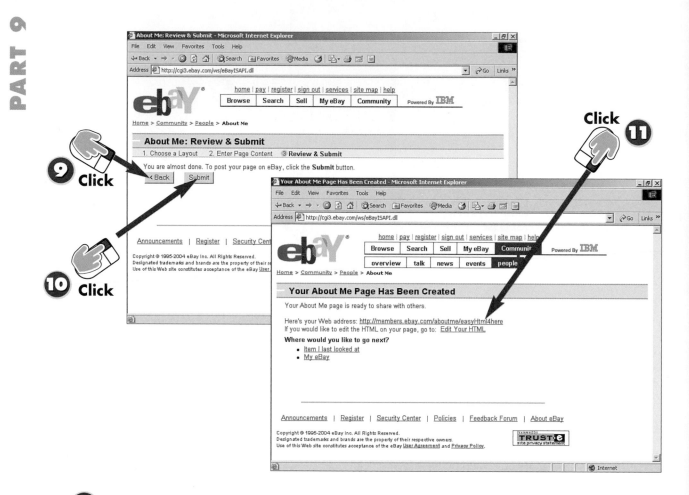

9 If you want to change anything, click **Back**.

10 Click **Submit** if you're ready to continue.

11 Click the link for your page to view it.

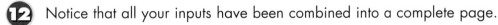

12 Notice that all your inputs have been combined into a complete page.

13 Scroll down and make sure that your listings and feedbacks are as you'd like them to appear.

End

Editing About Me HTML

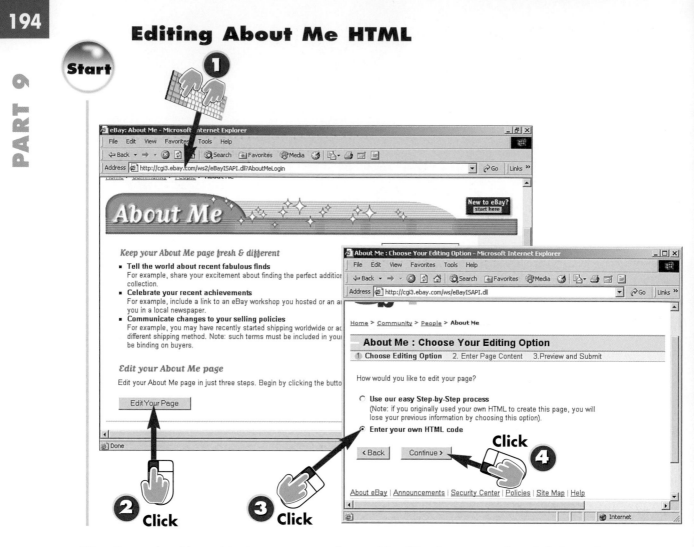

 1 Go to the About Me login page at **http://cgi3.ebay.com/ws2/eBayISAPI. dll?AboutMeLogin**.

 2 Click **Edit Your Page**.

 3 Select **Enter Your Own HTML Code**.

4 Click **Continue**.

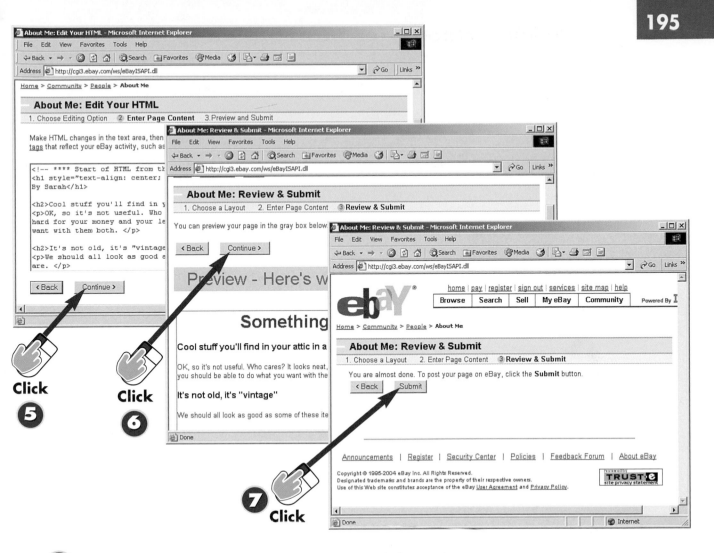

5 Change the HTML text to suit your liking and click **Continue**.

6 Click **Continue**.

7 Click **Submit** to save your changes.

End

Adding Your User Information to Your About Me Page

Start

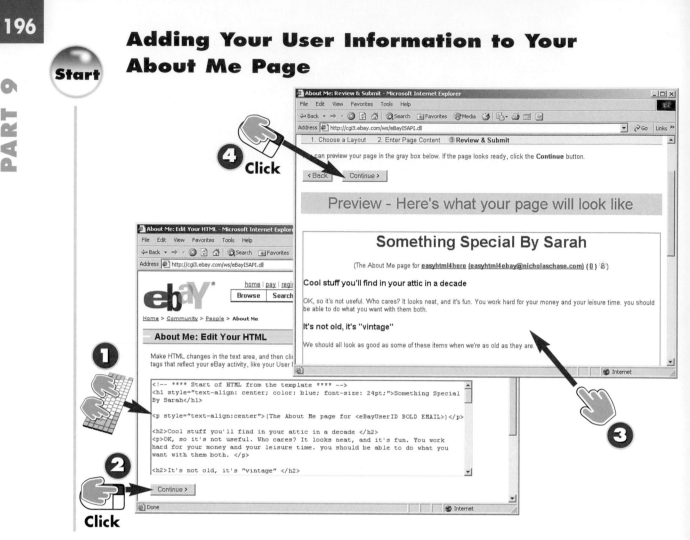

4 Click

1

2 Click

3

1 On the **About Me: Edit Your HTML** page, add text that includes the custom eBay user ID tag by typing **<p style="text-align:center">(The About Me page for <eBayUserID BOLD EMAIL>)</p>**.

2 Click **Continue**.

3 Check the preview.

4 Click **Continue**.

INTRODUCTION

Now let's look at the custom tags eBay provides. These tags enable you to arrange the page how you like but still keep the dynamic features. For example, you can add your user ID to the page anywhere you like and have it display your current feedback rating automatically, even when it changes.

TIP

What Does This Tag Do?
The **<eBayUserID />** custom tag is a way for you to tell eBay you want to display your user ID and any other relevant information, such as your feedback rating. Wherever you put it, eBay substitutes the relevant information when it displays the page. This way you don't have to manually keep the information up-to-date.

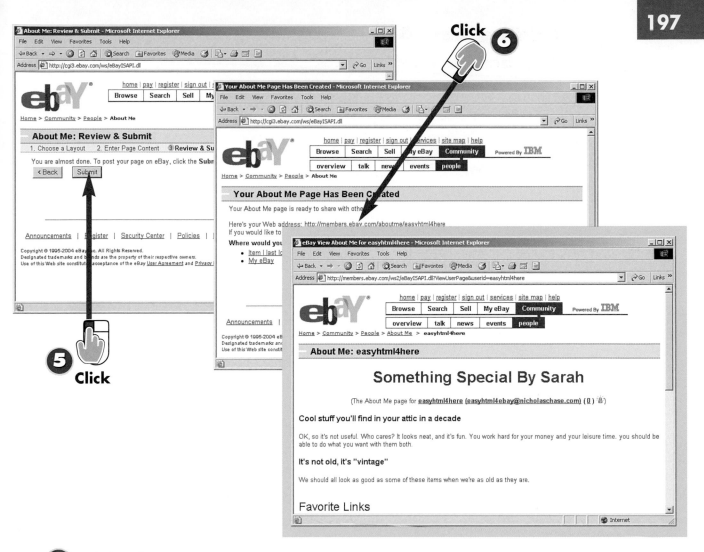

5 Click **Submit**.

6 Click to view your About Me page.

End

Adding and Grouping Your Items

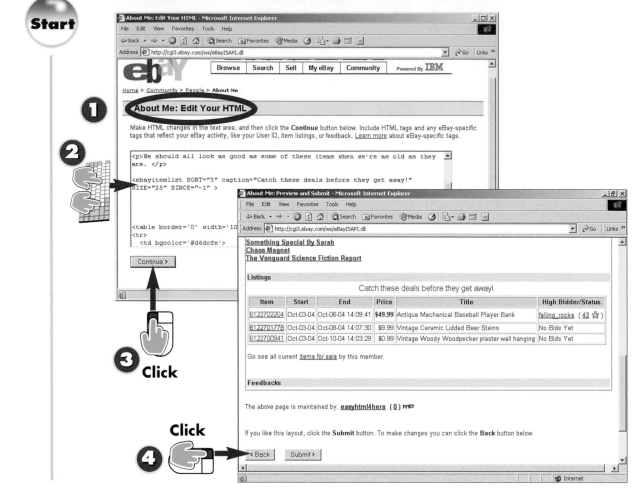

1 Send your browser to the About Me: Edit Your HTML page.

2 Add an **<eBayItemList>** tag by typing **<ebayitemlist SORT="3" caption= "Catch these deals before they get away!" SIZE="25" SINCE="-1" >**.

3 Click **Continue**.

4 View the effects in the preview and click **Back** to make more changes.

INTRODUCTION

One of the main purposes of an About Me page is to get people to buy more of your items. Fortunately, you can easily add your items to your About Me page, as well as control some aspects of how they're displayed, using the **<eBayItemList>** tag.

Some List Options

You can control the display of your items by using attributes on the **eBayItemList** tag, including **SIZE**, which limits the number of items to appear; **SORT**, which controls their order (8 is the newest first, 2 is the oldest first, 3 is the ending first, and 4 is the cheapest first); and **CATEGORY**, which takes a category ID.

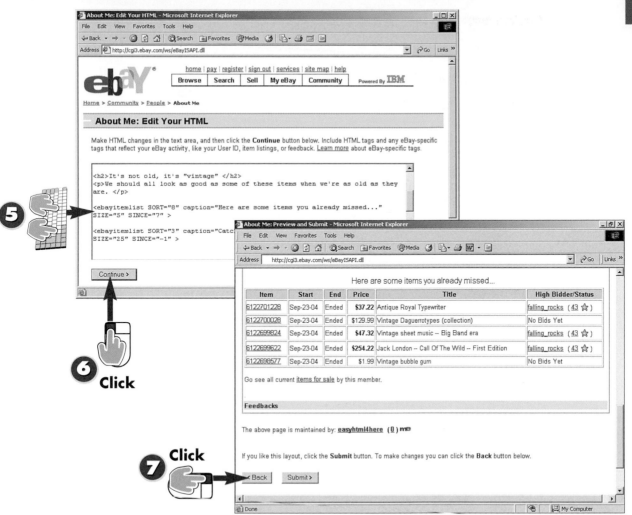

Add a list of items that includes items that have ended in the last seven days. Type
5 **<ebayitemlist SORT="8" caption="Here are some items you already missed..." SIZE="5" SINCE="7" >**.

6 Click **Continue**.

7 View the preview and click **Back** to make more changes.

End

How Can I Show Only Ended Auctions?
Keep your current auctions off of the list by adjusting the **SIZE** attribute. For example, if you've had five auctions end in the last seven days, set the **SIZE** to **5** so only those items show. Note that this approach requires active management on your part.

More List Options
The **eBayItemList** tag also includes **SINCE**, which sets the number of days an item stays on the list after ending, and **CAPTION**, which sets the text at the top of the table of items. The **BORDER**, **TABLEWIDTH**, and **CELLPADDING** attributes control the table itself. You can use the **BIDS** attribute to show a list of items you're bidding on.

Adding Your Feedback

Start

About Me: Edit Your HTML - Microsoft Internet Explorer

File   Edit   View   Favorites   Tools   Help

Back ▾ ⇒ ▾ ⊗ ⚙ ⚙ | Search ⓕFavorites ⚙Media ⚙ | ▾ ⚙ ⚙ ⚙

Address http://cgi3.ebay.com/ws/eBayISAPI.dll

home | pay | register | sign out | services | site map | help

eBay®   Browse   Search   Sell   My eBay   Community   Powered By IBM

Home > Community > People > About Me

① **About Me: Edit Your HTML**

Make HTML changes in the text area, and then click the **Continue** button below. Include HTML tags and any eBay-specific tags that reflect your eBay activity, like your User ID, ite...

```
<ebayitemlist SORT="8" caption="Here are
SIZE="5" SINCE="7" >

<ebayitemlist SORT="3" caption="Catch th
SIZE="25" SINCE="-1" >

<eBayFeedback CAPTION="Check out our fee
COLOR="WHITE">

<!-- **** End of HTML from the template
```

Continue >

Done

② **Click**

③

About Me: Preview and Submit - Microsoft Internet Explorer

File   Edit   View   Favorites   Tools   Help

Back ▾ ⇒ ▾ ⊗ ⚙ ⚙ | Search ⓕFavorites ⚙Media ⚙ | ▾ ⚙ W ▾ ⚙

Address F:\Documents and Settings\Administrator\Desktop\About Me Preview and Submit2.htm

Feedbacks

Check out our feedback

User:flojollie (1244 ★) Date:Aug-09-04 16:43:33 PDT

Praise: GREAT CUSTOMER, A PLEASURE TO DO BUSINESS WITH, THANK YOU.

User:buckroses (95 ★) Date:Jun-20-04 19:45:49 PDT

Praise: Fantastic buyer! / quick pay / easy to work with, hope to do more biz with.

User:mathquiltssmocking (180 ☆) Date:Jun-03-04 09:00:21 PDT

Praise: Fast ship. Thanks.

To see all feedback for this member, go to the Member Profile page.

The above page is maintained by: **easyhtml4here** (0) me

If you like this layout, click the **Submit** button. To make changes you can click the **Back** button below.

Submit >

Done   My Computer

④ **Click**

End

① Add the **<eBayFeedback>** tag to your page by typing **<eBayFeedback CAPTION="Check out our feedback" ALTERNATECOLOR="lightpink" COLOR="WHITE">**.

② Click **Continue**.

③ Notice that your most recent feedback comments appear on the page.

④ Click **Submit** to save your changes.

Creating a New Store

Start

Click ②

Click ④

① Point your browser to **http://stores.ebay.com**.

② Click **Open Your Store Now**.

③ Enter your user ID and password.

④ Click **Sign In**.

See next page

INTRODUCTION

A store is a step above an About Me page in that it enables you greater functionality. You can create (and link to) your own categories, create a store "header" that appears at the top of your listings, and even create multiple pages and have them link seamlessly together. What you can't do is completely control the HTML that makes up your store, but there are still opportunities for customization. Let's start by creating the actual store.

TIP

Why Can't I Create a Store?

If you have a newly created account, you might not be able to create a store. To create a store, you must have your credit card information on file for your seller's account and have a feedback rating of at least 20.

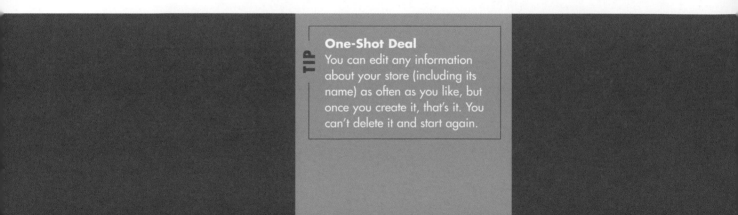

 5 Click **Review the eBay User Agreement**.

6 Click **I Accept the eBay User Agreement**.

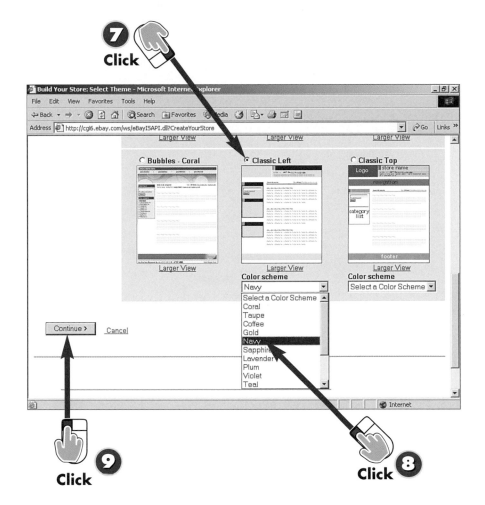

Click ⑦

Click ⑨

Click ⑧

⑦ Select a radio button to pick a theme, such as **Classic Left**, which puts the navigation on the left side of the page.

⑧ Click the pull-down menu underneath the theme and select a beginning color scheme.

⑨ Click **Continue**.

See next page

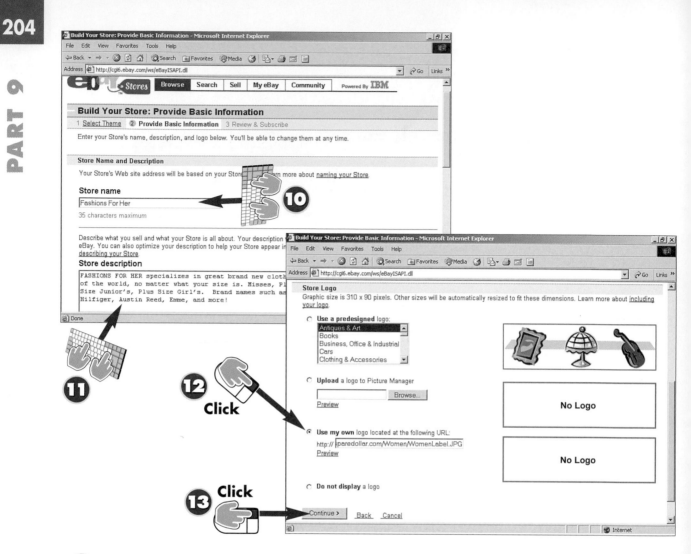

10 Enter your store name.

11 Enter your store description. eBay limits this description to 300 characters.

12 Choose the source for your logo. You can choose a predesigned logo, upload a logo, or point to an existing logo by entering the URL.

13 Click **Continue**.

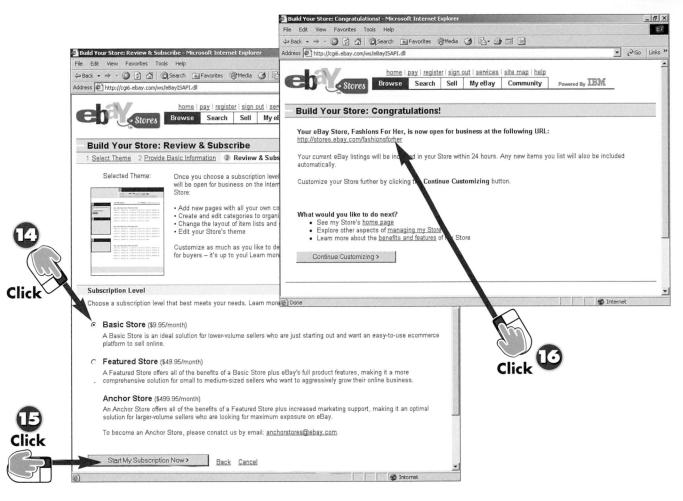

14 Choose a subscription level based on your needs.

15 Click **Start My Subscription Now**.

16 Click your store URL to view the store as it currently exists, or see the next task to continue customizing it.

End

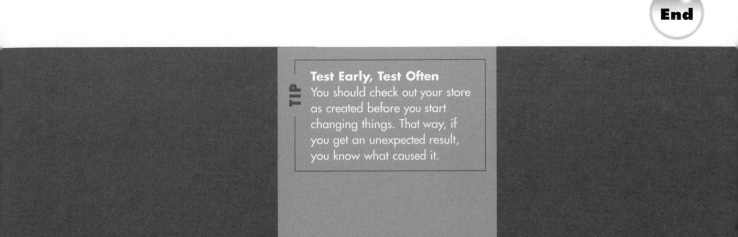

Test Early, Test Often
You should check out your store as created before you start changing things. That way, if you get an unexpected result, you know what caused it.

Customizing the Store Theme with HTML

Start

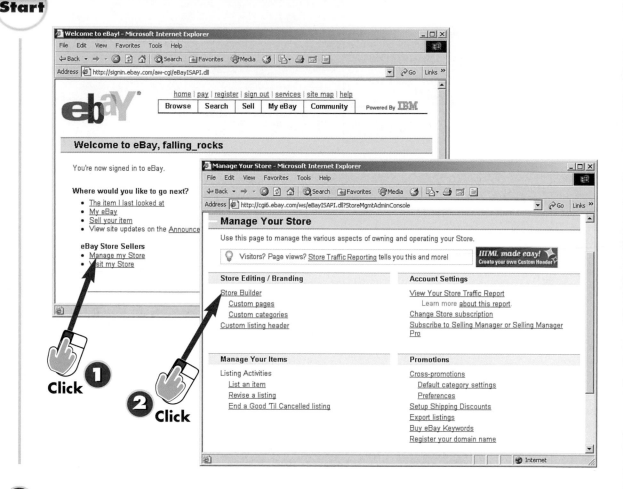

1 Sign in to eBay and click **Manage My Store**.

2 Click **Store Builder**.

Although it's true that eBay doesn't provide you with the opportunity to completely control the appearance of your eBay store, it does enable you a good deal of control over what actually appears on the page. In this task, we'll customize the existing template and add a custom HTML header.

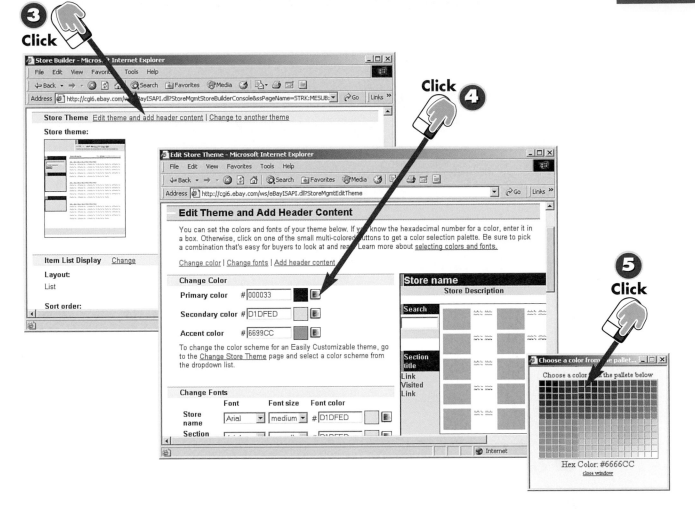

3 Click **Edit Theme and Add Header Content**.

4 Click a palette button to see more color choices.

5 Click a color to select it.

See
next
page

What Can I Edit?
This page enables you to edit
colors, fonts, sizes, and header
information. Except for layout and
content, there isn't much you can't
control from here.

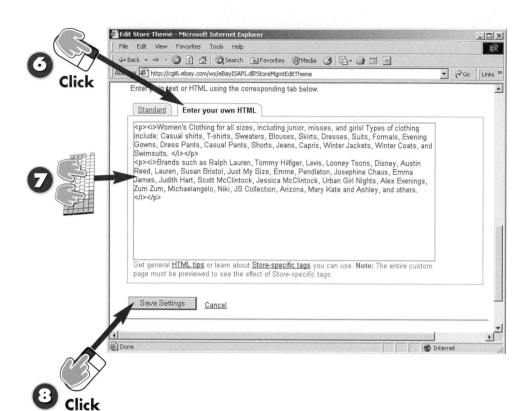

6 Click **Enter Your Own HTML**.

7 Add HTML text to the box.

8 Click **Save Settings**.

TIP

A Quick Preview
You can see how your HTML text will look by clicking the **Standard** link. Click **Enter Your Own HTML** to go back to the HTML edit box.

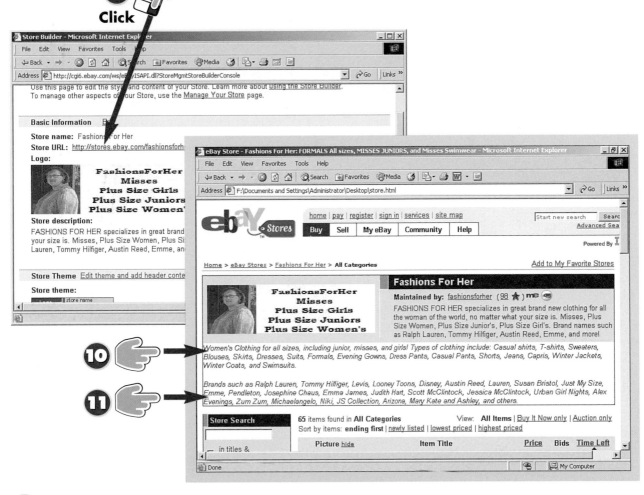

9 Click to view your store.

10 Notice that the text you added appears below the main header for the store.

11 Notice also that the HTML you added takes effect in this new area.

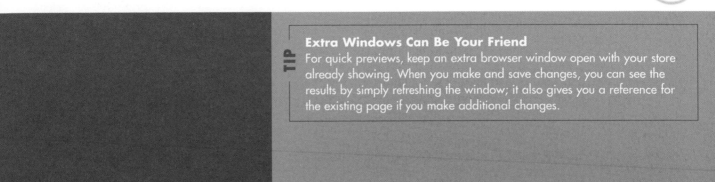

Extra Windows Can Be Your Friend

TIP For quick previews, keep an extra browser window open with your store already showing. When you make and save changes, you can see the results by simply refreshing the window; it also gives you a reference for the existing page if you make additional changes.

Creating a Custom HTML Store Page

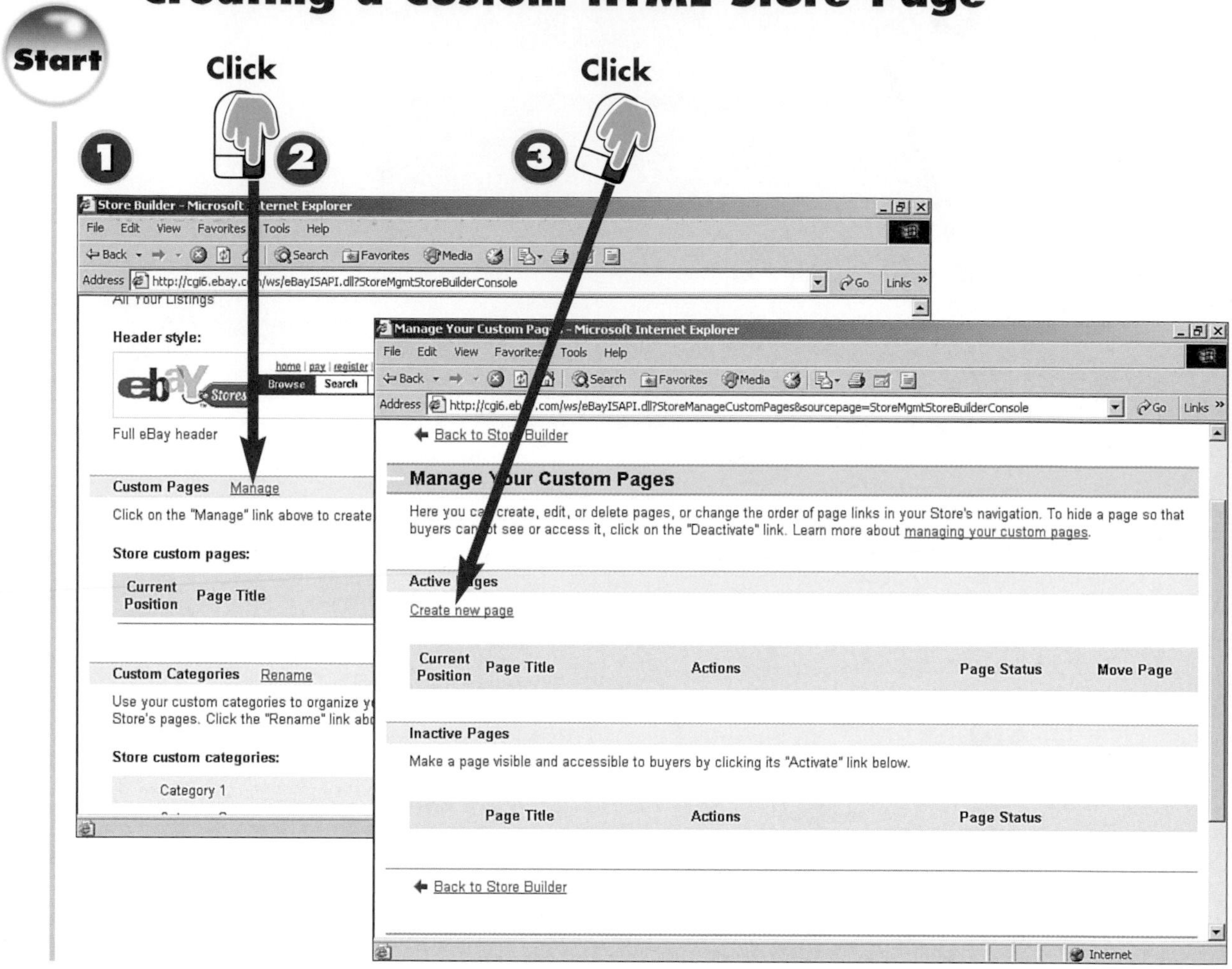

Start

Click

① **②**

Click

③

① Go to the Store Builder.

② Scroll down to Custom Pages and click **Manage**.

③ Click **Create New Page**.

Although you can't control the HTML template for your eBay store, you do have the option to create additional store pages in predetermined formats. These formats have predetermined image sizes and positions and enable you to use a form to enter the text for each paragraph the layout accommodates. Fortunately, one of the templates is simply a blank page to which you can add any HTML you like.

TIP

Not Completely Flexible
Although you can enter any HTML you like within the confines of the custom page, remember that anything you add is displayed within the overall template.

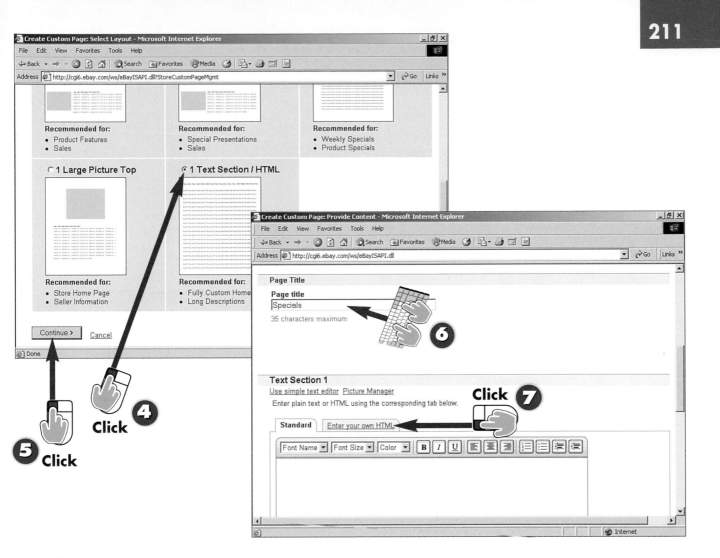

4 Select **1 Text Section/HTML**.

5 Click **Continue**.

6 Enter a page title.

7 Click **Enter Your Own HTML**.

See next page

TIP

Creating a First Draft
Ease your development by first creating your HTML in a separate page you can easily view in a browser. When you're satisfied with it, copy and paste it into your store.

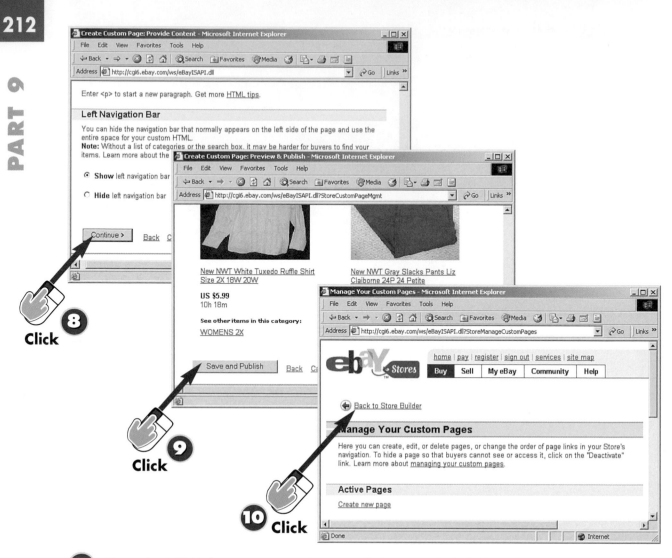

8 Enter the HTML for your page; then scroll down and click **Continue**.

9 Click **Save and Publish**.

10 Click **Back to Store Builder**.

Page Order
You can control the order in which your custom pages appear in the navigation bar by moving them up and down in the list in the Manage Custom Pages section.

Store-specific Tags
eBay recently added new tags specifically for stores. These tags are not in the HTML form—they use curly braces ({}) instead of brackets (<>), but they can provide useful capabilities. See http://pages.ebay.com/help/stores/stores-specific-tags.html for more information.

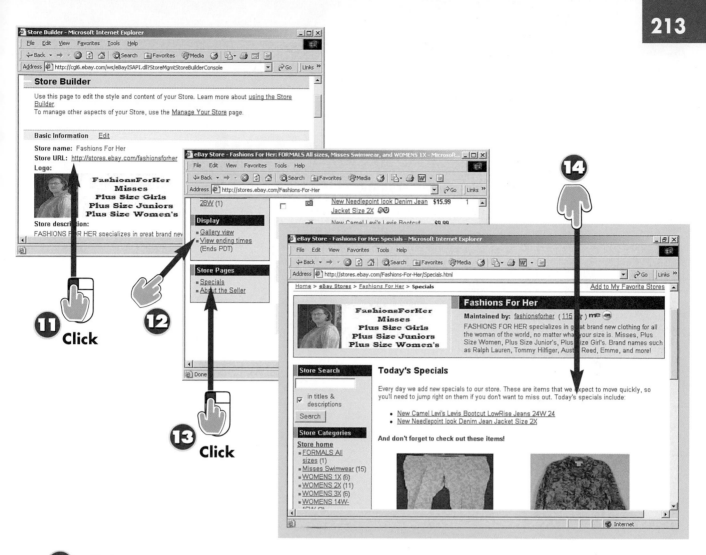

11 Click to view your store.

12 Notice that your page is automatically added to the left side navigation.

13 Click to view your page.

14 Notice that your page is automatically included in the overall store layout.

End

TIP

Changing Your Home Page
You can make one of your custom pages your store's home page by changing the Store Home Page and eBay Header Style in the Store Builder.

PART 10

Making Your Listings Stand Out

At this point, you know everything you need to know to run an eBay business. (Well, everything about HTML, anyway!) You can create a listing, make it look nice, and link to emails and other information. You even know how to create and maintain your own eBay Store and About Me page.

This section is different. This section is where you learn how to do those little things that don't come easy to your average eBay seller because they're not obvious. Some, like enabling users to search among your items, involve HTML that is just one step above simply manipulating the look of a page. Some, such as supersizing photos, are designed to get around restrictions eBay has in place specifically to keep you from doing them.

Overall, this part shows you how to add those little niceties that make it clear you've put time and thought into making your auctions look as good as they can, which hopefully translates into increased buyer confidence and higher bids.

Making Your Page Stand Out

You are bidding on an unusual Lord Nelson porcelain potpourri basket. Made in England, it is made up of two pieces and imprinted "Lord Nelson England" on the bottom. The top piece is decorated with beautiful multi-colored flowers and the bottom piece is the "basket". This is a unique piece that has been lovingly cared for and except for some light crazing, it is in wonderful condition. It would be a great addition to anyone's collection. The piece stands seven inches tall by four inches wide.

Search my other auctions

Close Window

Enable users to search your other auctions

condition. It would be a great addition to anyone's collection. The piece stands seven inches tall by four inches wide.

side

top

bottom

inside

Close Window

Creating your own click-to-enlarge images

Enabling Users to Search Your Other Auctions

Start

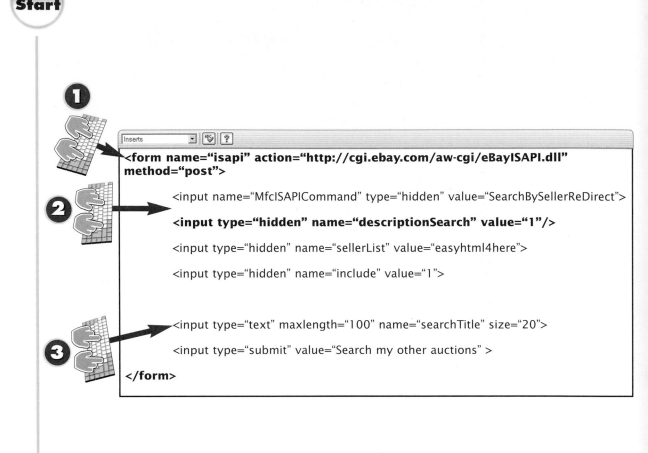

```
Inserts

<form name="isapi" action="http://cgi.ebay.com/aw-cgi/eBayISAPI.dll"
method="post">

    <input name="MfcISAPICommand" type="hidden" value="SearchBySellerReDirect">

    <input type="hidden" name="descriptionSearch" value="1"/>

    <input type="hidden" name="sellerList" value="easyhtml4here">

    <input type="hidden" name="include" value="1">

    <input type="text" maxlength="100" name="searchTitle" size="20">

    <input type="submit" value="Search my other auctions" >

</form>
```

① Add the actual form to the description by typing the **<form>** and **</form>** tags and the necessary attributes.

② Add the "hidden" values eBay needs to perform the search properly by typing the first set of **<input>** tags and corresponding attributes.

③ Add the input box where users will enter their search terms by typing the second set of **<input>** tags and corresponding attributes.

INTRODUCTION

If possible, you want to get bidders to buy additional items you have for sale. In this task, you learn how to let people do an eBay search that looks only at your items. Before starting this task, create a new auction, enter the description, and then select **Enter Your Own HTML**. (See Part 1, "Creating an Auction Listing," for help.)

HINT

Change easyhtml4here In the fourth line of code, replace **easyhtml4here** with your own eBay ID.

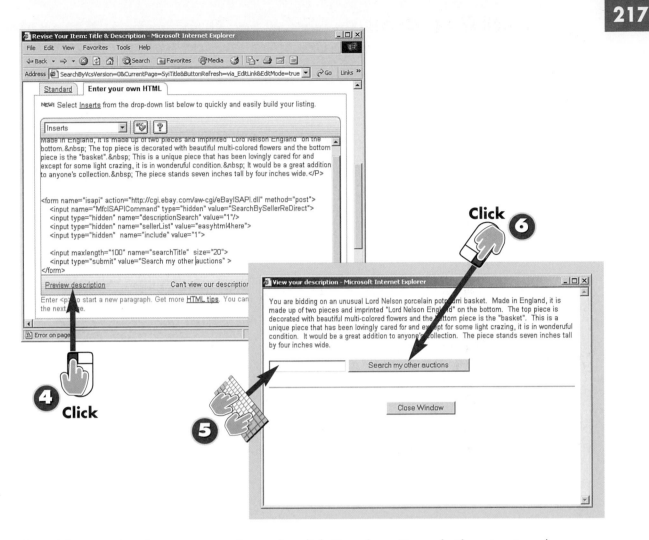

4 When you're done entering the code, click **Preview Description** to view the new form.

5 To test the form, enter a search term.

6 Click **Search My Other Auctions**.

End

On the Outside Looking In
You can also use this technique to let users search your items from an external web page, such as your weblog. Just insert the form code into the external page's HTML.

Using Click to Enlarge to Maximize Attention

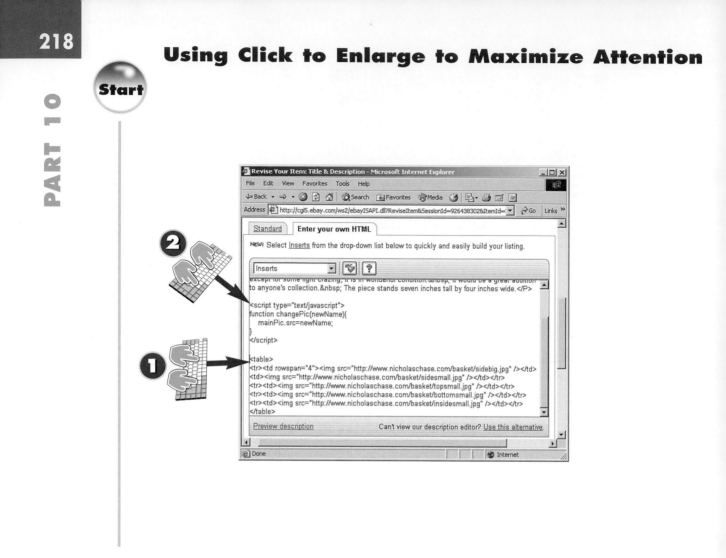

1 Enter the code to create a table that lays out the original images.

2 Add a **script** section to the description, above the code for the table.

INTRODUCTION

An auction listing with a number of large photos can be hard to navigate and slow to load. This task shows you how to duplicate eBay Picture Services' Supersize Picture function with your own images so the user can click a small version to see the large version. Before starting this task, create a new auction, enter the description, and select **Enter Your Own HTML**.

Enter Your Own URLs
In the **<img>** tags, replace the URLs listed with the complete URLs for your own pictures.

TIP

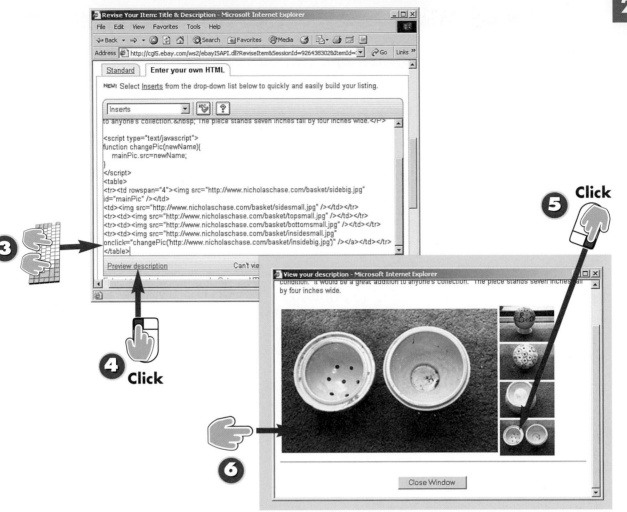

3 Call the script when the user clicks one of the small images by adding the **onclick** code to each of the **<img>** tags.

4 Click **Preview Description**.

5 Click the bottom thumbnail.

6 Notice that the main picture, which you did not click, changes to the new image.

See next page

What's a Function?

TIP

A *function* is a set of instructions that has a name, such as **changePic**, that lets you call it from another location. In this case, the function takes an argument, **newName**, so when you type **changePic('topbig.jpg')**, it's the same as typing **mainPic.src='topbig.jpg'**. This way, you can get one function to do a lot of different things.

```
<script type="text/javascript">

function changePic(newName){

newPicURL = "http://www.nicholaschase.com/basket/"+newName;

  mainPic.src=newName;

}

</script>
```

```
<table>

<tr><td rowspan="4"><img src="http://www.nicholaschase.com/basket/sidebig.jpg"
id="mainPic" /></td>

<td><img src="http://www.nicholaschase.com/basket/sidesmall.jpg" onclick="changePic('
sidebig.jpg')" /></td></tr>

<tr><td><img src="http://www.nicholaschase.com/basket/topsmall.jpg"
onclick="changePic('topbig.jpg')" /></td></tr>

<tr><td><img src="http://www.nicholaschase.com/basket/bottomsmall.jpg"
onclick="changePic('bottombig.jpg')" /></td></tr>

<tr><td><img src="http://www.nicholaschase.com/basket/insidesmall.jpg"
onclick="changePic('insidebig.jpg')" /></a></td></tr>

</table>
```

7 Simplify the calling of the script by putting most of the URL into the script itself.

8 Simplify the calls to the script.

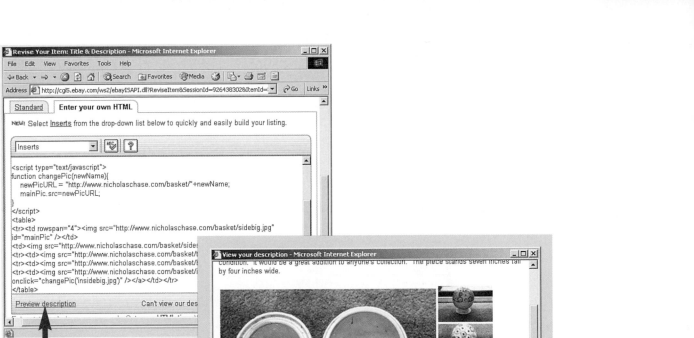

Click ⑨

Click ⑩

⑨ Click **Preview Description**.

⑩ Click any of the thumbnails. Notice that the big picture changes.

See next page

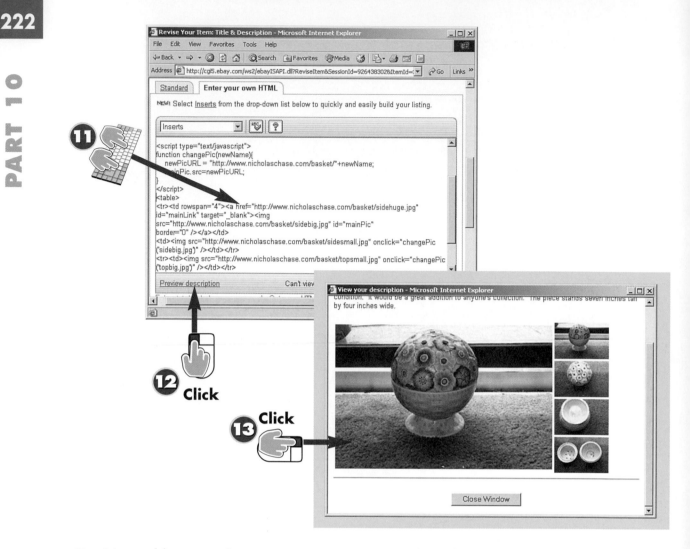

11. Now add an even bigger picture, in a new window, if the user clicks the big picture. Add a link to the main picture.

12. Click **Preview Description**.

13. Click the big picture. It should open a new window with a larger version of the photo.

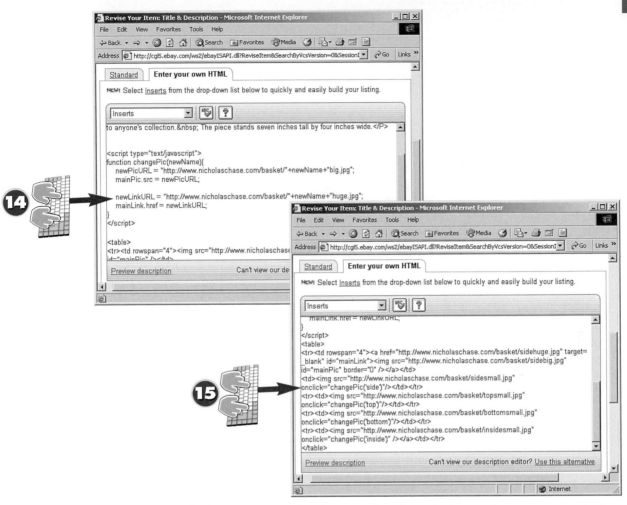

Now you have to find a way to make the URL the photo links to change to match the picture it's showing. Generalize the script even more, so that it changes both the **src** of the image and the **href** of the link.

Change the **onclick** handlers to match the new script.

See next page

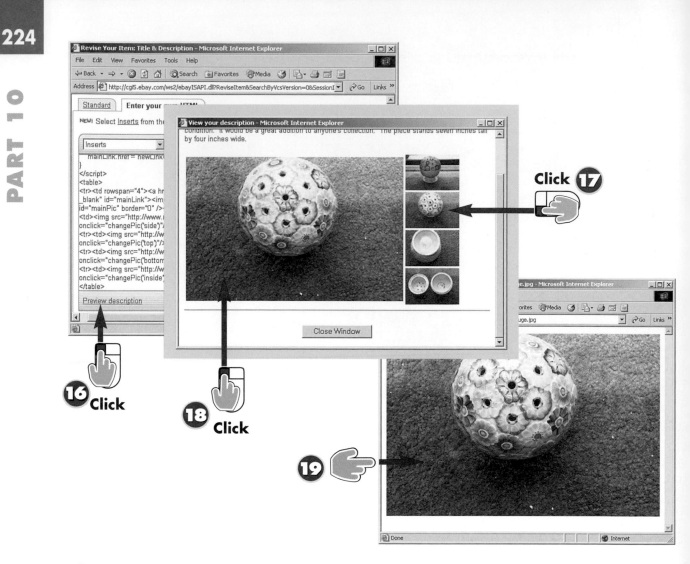

16 Click **Preview Description**.

17 Click a thumbnail to change the photo.

18 Click the large picture.

19 Notice that the new window always matches the big picture, even when the picture changes.

End

Preloading Images

Start

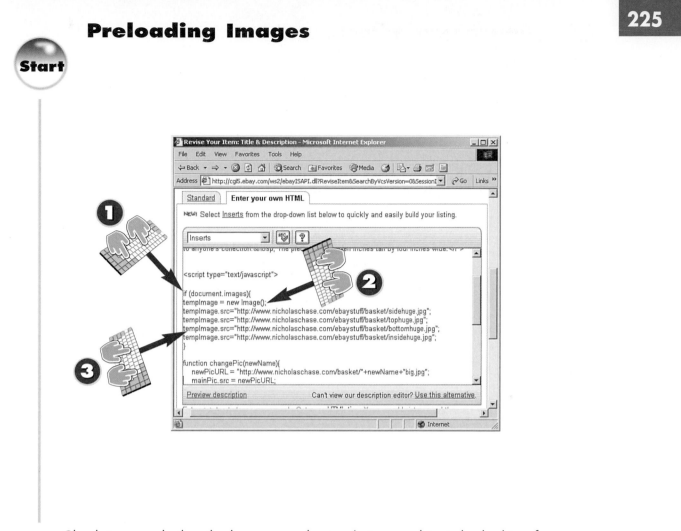

1 Check to see whether the browser understands image objects by looking for **document.images**. Add this part of the script directly to the **script** element so it executes when the browser first loads the page.

2 Create an image object.

3 Use the object to load each of the large images in turn.

End

TIP

What Is document. images?
Some older browsers won't understand what we're asking them to do here. On those browsers, **document.images** doesn't exist, so the script considers it "false" and skips that section of code.

TIP

Seeing It in Action
If you've already downloaded each of the images, you can see the effect this has by clearing your browser's cache and preloading only some of the images.

Mouseover Effects

Start

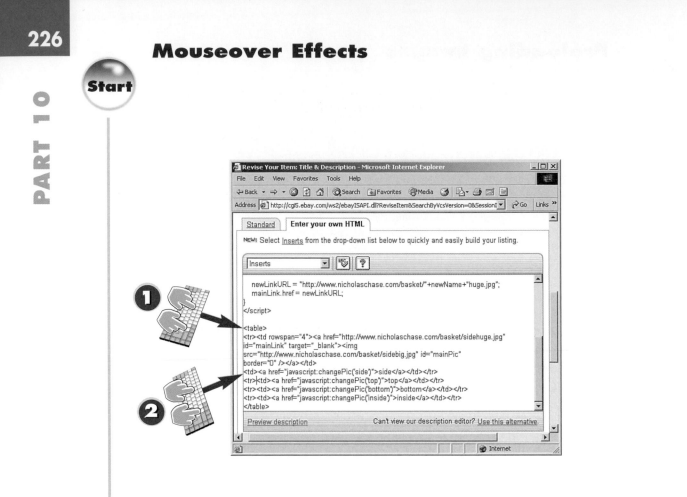

1 Set up the initial layout.

2 Make the text into links that call the JavaScript **changePic** function when clicked.

INTRODUCTION

When you roll your mouse over a link, the browser changes the cursor so you know it's clickable. Using Cascading Style Sheets, you can take control of this process to create elaborate effects, called *rollovers*. In this task, we'll replace the thumbnails from the previous task with text, but when the user rolls over the text, it will change colors and the thumbnail will appear behind it.

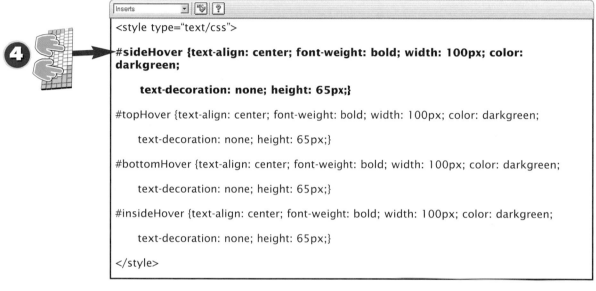

```
<table>

<tr><td rowspan="4"><a href="http://www.nicholaschase.com/basket/sidehuge.jpg" id="mainLink"
target="_blank"><img src="http://www.nicholaschase.com/basket/sidebig.jpg" id="mainPic"

border="0" /></a></td>

<td><a href="javascript:changePic('side')" id="sideHover">side</a></td></tr>

<tr><td><a href="javascript:changePic('top')" id="topHover">top</a></td></tr>

<tr><td><a href="javascript:changePic('bottom')" id="bottomHover">bottom</a></td></tr>

<tr><td><a href="javascript:changePic('inside')" id="insideHover">inside</a></td></tr>

</table>
```

3

```
<style type="text/css">

#sideHover {text-align: center; font-weight: bold; width: 100px; color:
darkgreen;

    text-decoration: none; height: 65px;}

#topHover {text-align: center; font-weight: bold; width: 100px; color: darkgreen;

    text-decoration: none; height: 65px;}

#bottomHover {text-align: center; font-weight: bold; width: 100px; color: darkgreen;

    text-decoration: none; height: 65px;}

#insideHover {text-align: center; font-weight: bold; width: 100px; color: darkgreen;

    text-decoration: none; height: 65px;}

</style>
```

4

3 Add **id** attributes to each link so you can set the style on them individually.

4 Set the initial styles for the links.

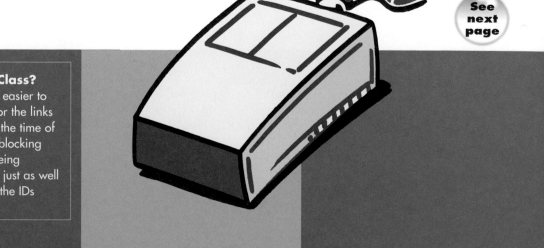

See next page

Why Not Use a Class?
It would certainly be easier to set the initial styles for the links using a class, but at the time of this writing, eBay is blocking certain styles from being applied this way. It's just as well because you'll need the IDs anyway.

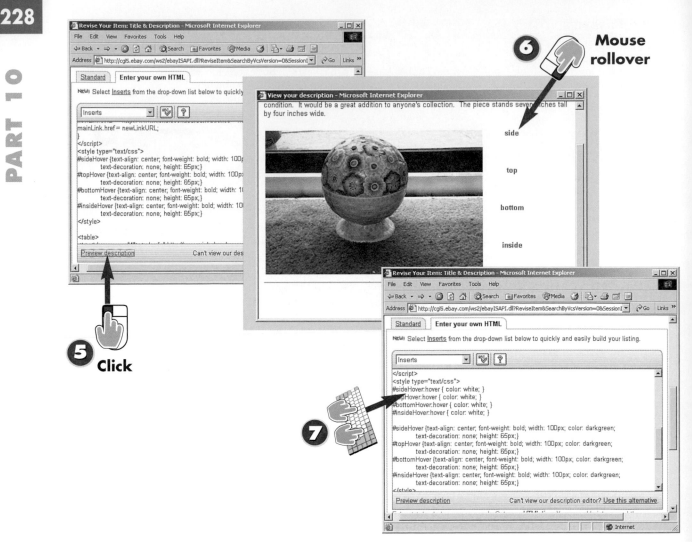

Mouse rollover

5 Click

5 Click **Preview Description**.

6 Roll the mouse over the links to verify that nothing happens.

7 Use the **:hover** "pseudoclass" to change the color of the links when you roll the mouse over them.

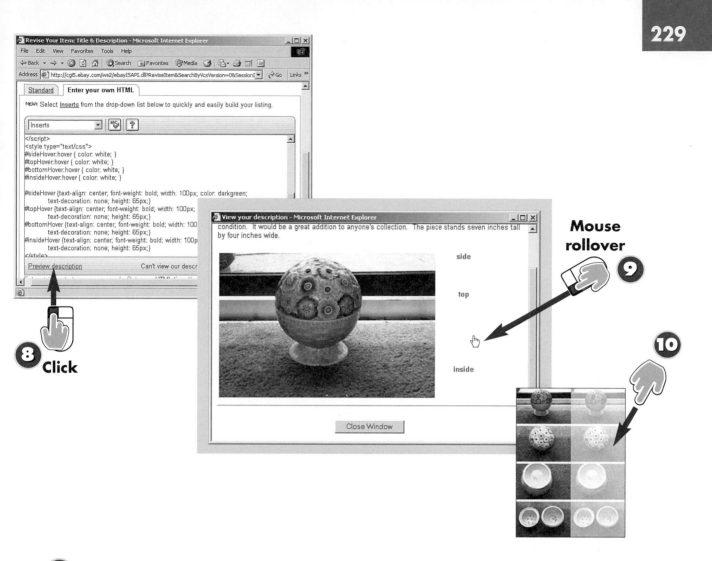

See
next
page

8 Click **Preview Description**.

9 Roll your mouse over one of the links. Because you've set it to white, it seems to disappear. That problem goes away when you get the images involved.

10 Create the background image. This image contains all the content necessary for all the backgrounds.

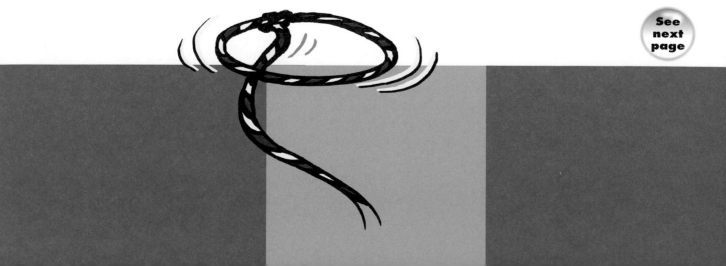

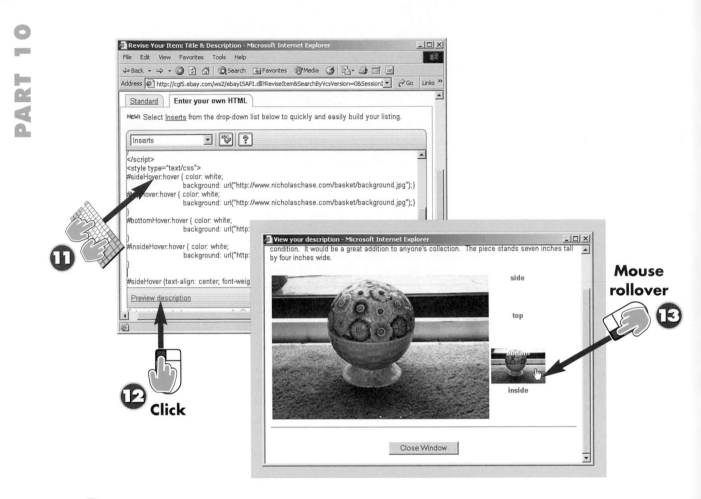

Mouse rollover

11 Click

12 Click

13

---

11 Set the **:hover** styles to add the background image to each link.

12 Click **Preview Description**.

13 Roll over the links. Notice that, for all of them, the background image appears but not necessarily correctly.

Why Don't I See All the Images?

Your first thought might be that you should see all the images when the background comes up, but the background shows up behind only the element it's the background for. Because you've explicitly sized the table data cells at 100 × 65 pixels, that's all you see of the background.

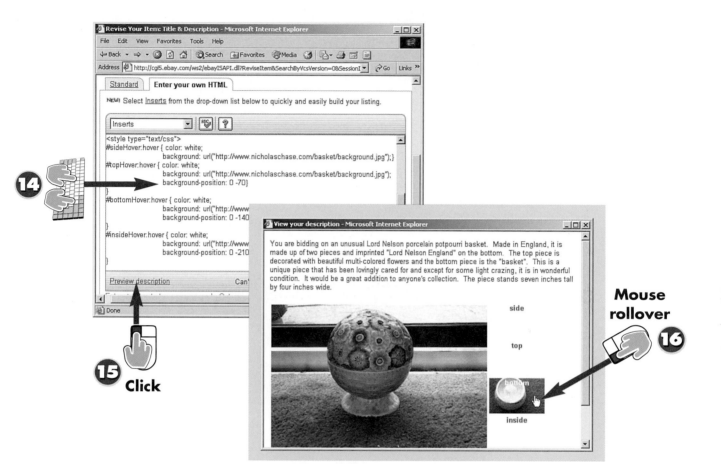

Mouse rollover

14 Correct the problem by offsetting the background image using the background position style.

15 Click **Preview Description**.

16 Move the mouse over the images to see the effect.

See next page

What Do Those Numbers Mean?

The first number in the background position is the movement to the left. Because all these images are along the left of the overall image, you don't need to change that. The others are the number of pixels down you want to move the image; each individual image (and border) is 70 pixels high. Because you're actually moving it up, you use negative numbers.

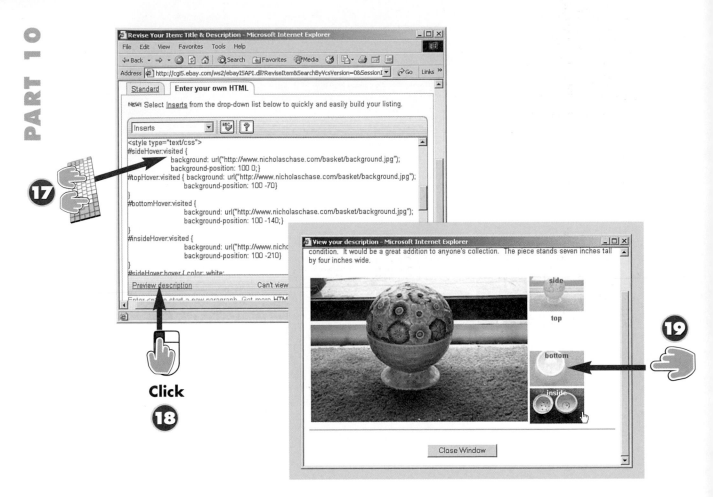

Click

18

19

17 Add the background for links you've already visited by using the **:visited** pseudo-class and showing the right side of the background image.

18 Click **Preview Description**.

19 Notice that the links you've already visited have a faded background but they get the full background when you roll over them. Links you haven't visited don't have any background at all.

End

The Four Link States

TIP

You can set the appearance for links in four states. For a normal, unvisited link, just set a style for the link itself. For the link after it has been visited, use the **:visited** pseudoclass. For the link while you have the mouse over it, use the **:hover** pseudoclass. For the link while you're clicking it, use the **:active** pseudoclass.

Adding Your Own Counter or Other Enhancements

Start

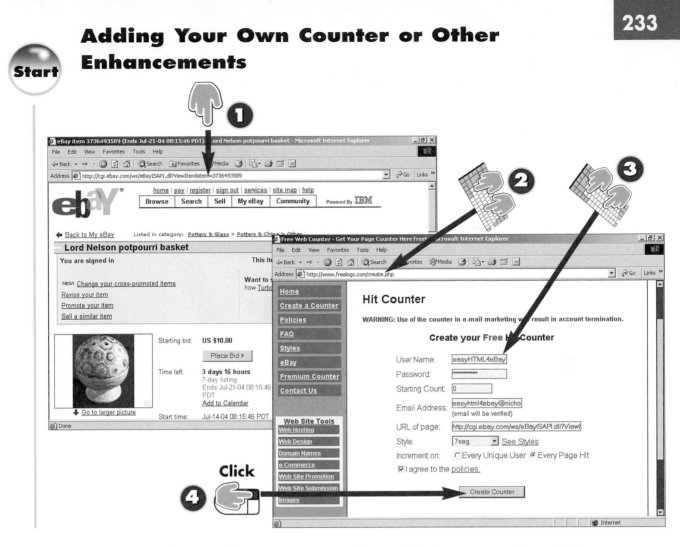

Click

See next page

1 To use a counter from Freelogs.com, you need the URL for the page it'll be added to. Create a new auction and get its URL.

2 Point your browser to **http://www.freelogs.com/create.php**.

3 Enter your information in the form.

4 Click **Create Counter**.

INTRODUCTION

You might wonder why you need to know how to add a counter to your auction. After all, eBay provides counters, right? Well, besides the fact that you need to pay Andale for anything but a basic counter, it's important to realize that the skill involved in adding a custom counter is the same for adding any enhancement from an outside source, such as an enhanced shipping calculator or other feature.

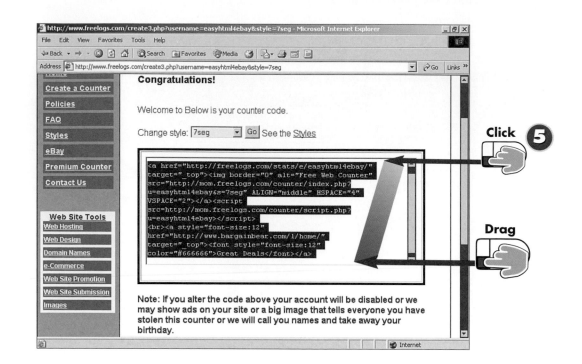

Click 5

Drag

---

 5 Select all the text in the text box by clicking the top and dragging to the bottom.

 6 Press **Ctrl+C** to copy the text.

Click

7

8

Click

7 Place the cursor where you want the counter to appear in your description and select **Edit**, **Paste**.

8 Click **Preview Description**; then save your auction as usual.

End

Index

M

N-O

P

How can we make this index more useful? Email us at indexes@quepublishing.com

text
adding HTML tags to, 38-39
aligning on description page, 94-95
bolding, 46
bulleted lists, creating, 130
colors, 121
emphasizing, <em> tag, 126
emphasizing, <strong> tag, 126
formatting, 30-37, 46-49
headings, creating, 38-39
horizontal lines, adding, 43
italicizing, 46, 124
kerning, 127
leading, 128
moving text, adding, 132
nesting elements, 49
numbered lists, creating, 131
paragraphs, creating, 42
separator lines, creating, 43-45
sizing, 120
span tag, 124
strikethrough, 125
text backgrounds, 129
typefaces, 122
underline, 126
unwrapping, 91
wrapping around images, 90-91
wrapping text around, 91
writing descriptions, 30-37

text tables, creating, 76-77
text-decoration property, 125
themes, 24-25
tiled backgrounds, creating,
110-117
titles, length, 33
tracking auction activity, 21
turning off borders, 102
tweening, 180
typefaces, 122

U

underline text, 126
removing, 126
unwrapping text from objects, 91
uploading photos to eBay, 66
URLs
adding, 218
querystring, 143
user IDs
display options, 197
displaying, 196
users, registering, 10-13

V-Z

variables
creating, 142
definition, 142
video, adding, 168

watermarking software, 70
watermarks
adding to images, 70-73
digital watermarks, 73
translucency, 72
webmail, 137
windows, opening, 148-149
word-spacing property, 127

Rather than having you read through a lot of text, Easy lets you learn visually. Users are introduced to topics of technology, hardware, software, and computersin a friendly, yet motivating, manner.

Easy Digital Cameras
Mark Edward Soper
ISBN: 0-7897-3077-4
$19.99 USA/$28.99 CAN

Easy Adobe Photoshop Elements 3
Kate Binder
ISBN: 0-7897-3330-7
$19.99 USA/$28.99 CAN

Easy Microsoft Windows® XP, Home Edition
Third Edition
Shelley O'Hara
ISBN: 0-7897-3337-4
$19.99 USA/$28.99 CAN

Easy Digital Home Movies
Jake Ludington
ISBN: 0-7897-3114-2
$19.99 USA/$28.99 CAN